Why Weren't We Told?

Why Weren't We Told?

A Handbook on 'progressive' Christianity

Compiled and edited by

Rex A. E. Hunt & John W. H. Smith

POLEBRIDGE PRESS

Salem, Oregon

Cover and interior design by Robaire Ream

ISBN 978-1-59815-111-4

In appreciation of some progressive heroes
who moved against the stream,
'down under' in Australia and New Zealand . . .

Charles Strong
(1844–1942)

Samuel Angus
(1881–1943)

Lloyd G. Geering
(1918–)

Contents

Reclaiming the Faith's FreeThinkers

'progressive' Christianity Alive

Some encouragement . . . because we are not alone!
Collated by Rex A. E. Hunt

Living the 'progressive' Dream
Stories from congregations and groups self-styled as 'progressive'

Resources Toolbox
Compiled by Rex A. E. Hunt

Acknowledgments

An earlier version of "Being a 'progressive' Christian", by Keith Rowe, was originally presented at the Common Dreams 2 Conference, Melbourne, (Australia) in April 2010.

"Biblical and Modern Worldviews of the History of the World and Human Life", by Roy Hoover, first appeared in *The Fourth R*, January–February 2004. Used with permission of the author and publisher, Polebridge Press.

"A Mystical Lord's Prayer", by Paul Alan Laughlin, and the Introductory words, are reprinted from *The Fourth R*, vol. 22, no. 6 (November–December 2009), with permission of the author and publisher, Polebridge Press.

"Musings 1–10", by Jim Burklo, have also appeared—some edited here—on his blog *Musings,* found at www.tcpc.blogs.com/musings. Selected and used with permission of the author.

The prayer "Dear One, Closer to Us than Our Own Hearts", by Jim Burklo, is used with permission by the author.

The blessing/benediction "May the Peace of God Surround You", by Jim Burklo, is used with permission by the author.

The prayer "Living presence, life fire of the universe", by Pam Raff, on behalf of the Rockhampton Progressive Group, is used with permission.

The songs "In What Strange Land"—words by © Colin Gibson, music by © Shirley Erena Murray—and "On a Cool and Autumn Dawn", by © Bill Bennett, were first published in *Hope is Our Song* book and CD, NZ Hymnbook Trust 2009/11, respectively. Used with permission of the publisher.

The six hymns based on "The Canberra Affirmation" were written and published by © George Stuart in 2009 in *Singing a New Song: Traditional Hymn Tunes with New Century Lyrics,* vol 2. Used with the permission of the author.

The Hymn "In the Sacrament with Water", by © George Stuart is used with permission by the author.

The Hymn "Love Now Ascending", by Jim Burklo, is used with permission by the author.

The Hymn "My Song Is of Love", by Pam Raff, on behalf of the Rockhampton Progressive Group, is used with permission.

Abbreviations

Gen	Genesis
Deut	Deuteronomy
Mic	Micah
Ps	Psalms
Isa	Isaiah
Matt	Matthew
	Mark
	John
Gal	Galatians
Rom	Romans
1,2 Tim	1,2 Timothy
Col	Colossians
Heb	Hebrews
Rev	Revelation

Foreword

Revd Professor Sir Lloyd Geering, ONZ, GNZM, CBE

In 1963 a considerable theological controversy was sparked off by Bishop John Robinson's little book, *Honest to God*. This became one of the most widely read theological books of the twentieth century, as witnessed by the fact that in Australia alone three special printings were issued in as many months. Before the year ended, the SCM Press had followed it with *The Honest to God Debate*. In the following year the more radical theologians were announcing 'The Death of God', and in April 1966 the weekly magazine *Time* devoted a whole issue to God's demise.

In New Zealand the controversy spilled out of the churches into the general community when I wrote an Easter article for our church journal. I posed the question, "What does the Resurrection of Jesus mean?" and suggested, as many scholars had already done, that the story of the empty tomb was a pious legend; it could therefore not be taken as historical evidence of a supernatural miracle. In the course of the nationally wide public debate that followed, a lawyer who had once been a fellow student of mine complained to me, "I have been a loyal churchman all my life, and I am a reasonably intelligent person. Why have I not been told all this before?"

His complaint was fully justified. I was simply discussing what scholars had been writing about for quite some time, but none of it had ever been heard by people in the pews. In fact, those of us who were then involved in theological teaching had not found anything very new in Robinson's book, for we had been reading for ourselves the writings of Rudolf Bultmann, Paul Tillich, and Dietrich Bonhoeffer. The reason Robinson caused a stir is that he brought out into the open some of the radical theological ideas that had begun surfacing in academic circles during the previous decades.

A great gulf had been opening up between the thinking of theologians and biblical scholars on the one hand, and what was still being preached in the churches on the other. It was not that preachers deliberately hid from their congregations what they themselves often learned about in their seminaries; it was rather that pastoral concern for their parishioners had led them to regard the weekly sermon as a way to encourage and comfort its hearers rather than upset them with new and challenging ideas. Unfortunately, this growing gulf between the pulpit and the pew left the congregations in ignorance, with the result the mainline churches are today suffering rapid decline, as increasing numbers have been drifting out of the churches, feeling that the 'old-time religion' is no longer relevant to today's life.

The roots of this malaise can actually be traced as far back as the nineteenth century. That was when biblical studies and religious thought first entered this modern period of radical change. In 1860 a group of Anglican scholars of Oxford University published their *Essays and Reviews*. It caused a much bigger uproar than Darwin's *The Origin of Species* of the year before. It was vigorously attacked by both priests and laypeople, with the result that two of its contributors were suspended from holy orders. When they were later reinstated by an appeal to the Privy Council, a protest was signed by 11,000 clergymen and 137,000 laymen.

In spite of this initial setback, the new theology had come to prevail in the major seminaries and theological schools by the end of that century and was known as Protestant Liberalism. It even surfaced in the Roman Catholic Church, where it was referred to as Modernism. But whereas the authority of the Vatican was able to crush Modernism very quickly, Protestant Liberalism went on to flourish, producing hosts of biblical commentaries and new translations of the Bible. It produced such great preachers as Leslie Weatherhead in London and Harry Emerson Fosdick in New York, and the churches remained full.

But not all Protestants were happy with the liberal theology, and reaction began to set in, quite slowly at first. It came to a head with the publication of a series of booklets called 'The Fundamentals' (published during 1910–15) that gave rise to the term 'fundamentalism'. Fundamentalists insisted on the literal inerrancy of the Bible and defended what they took to be the traditional positions, such as belief in a 'personal' God, the Virgin Birth, the efficacy of the Christ's atoning sacrifice on the cross and the bodily resurrection of Jesus.

Only slowly did the reactionary fundamentalism of USA spread to Australasia. So widespread was Protestant Liberalism that, when I was a student in the 1930s, I never heard sermons expounding these orthodox doctrines in their traditional way. Rather, Jesus was held up as the role model par excellence and his teaching was presented as the way to live a fulfilling life. Among my fellow theological students only a tiny number espoused the fundamentalist position. Most of us saw fundamentalism as the dying remnant of a past orthodoxy that had now become obsolete, along with a historical Adam and Eve. We certainly did not see it as a growing movement. How wrong we were!

We should have listened to Kirsopp Lake, a New Testament scholar who, in 1925, wrote a book entitled *The Religion of Yesterday and Tomorrow*. He showed that the denominational divisions had lost their relevance and been replaced by three new streams that divided Protestants into the Experimentalists, the Institutionalists and the Fundamentalists. Then he made this remarkable prophecy: "The Fundamentalists will eventually triumph. They will drive out the Experimentalists and then reabsorb the Institutionalists who, under pressure, will become more orthodox. . . . The church will shrink from left to right."

And so it has turned out. While liberals were busy promoting ecumenism and a positive understanding of the non-Christian religions, the conservatives gathered momentum. By the 1960s they had grown strong enough to challenge Liberalism, which they rejected as a spent force. This conservative thrust gave rise to the 'No Other Gospel' movement in Germany and to widespread public controversy in New Zealand. In the USA the conservative churches were expanding and the fundamentalist televangelists began to flourish, while the liberal churches were declining.

In the academic world, however, a wave of even newer theology was beginning to emerge out of the declining liberalism. Though it may be said to have started with Bultmann, Bonhoeffer and Tillich, it went on to Harvey Cox, John Cobb, Gordon Kaufmann and Don Cupitt, with the Catholic Church producing Hans Kung, liberation theology and some feminist theologians. These more radical voices have stimulated some to form small tentative networks independent of church control, such as the Sea of Faith Network in the United Kingdom, New Zealand and Australia, and the Snowstar Institute in Canada. In the academic world it gave rise to the Westar Institute, a group of scholars that found it desirable to carry out its biblical work free of all interference by ecclesiastical or university institutions.

Some within the existing ecclesiastical institutions, encouraged by the new theological voices, have set out to counter the spread of fundamentalism. They have begun to speak of themselves as 'progressive' Christians. A growing number of congregations in the United States and Australasia have chosen to define themselves as 'progressive', while a network of 'progressive' groups have held two large conferences in Sydney and Melbourne, known respectively as Common Dreams 1 and Common Dreams 2.

The purpose of this publication is twofold. First, it aims to make more widely known, both within the churches and outside of them, what this 'progressive' movement stands for. Progressives have no wish to replace the traditional though now outmoded orthodoxy with a new creed or statement of faith. They find no set of 'right' beliefs that all Christians should be expected to embrace, especially since there never has been a time when all Christians shared the same beliefs, though from time to time church authorities did try to enforce creedal unanimity.

Progressives see the Christian cultural tradition as an ever-evolving one, in which individuals are free to think through and enunciate for themselves the beliefs they find most satisfying. The one thing all Christians have in common is they draw from the same cultural past, of which the Bible remains an unchangeable core. But along with this comes the extraordinarily complex history of the Christian tradition, including its often contradictory and even hostile expostulations. For just as the Bible is a collection of books and does not speak with one voice, so those who draw inspiration from this rich cultural source, not only select from it what they find speaking to them most urgently, but freely relate it to the knowledge and experience they are continually gathering in this fast-changing world.

The second purpose of this book is to provide material that will promote further study, stimulating readers to clarify their thinking on a great variety of issues. None of this material claims to be definitive. Rather, it provides examples of work in progress. To this end there are short, concise cameos on ethics, eco-spirituality, atonement, Christmas, science and religion, and a host of other topics. This is not a book to be read straight through from beginning to end, but to be picked up, studied, thought about and returned to from time to time.

Lloyd Geering: A Tribute

James Veitch

Born in 1918, Lloyd Geering was educated at the University of Otago (MA) and at the Theological Hall, Knox College, in Dunedin. He was unable to continue his studies because of the War and, on graduating in 1942, took up a parish deputising for its minister, who had become a military chaplain.

While in a parish work he completed a Bachelor's degree in Divinity with distinction in Old Testament Studies from the Melbourne College of Divinity. Following ministry in two further parishes, he was appointed in 1956 Professor of Old Testament Studies at Emmanuel College Brisbane, Australia. Three years later he was elected Professor of Old Testament at the Theological Hall Knox College in Dunedin. He took up the appointment in 1960 along with a lectureship in Hebrew at the University of Otago. In 1963 he became Principal of the Theological Hall.

Between 1965 and 1970 he was involved in debate over theological matters and at one stage, in 1967, was charged with doctrinal error— a charge that was dismissed after a trial and vote at the General Assembly of the Presbyterian Church. But the debates had thrust him into the spotlight, and 'Geering' became a household name from that time onwards. The debate itself lingered on and, after appearing on a TV program in Brisbane in 1970 in which he repeated views on which he had been earlier cleared, the General Assembly disassociated itself from his views.

Lloyd became Professor of Religious Studies at Victoria University Wellington in 1971, until his retirement in 1984. From 1983 he became lecturer for the St Andrews Trust for the Study of Religion and Society and was for a time honorary minister of St Andrews-on-the-Terrace. The controversy of 1966 and 1967 established him as a public figure.

For many years, he wrote a weekly column for an Auckland newspaper and for a weekly magazine and this kept him in the public eye. He was a regular lecturer for the Trust where his lectures were published. He lectured regularly in New Zealand and Australia, appeared on TV and often spoke on radio. After meeting with Robert Funk in 1995, he soon became a Fellow of the Westar Institute and a holder of the D. F. Strauss Medal. He lectured in the United States with Westar and his main books were published by Polebridge Press, the publishing arm of the Westar Institute.

The controversy which made him a public figure centred around two phrases. First, a quotation from Ronald Gregor Smith, then at Glasgow University, who had written, "So far as historicity is concerned . . . we may freely say that the bones of Jesus lie somewhere in Palestine."[1] This phrase, quoted approvingly in an Easter article on Resurrection the same year, sparked widespread debate and reaction in and outside the church, which was by no means diminished by the publication of further articles to explain the background to his thinking. This was followed the next year by a second quotation; five words that made front page newspaper headlines from a sermon (based on a verse in Ecclesiastes)—*man has no immortal soul* (the remainder of the sentence reads, *and we are forced to agree that man is an animal*).

The row these words sparked was unprecedented in New Zealand history then as of now. But he survived to develop his thinking in ways that have made him New Zealand's premier progressive Christian religious thinker.

At the age of 93 he is delivering two lecture series, one on Carl Jung and the second, *Ethics for the Sexually Perplexed*. He is without a peer.

Notes

1. R. G. Smith, *Secular Christianity*.

Further Reading

Selected titles by L. Geering: *God in the New World* (1968); *A Faith Odyssey* (2001); *Coming Back to Earth: From Gods, to God, to Gaia* (2009); *Such is Life: My Encounter with Ecclesiastes* (2010).

J. Veitch, *Nothing Will Ever Be the Same Again: New Zealand Presbyterians in Conflict September 1965–November 1967* (unpublished ThD thesis, 1999).

Introduction

It was Saturday morning. The weekend newspaper had just arrived. Great wads of it! With coffee in hand a hopeful relaxed read was commenced.

As one does most weeks, the *Letters* pages were the first to be checked out. One stood out. "That's it. The connection between Coca-Cola and Christianity is that they've both been 'marketed' as 'the real thing'. And the real thing is: Coke rots your teeth, and Christianity might do something similar to your mind. Better celebrate life, here and now in the real world — with some fine French champagne" (RD, Castle Hill).

Turning over a couple of pages, one of the many *Feature* articles — this one by a political campaign consultant — attracted a quick read. Six lines into the article these words appeared: "I remember my first lesson from [one of] Ronald Reagan's long-time pollsters . . . who sagely said: 'Yes, persuade by reason, but remember that motivations are about emotion.'"

'Progressive' religion, like politics, and in fact all human living, is an interplay of reason and emotion. Neurophysicists remind us, while there are regions within our brains that generate and process both emotions and analyses, they are incredibly interwoven. The flowering of the progressive movements within Christianity is testimony to that interweaving pattern, most visible at the 'grass roots'.

A progressive Christianity is not new. In one form or another it has been around for two hundred years or more. A reading of Paul Laughlin's chapter on 'Heretics or Heroes' illustrates this point. What is new about its current expression now intentionally called 'progressive', is this open and inclusive faith is 'coming out' in unexpected ways, or resurfacing in hundreds of congregations in mainline churches around the world. That is, a dynamic grass roots movement where the initiative is often taken by a lay person! As a member of a grassroots group has said: "Our group meets before the service each Sunday and walks to church. It travels 100 meters and goes back 150 years."

Researcher Hal Taussig[1] says progressive Christianity has within it five characteristics:

1. A spiritual vitality and expressiveness
2. An insistence on Christianity with intellectual integrity
3. A transgression of traditional gender boundaries
4. Belief that Christianity can be vital without claiming to be the best or the only true religion
5. Strong ecological and social justice commitments

Those who have encountered progressive Christianity only recently—through courageous preaching and inclusive liturgies, or when joining a 'church alumni' group where the work of the scholars of Westar Institute/Jesus Seminar are more often than not on the study agenda—their expressed anger and disappointment is palpable: "Why weren't we told?" This international collection of cameos and articles on the themes and issues addressed by that progressive Christianity is a response to that cry. It is designed to support those who are already on the progressive journey. Or would like to share something of what they have found, with others still searching. And to celebrate the life of this emerging, . . . well, it has been described as a 'movement', but as one of our contributors has recently been overheard to say, it is not so much a movement as "a stream of thinking that is slowly but inexorably spreading over the religious landscape like a river spreading on a flood plain".

The authors represented in this volume come to progressive Christianity with various experiences: as laypeople, academics, clergypersons, theologians, liturgists, poet/hymn writers, scientists, ethicists, retreat leaders, and sociologists—all committed to progressive Christianity. Some come from within Church Christianity while others come from the fringes to where they have been pushed by an unsympathetic or stubborn church hierarchy. There is even a supposed 'heretic' or two!

Collectively, they are like musicians in a jazz band. Sometimes it is the bass that leads. At other times it is the clarinet or guitar that features. Basic rhythm or beat along with lead instruments, continually interacting and playing with one another, outside a fixed script. Like life, the universe, and constructive theology, progressive Christianity is a process of composition and improvisation. Nothing fixed or final. And that's good.

The down side is that while this contemporary progressive thinking is world-wide, it is in the minority in most places, with many people having left Church Christianity to join the church alumni associations. Orthodoxy and scared church leaders have seen to that! Such establishment leaders seem blind to, or afraid of, this progressive thought. It challenges too many 'sacred cows'. So instead of working to change theology or embrace the progressive streams of biblical literacy and criticism, they try to make old thought, creeds, and concepts from the past, fit new realities. It doesn't work and people continue to leave the church. Inspired by Jesuit Andrew Hamilton's[2] metaphor in another context, we would want to claim progressive Christianity is the canary in the Church Christianity mineshaft. Its evolving and growing witness could be dismissed by the mine managers and overseers, who wish for nothing other than 'peace and unity within the ranks', but that dismissal will not make the mineshaft a more relevant and safe living space. To reform—even reconstruct—the enterprise, it will prove better in the long run to feed the canaries and to listen to their song!

Yet local and sometimes individual progressives—the grassroots progressives—need to know they are not alone. Some of the most exciting theological and religious reflection is being done within global progressive Christianity. In Australia, New Zealand, Canada, USA, England, Ireland, Scotland to name just some—where resources and personnel are shared across state and national borders. This collection taps into some of this rich, creative source.

As we compiled this book and engaged in research and writing, we were again reminded of some of the courage and wisdom of 'heroes' from the past. Ralph Waldo Emerson expressed the progressive spirit well: "Do not be timid and squeamish. All of life is an experiment. The more experiments you make, the better."

Our grateful and personal thanks to all the authors, contributors and those with whom we have consulted—some working against very tight deadlines. Warm appreciation to Larry Alexander, Char Matejovsky, and the staff of Polebridge Press for guiding us through the publishing process. We are also grateful to Emeritus Professor Peter Fensham, Adjunct Professor, Faculty of Education, Monash University, for his guidance in the drafting of the research instrument "Request for Information". This instrument was used to gather data for the section on *Progressive Christianity: A Grassroots Response*. Peter's extensive experience in Christian Education was most valuable.

We are especially grateful to Sir Lloyd Geering who agreed to write the Foreword to this collection. He has been and continues to be, an absolute inspiration to all progressives around the world, but especially in New Zealand and Australia.

We live in a time of transition rather than tradition. People are exploring. People are waking. May our progressive journeys continue to be both exciting and changing. It is only when one refuses to think about religion in general, or Christianity in particular, can it remain closed and unchanged. Progressive Christianity on the other hand, is a much more adventurous life!

Rex A. E. Hunt
John W. H. Smith
2012

Notes

1. H. E. Taussig, *A New Spiritual Home*, 7–52.
2. A. Hamilton, "Democracy in the Church".

Asking the Question . . .
Why 'progressive'?
Aren't We All Christians?

Fred Plumer

Frequently, after a lecture or seminar, someone will ask me: "Why do you have to call it 'progressive' Christianity? Aren't we all Christians?" These were usually people who seemed to be a little on edge, and sometimes even angry, but their questions were sincere and, frankly, they are good ones.

I think it is important to note that the term progressive was part of the Australian and American Christian dialogue over a hundred years ago. Toward the end of the nineteenth century there was, in America for instance, an active group of well-respected clergy who initiated a movement that had a profound impact both short and long term.

In his fascinating book, *The War for Righteousness*, Richard M. Gamble writes:

> The self-described 'progressives' among America's Protestant clergy at the turn of the twentieth century were well known in church circles and beyond for their advanced thinking on theology, politics, and foreign affairs. As they faced the prospect of a new century, these ministers and academics thought of themselves as broad-minded, humane, and cosmopolitan, in harmony with the very best scientific, political, and theological wisdom of the age. In short, they were among the 'right thinking' leaders of their day. These reformers have since been labeled 'liberal' or modernist by historians, but the word 'progressive' suited their character and their times.[1]

This group of reformers included such well-known names as Congregational ministers Lyman Abbot, Washington Gladden, George A. Gordon, and William Jewett Tucker, who was also president of Dartmouth College. Harry Emerson Fosdick, Shailer Matthews, and Henry Churchill King often served as highly visible and quotable spokesmen for the group.

Gamble points out in his book in some detail that this movement had a strong social influence, but not all of it good. However, I believe it is important to point out that even back then, over one hundred years ago, the movement was firstly about rethinking theology and attempting to move Christianity into the twentieth century. William Jewett Tucker wrote back then that the first effect of the progressive departure in this 'rethinking theology' was to bring about a change in the prevailing conception of God!

Likewise, Henry Emerson Fosdick once reflected that progressive leaders of those times,

> deliberately, sometimes desperately worked to adapt Christian thought and to harmonize it with the intellectual culture of our time. . . . Adaption was the only way we could save our faith, and its achievement was a matter of life and death.[2]

From the very beginning, the leadership of The Center for Progressive Christianity (now known as ProgressiveChristianity.org) believed, like our predecessors, that as progressives, our primary purpose was to actively engage in examining what we mean by God, Christ and Jesus by utilizing the abundance of science, historical and archeological information that we now have available, information we did not have even a hundred years ago. Although the progressive Christian movement is considered new by most people today, it has a long history dating back to some of the first-century disciples of Jesus and a few of the early theologians, particularly in the Eastern Church and the contemplative tradition of the faith. It was always a faith that was more interested in behavior rather than beliefs, compassion rather than creeds and the Mystery rather than absolutes.

So how do I answer that person who wants to know why we need the term 'progressive Christianity'? "Aren't we all Christians?" My short answer is that there are three good reasons.

I believe, as individuals, we need terms like 'progressive Christian' to remind us that we are on a spiritual journey into the Great Unknown. The idea that we are always progressing helps us not only from becoming complacent about our faith, but hopefully it keeps us from assuming that we have arrived. Reminding ourselves that we are progressive Christians can help us stay awake so that we might see who we really are at that moment as a divine creature that is part of something so large, it is beyond our imagination. Being a progressive assumes we are all connected at some ontological level. And we are constantly moving, with a faith that assumes we are moving toward something good, something holy and something divine.

I believe we need the term 'progressive Christian' so we can talk to others about our faith in ways not often heard in typical Christian settings. It is frankly a great way to start a conversation or end one, but it allows us a way to describe ourselves with a new vocabulary and new metaphors. For those who still care about the church, we need to practice our faith, and model it for others rather than telling others what they ought to believe.

And, finally, I agree with Henry Emerson Fosdick. I believe the church needs progressive Christianity for survival. As he eloquently said, progressives "deliberately, sometimes desperately, worked to adapt Christian thought and to harmonize it with the intellectual culture of our time. . . . Adaption was the only way we could save our faith and its achievement was a matter of life and death." And yes, that was over one hundred years ago. Don't you think it is about time?

Notes

1. R. M. Gamble, *The War for Righteousness*, 3.
2. H. E. Fosdick, quoted in R. M. Gamble, 43.

Further Reading

M. J. Borg, *The Heart of Christianity.*
R. M. Gamble, *The War for Righteousness.*
L. Geering, *Is Christianity Going Anywhere?*
C. W. Hedrick, *When Faith Meets Reason.*
H. Taussig, *A New Spiritual Home.*
S. McLennan, *Jesus Was a Liberal.*

'progressive' Cameos . . .

COLLATED BY REX A. E. HUNT

Art

Val Webb

While doctrines and creeds seem to take centre-place in Christian traditions as ways to teach the faithful, the visual image has had a far greater impact on how ordinary people 'see' the Divine. This is despite the fact the Divine has no form or image as God's command to Moses made clear: "Take care and watch yourselves closely, so that you do not act corruptly by making an idol for yourselves in the form of any image" (Deut 4:15–16).

By Medieval and Renaissance times, however, Europe's walls were covered with paintings by the great masters (great mistresses were strangely absent), depicting exactly how the Trinity looked—an old grey-beard on a far-off cloud, a younger fair-skinned 'look-a-like' and a dove. These humanly-constructed images were imprinted on every mind, along with detailed visions of heaven and hell which disseminated fear and hope more successfully than any theological tome. Specific symbols were used to identify biblical characters and saints so their 'story' could be read. These paintings and murals were not casually executed—they adhered to strict guidelines laid down by clergy in order to 'teach' correct dogma. Consequently, changes in theological ideas down the centuries, such as understandings about Jesus and the atonement, can be traced in Christian art.

For progressives, such perpetuation of a male Divine Being reinforces the theistic God—a Being external to the world, unaffected by the world but intervening in its mechanics in answer to prayers. Even though the Creation myth describes Divine action as Wind or Spirit moving over the waters and creation spoken into life, Christian art invariably depicted God as a male Being creating with human hands.

Progressive Christianity sees the Divine as formless Energy, Life and Spirit within the universe, the Ground of Being, Source of all things, the Divine within. Such imagery offers a great challenge to progressive artists to imagine 'Formlessness' in visual ways without locking the Divine into limiting shapes. Modern and abstract art offers more opportunities for this, as do other art forms such as dance, music and temporary art forms like sand paintings, where Divine Energy 'acts' within the created piece.

Progressives also emphasize a theology of beauty and celebration of life, rather than absorption with sin, evil and escape from this world. If the Divine is within everything, this opens the whole creation to wonder and awe as a 'holy place', a living, interconnected art-form of which we are a tiny part. Matthew Fox said,

> A lifestyle is an art form. It brings life and wonder, joy and hope to persons otherwise condemned to superficial living. Our times call for the creation of lifestyles of spiritual substance.[1]

Notes

1. M. Fox, *Cosmic Christ*, 209.

Further Reading

R. Crumlin, *Images of Religion in Australian Art.*
H. De Borchgrave, *A Journey into Christian Art.*
J. Drury, *Painting the Word.*
V. Webb, *Stepping Out with the Sacred.*

Atonement

David Clark

There are a number of interpretations of the doctrine of the atonement, but the one dominating Western theology, spirituality and liturgy is the doctrine of substitutionary atonement. It was spelt out by the medieval theologian Anselm in a treatise on the incarnation.

Anselm asked, "Why did God become human?" His answer was that God became human in Jesus Christ in order that Jesus might die on the cross in place of all humanity, who ought to die because of their sins. Thus, God's anger and offended honour are appeased. Only a perfect sacrifice, the death of the sinless Son of God, could satisfy the righteous God. Ask any Westerner with some knowledge of Christianity, "Why did Jesus die?" and the answer is likely to be something like, "To save us from our sins."

With Borg and Crossan (2006), I will argue that substitutionary atonement is bad history, bad anthropology and bad theology. I would also say it is bad psychology.

Historically, substitutionary atonement presents Jesus' death as a divine necessity to achieve 'at-one-ment' between God and humans. In fact, Jesus' crucifixion was inevitable as Roman overlords and Jewish priestly aristocracy reacted to Jesus' challenges to the temple system and to the social and economic inequities of Roman and Herodian rule. This became a focus in the last week of his life in Jerusalem, resulting in his crucifixion—a punishment reserved only for runaway slaves or for those challenging Roman rule.

Anthropologically, substitutionary atonement literalises the Garden of Eden myth. It assumes the 'fall' of the two first humans in Eden who, fallen, pass on their sinfulness to every successive human being. There simply was no 'Adam' and 'Eve'. Rather, human beings physically evolved over tens of thousands of years, more recent millennia seeing the dramatic evolution of human moral and spiritual sensibilities and growing capacity both to comprehend the divine and to act morally and selflessly.

Theologically, substitutionary atonement makes God a child abuser on a cosmic scale, requiring the brutal death of God's only child to satiate the divine anger. It presents a limited God, incapable of devising any other means of divine-human reconciliation. It misrepresents the Jewish sacrificial system in which animals were humanely, not brutally, killed, then cooked and consumed as a fellowship meal with God—a true at-one-ment. It perpetuates the notion of 'original sin' developed by Augustine of Hippo as he reacted to the Christian Roman Empire falling to godless hordes from the north.

Psychologically, substitutionary atonement has been the basis of generations of Christian self-loathing, reinforced by liturgical emphasis on the atoning death of Jesus and human unworthiness, and spiritualities focused on the agonies and blood of Jesus requiring Christians' self-abnegation and mortification. This practice projects a punitive God who will punish those who do not accept Jesus' atoning death, rather than the loving God of Jesus who seeks to draw out the best from us and welcome us home. Contrary to having original sin within us, we humans have the 'original blessing' of an innate capacity of great goodness. We are also capable of great evil.

Substitutionary atonement presumes sin as that which separates humans from God, but there are other experiences and explanations of human distance from God not addressed by a theology of sacrifice.

While the doctrine of substitutionary atonement has dominated Western theology, spirituality and liturgy, it is unknown in the Eastern Church; likewise, the doctrine of original sin. Parallel to the West's development of original sin and substitutionary atonement was the Eastern development of the doctrine of *theosis*. Theosis is best expressed in the statement "God became a human being in order that human beings could become divine."

Theosis is a psychologically and spiritually healthier way of understanding human and divine at-one-ment. Theologically, it puts God in a much more positive light. Theosis includes the notions of step-by-step development, that life is a journey of learning in all areas of human endeavour, and that the Christian life is responding to the love of God. At-one-ment is achieved as each of us opens ourselves to becoming more and more godlike.

Further Reading

K. Armstrong, *The Case for God.*

M. J. Borg and J. D. Crossan, *The Last Week.*

J. B. Cobb, Jr., "In What Ways Can Whitehead's Process Philosophy Assist Process Theologians to Understand the Doctrine of Atonement?"

S. Finlan, *Options on Atonement in Christian Thought.*

S. J. Patterson, *Beyond the Passion.*

L. Tatman, "Atonement" and "Crucifixion", in L. Isherwood and D. McEwan, *An A to Z of Feminist Theology.*

P. Williams, "The Jesus Agenda: Christianity for a New Century".

Holy Heresy

Jim Burklo

It's part of my job as Associate Dean of Religious Life at the
University of Southern California
to read prayers.
Our The Little Chapel of Silence on campus
is a beautiful old space where anyone can sit for a while on one
of the pews
and quietly pray or meditate.

On the unadorned altar is a wooden box with a slot in it,
with pieces of paper and pens next to it. Students, staff, and visitors

write their prayers, in English, Spanish, Mandarin, and other languages,
and put them into the box.
No indication is made about what will become of the prayers.
There they sit until I retrieve them.

I find myself moved nearly to tears
by the soulful expressions on these little pieces of paper.
Longings for love. Broken hearts. Family crises.
Health challenges. Deaths and divorces. Gratitude.
Awe for the divine mystery.

Several of the prayers in Spanish
began with this address to God:
"Diosito mio . . ."

I have heard this phrase in Hispanic Protestant churches in the past.
Literally it means "my little God".
"Ito" is the diminutive form at the end of words used so often in Spanish
to address someone or to describe something dear.

It might seem a heresy to address God as "little" and as "mine".
It might seem like an attempt to shrink ineffable, transcendent divinity
down to something that can be kept in a teacup cabinet.
Yet the sincere prayers directed to "Diosito mio" belie that suggestion.

My dear little God, to those who thusly start their prayers, is, to them,
not a God they made small, but the God
who became small and dear for them.

I'm pretty sure that this phrase, "Diosito mio",
was not developed by a theologian.
I'm pretty sure that the Catholic Church didn't invent it.
I would venture the guess that this phrase comes from
the depths of the human soul.

So while it might seem to contradict the theology in Christian catechisms,
"Diosito mio" reveals something deep and basic
about our innate spirituality.
To be sure, it's a paradox to suggest
the essence of the cosmos is "little and dear".
But maybe it's a paradox with which we can live,
and let live, for the sake of bringing us closer
to the heart of ultimate reality.

Autonomy

Paul Alan Laughlin

Autonomy is perhaps the most fundamental, defining value of progressive religious thought, Christian and otherwise. The word derives from the Greek word *autonomia* ('independence'), itself a combination of two Greek words meaning 'self' and 'law', respectively. Autonomy, therefore, connotes self-governance, self-determination and independence of mind.

In a religious or theological context, being autonomous identifies oneself as the final authority in matters of belief, doctrine, and biblical interpretation, all of which must be based on one's own reason or experience or, more likely, a combination of the two. The opposite of autonomy is *heteronomy*, which means "ruled by another or others" and entails a more passive deferral in matters of belief to any of a host of outside authorities, including scripture, tradition, councils, creeds, doctrines, clergy, prophets, scholars, teachers, and even family members and friends. A progressive religious orientation is typically open to input from such external sources, but in the end is autonomous in that it insists on the right of individuals and groups to determine for themselves what to believe or think, rather than to defer to the assertions of others, however official or authoritative they may appear or claim to be.

Throughout the history of Christianity, adherents of the faith who thought for themselves and often came to conclusions contrary to those in positions of authority were often accused of *heresy* or *heterodoxy*, both of which mean "false, unorthodox, and deviant belief". But autonomy in matters of faith began to take hold and to grow in popularity and influence in Europe among the humanists of the Renaissance and framers of the Reformation in the fourteenth through sixteenth centuries. It especially flourished in the following two centuries in the form of the rationalism of the Enlightenment, often to the chagrin of ecclesiastical leaders, who rightly saw their claimed authority being challenged.

Progressive Christianity, then, can be considered an important by-product of these great movements, the modern scientific method and worldview that they produced, and above all the autonomy that they encouraged.

Further Reading

P. Rasor, *Faith without Certainty*.
N. Reynolds and W. C. Durham, *Religious Liberty in Western Thought*.

Believing

Keith Rowe

Progressive Christianity represents a mode of Christian living and believing that seeks to relate Christian believing to contemporary knowledge of life and to the questions that belong to our time and place. I
offer three images that might help us in reflecting on the nature and
form of progressive Christian believing.

The *first image* is that Christian believing is more like flowing within a living stream than defending a castle of unchanging creeds, ethical norms or ecclesiastical structures. The great words of faith and the
realities to which they point—God, Christ, Spirit, Love, Faith, Hope,
Peace—need to be explored afresh and restated in every age and every
cultural setting. Henry Nelson Wieman (1884–1975), a pioneer progressive thinker, made a helpful distinction between 'Creative Good' and
'Created Good'. Creative good is the divine energy and love flowing
through human history, healing what no longer serves human well-
being, binding humanity together, transforming what is tired, luring
creation toward deeper expressions of cooperative existence. Created
good refers to time- and culture-bound and provisional expressions of
what is believed within a particular human community. Our problem,
says Wieman, is that we become wedded to created good, while failing
to respond to the invitation of creative good to contribute to the birth
of fresh expressions of human becoming.

Progressive Christianity honours those who explore the edges
of life, challenge inherited orthodoxies or seek new words to name
emerging truth. Alfred North Whitehead (1861–1947) complained that
while changes in scientific understandings are welcomed as a triumph
of the enquiring mind, any change in religious thinking in response
to new times tends to be described as a defeat for the Christian way.
It's a triumph of the Christian spirit that in our generation we have
become more aware of what it means to be Christian in the presence
of the poor, how gay and lesbian people have a secure place within
the love of God and the life of the church, how our picture of God is
changing in response to an expanded understanding of life, how our
understanding of the Bible has expanded because of disciplined study
by biblical scholars.

The *second image* is that we are like people standing on small is-
lands of secure knowledge surrounded by a great sea of mystery. For
some awareness of mystery is simply recognition of problems yet to
be solved by human ingenuity. For progressive Christians, however,
sensitivity to mystery is a form of knowing that belongs to the deepest

dimensions of human existence. Sensitivity to mystery and to the deep down intuitions that give meaning and purpose to human living, often in spite of tough times and of superficial evidence to the contrary, is the aspect of human living and believing where the word 'God' comes alive yet without losing its somewhat elusive character. Sensitivity to wonder and mystery is a vital accompaniment to Christian believing. It's not surprising that progressive Christians tend to favour worship and music that is thoughtful, meditative, uses evocative/poetic language and evokes a sense of wonder and of mystery.

The *third image* is that Christian believing is like a conversation among explorers travelling in unexplored territory. Progressive Christianity represents a conversational style of human existence. Collectively and individually we dwell in ongoing critical conversation with the various areas and practitioners of human knowing and living that surround us; with artists and scientists, musicians and philosophers, sceptics and over-believers; psychologists and social activists, economists and historians, people of cultures other than our own and most importantly with adherents of faiths and religions other than the one by which we are shaped. God is present beyond the boundaries of the Christian Church and life-giving truth can be found in every area of human living and knowing. Various forms of progressive theology have emerged from particular conversations: process theology from conversation with developments in physics and an evolutionary world view; liberation theology asking what it means to be Christian in conversation with the poor and socially marginalised; feminist theology enquiring into the shape of Christian living and believing in conversation with women's experience; queer theology from conversation with and within the lesbian, gay, bisexual, transgendered and intersex (LGBTI) community. No one person can be in conversation with all life's diversity—that's one good reason why progressive believing is a communal enterprise.

Further Reading

M. J. Borg, *Speaking Christian.*
————, *The Heart of Christianity.*
P. Clayton, *Transforming Christian Theology.*
D. R. Griffin, *Two Great Truths.*
M. Polanyi, *The Tacit Dimension.*

A Creed for Christians

Jim Burklo

God is Love, the cosmic creativity present everywhere and in everything,
Gently urging all toward the good.

To Love we raise our awestruck praise!

Jesus embodied the Love that is God.
He loved the poor, the sick, the outcast,
He loved the unpopular, and even his own enemies.
He loved so completely, he loved so dangerously,
That it cost him his life.

As Christians we aim to serve humbly, as he did,
Resurrecting his life of Love through communion with others.

The texts and traditions of Christianity give voice to our souls,
so that we may support each other in our quests of compassion.
Love is the measure of what is worth following,
And what is not, in all religions.
So we pray for a Holy Spirit of discernment
To express our faith afresh in new times and places.

Biblical Scholarship

Gregory C. Jenks

Biblical scholarship is a distinctive set of academic approaches to the Bible that has been formed in the academy rather than the life of the church. While relevant to the teachings and practices of the church, biblical scholarship is especially focused on finding the most appropriate ways to interpret the Bible.

At the heart of contemporary biblical criticism is a commitment to the critical evaluation of evidence rather than seeking truth by appeal to special knowledge derived from revelation or enunciated by authoritative religious figures. Over the past couple of centuries, biblical criticism has been especially influenced by the European Enlightenment and—more recently—by trends in both the humanities and the sciences.

Biblical scholarship is often described under three headings, each of which represents a phase in the historical development of the discipline even though all three categories may be operating concurrently in the activities of a contemporary biblical scholar.

The first category comprises those academic methods that are essentially historical and tend to focus on some aspect of how the biblical text came to exist. These methods include textual criticism, source criticism, form criticism, redaction criticism, and social-science studies of the ancient world. The historical-critical approach has been highly influential in the development of biblical scholarship over the past 250 years, but is increasingly losing ground to approaches that focus on the text as we have it, or even the reader rather than the text and its author.

While historical-critical methods have assisted greatly with our study of the Bible, they tend to focus on the world behind the text. They can give the appearance of scientific rigor, but are essentially deconstructive as they seek to analyse the component elements of the text rather than its extant literary form. Partly for this reason the last few decades have seen the flowering of literary criticism that pays particular attention to the form in which the text now exists.

Literary criticism puts the focus on the world of the text. The text includes not just the specific passage or individual book, but the Bible as a whole. This can be seen as a flight from history, or even a tactic to avoid the problems that arise when historical-critical studies expose the ambiguities around the composition and transmission of the biblical texts. However, more positively, literary criticism takes very seriously the reality that the Bible is literature. In particular, the Bible is sacred literature and the canonical form of the Bible generates a text that is greater than the sum of its parts.

Even more recently there has been a shift of focus from the text to the reader. How is the meaning of the Bible affected by the circumstances and expectations of the reader? What insights can a feminist reading of the Bible, or a Queer reading, or a Green reading, offer to a wider community that may not routinely pay attention to these concerns when reflecting on holy living?

Further Reading

K. Armstrong, *The Bible.*
G. C. Jenks, *The Once and Future Bible.*
R. Kugler and P. Hartin, *Introduction to the Bible.*

(Biblical) Storytelling

John Shuck

Every story in the Bible and in any religion is human made.

Human beings created the story of Moses coming down the mountain with the Ten Commandments. Human beings created the story of Krishna speaking to Arjuna on the battlefield. Human beings created the story of God creating the heavens and the earth. Human beings created the story of the Risen Christ appearing before the disciples.

Once we realise all religious stories are made by human beings, the balloon pops. This doesn't lessen the value or the importance of the stories. It shifts them. Rather than external realities, they become internal creations. Now we are contemplating, marvelling, and celebrating human creativity and imagination. The stories of God or of the gods are our stories projected outward.

A philosopher whom I have come to appreciate is Don Cupitt. He writes in very clear language for non-professionals. He calls himself a radical theologian. In his book *The Meaning of the West*, he writes:

> In religion and philosophy there is a perennial dispute between two parties. There are those who think that our greatest need in life is to gain security and blessedness by attaching ourselves permanently and securely to something very much greater, stabler and more perfect than ourselves, something that transcends the passing show of existence. I'll call these people the party of metaphysics. They are philosophical realists, for whom our salvation depends upon our relation to something Big out there.
>
> The other party includes all those who think that our chief need is to be cured of the errors and discontents that rob us of our ability to enjoy life and live it to the full. I'll call these people pragmatists, or even nihilists. They say that we don't need to attach ourselves to some great big saving Fact out there; we just need deliverance from our own anxieties, our illusions and our self-concern. We just need pure freedom and life-skills.[1]

Cupitt is of the second party. For him there is no 'outside'. The self-evolving universe is, he puts it, 'outsideless'. Rather than find our purpose, search out a guide, or find our path on God's great Google Map, we instead create it.

The stories of the Bible are not stories of external realities, but stories of human beings finding themselves, and when we put ourselves in these stories they are stories of our own self-discovery. So in Genesis 1 when God creates order out of chaos, that is our task. We are the ones to create order out of chaos.

Notes

1. D. Cupitt, *Meaning of the West*, 31.

Further Reading

T. Boomershine, *Story Journey.*
D. Cupitt, *What Is a Story?*

Eraser Moon

Jim Burklo

Pale sliver moon dangling
in the turquoise dusk.
No, it's better than that!

It's all that is left of the rubbery stub
at the top of my pencil,
worn down to a thin white curve
by erasing the inadequate words
I used to try to describe it.

Christmas

Rex A. E. Hunt

The Christmas many people celebrate today seems like a timeless weaving of custom and emotion beyond the reach of ordinary history. Yet the familiar mix of cards, carols, parties, presents, tree and Santa that have come to define December 25, especially in the Southern Hemisphere, is little more than 130 years old.

Since its inception Christmas has been debated, ignored, celebrated, banned, and reshaped. As a pre-Christian festival, its traditions go back in time to changes in the seasons and the affects these changes had on people, their social life and work situations.

As a Christian event, the 'Feast of the Nativity of our Lord' (rather than 'Christmas') didn't make the Church calendar until well into the fourth century and then as a result of a series of mixed motives, including the take-over of a number of rival so-called 'pagan' festivals such as the Norse ceremonies for Odin, the birth of the Persian god Mithra and the Roman Saturnalia. Such a 'take-over' seems to be the pattern of Christianity. Expansionist religions like Christianity, writes Australian theologian Roland Boer,

> work by taking over and appropriating the symbols and practices of a whole range of non Christian belief systems.[1]

So why did this festival become popular? The conclusion seems to suggest the pre-Christian folk festivals were essentially life affirming. They said 'yes' to life while the Christianity of that time, essentially a religion of the monks, was pessimistic as regards this earth, and valued it only as a place of discipline for the life to come, which meant it was a religion of saying 'no' to the world.

In popular Christian belief it is said the foundational stories of Christmas can be found in the nativity stories of the anonymous story-tellers we call Matthew and Luke, in the Christian Scriptures. Both stories, very different from each other in general shape, atmosphere and content, came rather later in the biblical tradition—probably anything from 85 CE–100 CE. And in spite of the modern tendency to homogenise them into one classic tale, they are very different:

> . . . Luke's account is full of strong, vibrant, bright colours with just a hint of umbers in the background. The other, Matthew's account, is rich but sombre, darkly hued, and strangely shaded. Luke tells a cheerful tale, a buoyant, hopeful, joyous tale. Matthew tells a gothic tale, fascinating, disturbing, disquieting.[2]

For many Christians, Luke's story is *the* Christmas story, even though the birth itself is only briefly mentioned and is not really the focus of the story. So why these stories? One suggestion comes from the comparative study of Hellenistic biographies.

The nativity stories mimic the pattern of Hellenistic biography, where the stories of their heroes' lives were read and interpreted backwards. Each biography followed a set structure of at least five elements:

1. a genealogy revealing illustrious ancestors,
2. an unusual, mysterious, or miraculous conception,
3. an annunciation by an angel or in a dream,
4. a birth accompanied by supernatural portents, and
5. praise or forecast of great things to come, or persecution by a potential competitor.[3]

In general terms these five elements can be found in both Matthew's and Luke's infancy stories.

Liturgically, the Christmas feast first appears on the Church's calendar in Rome in 336 CE, ten years after Nicea, although it did not appear in the East until the late fourth century. Prior to that, Epiphany (or 'old Christmas', celebrated on 6 January) was seen as more important than Nativity (celebrated on 25 December). The conflict was finally smoothed over with a decision to combine Christmas with Epiphany, which liturgically became known as the 'Twelve Days of Christmas'.

So, no matter how vehemently some might decry it, Christmas is firmly established in its socio-cultural environment, in terms of that environment. And while it seems there will always be people for whom Christmas is a pious devotion rather than a festival or carnival, such people were always in the minority. The Church's so-called 'hold' over Christmas was and remains, rather tenuous. Indeed,

> it may not be going too far to say that Christmas has always been an extremely difficult holiday to *Christianize*.[4]

Notes

1. R. Boer, "Bilbies, Gumnuts and Thanksgiving", 41–42.
2. G. Griffin, "The Colour of Joy", 55.
3. L. McGaughy, "Infancy Narratives in the Ancient World".
4. S. Nissenbaum, *Battle for Christmas*, 8.

Further Reading

M. J. Borg and J. D. Crossan, *The First Christmas.*
C. A. Miles, *Christmas Customs and Traditions.*
R. J. Miller, *Born Divine.*
S. K. Roll, *Toward the Origins of Christmas.*

Christology
(in an Evolutionary World)

Keith Rowe

The Christian conviction is that in Jesus the purposes of God are expressed within human history in a unique and compelling manner. He is 'the human face of God'. Paul understood Christian life to be life 'in Christ', what John Cobb describes as "life in a field of force generated by Jesus' life, death and resurrection".[1] Those who live within the memory and continuing influence of Jesus Christ become part of the

'Christ event', a cluster of happenings that have their focus in first-century Palestine and continue to echo down the corridors of history.

Christology is the attempt to speak of the significance of Jesus Christ and what it means for human living and believing to be shaped by the way disclosed in the ministry and continuing influence of Jesus. While respecting classical christological formulae that emerged from the life of the early church and later ecumenical councils, progressive Christians claim the question of who Jesus Christ is for us, is one needing to be explored afresh in every era. For Catholic theologian Ilia Delio, "Christology can no longer be a reflection on how Jesus Christ is truly God and truly human, but now we must also reflect on how Christ is truly cosmic." The christological question as posed by progressive Christians enquires into the significance of Jesus Christ and existence 'in Christ' within an evolving universe and a human family shaped by differing understandings of life and distorted by division, violence and disrespect for creation.

Though the titles 'Jesus' and 'Christ' tend to be used interchangeably, theologically they refer to different realities. 'Jesus' is the name given to a historical figure. The term 'Christ' draws on imagery belonging to first-century Jewish hope for the coming of one who would usher in the reign of God. John Cobb suggests the first Christians may have erred in applying this title to Jesus for the world of peace associated with the title did not and has not arrived. However, as Christianity spread in the gentile world the meaning of the title expanded and came to refer to the creative and transforming energy of God present in all of life and breathing the way of life pioneered by Jesus into the human family.

A theologian who has explored what it means to speak and live for Christ in an evolving universe is the Jesuit palaeontologist Pierre Teilhard de Chardin (1881–1955) whose writings were refused publication by the Vatican till after his death but who today represents a rich resource for progressive Christians. Following his lead, we may say of Jesus that in his teaching, living and dying he represents an evolutionary possibility for humanity. If humanity, collectively and individually, were to learn to live within the possibilities for life pioneered by Jesus and allow them to be re-expressed within the differing cultures and faiths of our world, humanity would move to a higher stage in the evolution of life and the fulfilment of the purposes of God.

Progressive Christians take seriously the findings and emerging consensus of biblical scholarship that in his teaching and living the historical Jesus invited people to a new consciousness and a mode of living described as life within the commonwealth or kingdom of God, a life marked by generosity, hospitality, forgiveness, peacemaking and immersion in the life of God. This rediscovery of the essentially counter-cultural and life-changing impact of his living and dying, teaching and continuing significance impacts on the progressive Christian understanding of what it means to live 'in Christ'.

For Teilhard, Christ is the very energy of God, "a sort of blood stream or nervous system running through the totality of life".[2] Jesus is an incarnation of the Christ but Christ is more than the historical Jesus. Christ is the very heart of the universe, the energy of creative change, drawing the universe together into new expressions of community and immersion in the love of God. Christ is present at the heart of the material world, the divine clue as to the structure and meaning of the entire universe, "animating the whole range of things from top to bottom".[3] Creation ceases to be a garden from which we have been ejected because of the sin of an ancestor, and is welcomed as a work in process of completion, indwelt and energised by the presence of Christ. John Cobb uses similar words when he describes Christ as "the principle of life and light, creation and redemption which is the presence of God in all things". Teilhard describes the evolution of the universe as Christogenesis—the development of the influence of Christ in all things guiding all creation toward unity motivated by love.

The human destiny is to participate in the ongoing work of Christ in an evolving universe, sharing in the building of community, peace, hospitality and understanding in a violent and divided world. Jesus was a human, like us, whose faithfulness to this servant way emerged from struggle and tough choices. But he served the purposes of God with such consistency and grace that it's appropriate to describe him as unique. His sensitivity to divine possibility and his courage in living into those directions is an example that inspires us, yet remains beyond the reach of our best efforts. In this sense there is a great gulf between Jesus and us, yet we are on the same road, co-creators in an evolving universe and growing in sensitivity to the presence and call of Christ.

Notes

1. J. B. Cobb, Jr., and D. R. Griffin, *Process Theology*, 103.
2. P. Teilhard de Chardin, *Hymn of the Universe*, 41.
3. P. Teilhard de Chardin, *Christianity and Evolution*, 89.

Further Reading

M. J. Borg, *Meeting Jesus for the First Time.*
I. Delio, *Christ in Evolution.*
P. Teilhard de Chardin, *Christianity and Evolution.*

The Clergy Letter Project

Michael Zimmerman

The Clergy Letter Project is a grassroots organization of thousands of religious leaders and scientists from around the world who have come together to demonstrate that religion and science can comfortably co-exist.

The Project began in 2004 when Michael Zimmerman began circulating what has become known as *The Christian Clergy Letter*—a two-paragraph statement encouraging the teaching of evolution. The Letter, signed by more than 12,600 Christian clergy members in the United States as of January 2011, urges school boards "to preserve the integrity of the science curriculum by affirming the teaching of the theory of evolution as a core component of human knowledge". It also explains the relationship between religious understanding and scientific knowledge: "Religious truth is of a different order from scientific truth. Its purpose is not to convey scientific information but to transform hearts."

Companion Letters have been developed for American Rabbis and Unitarian Universalist clergy members in the United States. Like the Christian Clergy Letter, these two Letters also promote a better understanding of the relationship between religion and science.

The Clergy Letter Project was designed with three primary goals in mind:

- To demonstrate that religion and evolutionary biology are compatible;
- To demonstrate that fundamentalist ministers who demand that people choose between religion and modern science are not speaking for all religious leaders; and
- To raise the quality of the discourse on this important topic.

In an attempt to reach more people with the positive message that it is perfectly possible to be religious and scientific, The Clergy Letter Project created *Evolution Sunday* in 2006. This event, scheduled on Sunday, 12 February, the 197th anniversary of the birth of Charles Darwin, was an opportunity for congregations all around the world to discuss the ways in which their faith and scientific understanding could strengthen each other. In 2008, in an attempt to be more welcoming to those who worship on days other than Sundays, the name of Evolution Sunday was changed to *Evolution Weekend*. Since its inception, thousands of congregations representing twenty countries on six continents have participated in some fashion. The Clergy Letter Project's website lists hundreds of sermons delivered on the relationship between religion and science.

Scientists have joined The Clergy Letter Project as well via a robust list of scientific consultants. These scientists, more than 950 strong as of January 2011, represent thirty different countries from six continents. They have agreed to answer questions posed in their areas of expertise by clergy members. The collaborative efforts of clergy and scientists demonstrate productive ways in which members of these two disciplines can work together.

One of the most important messages The Clergy Letter Project transmits is that the struggle some portray as being between religion and science, is actually a battle between different religious worldviews. Those who believe in a literal interpretation of the Bible may well be uncomfortable with evolutionary theory—but thousands of religious leaders representing the majority of religious traditions have absolutely no such discomfort.

Further Reading

The Clergy Letter Project website: www.theclergyletterproject.org
M. Dowd, *Thank God for Evolution*.
National Academy of Sciences, *Science, Evolution, and Creationism*.
M. Zimmerman, "Redefining the Creation/Evolution Controversy".

(Competitive) Piety

Gary Bouma

Competitive piety takes many forms, nearly all unhelpful and many positively dangerous.

When I was growing up, my continuing experience with people of faith has honed my sensitivity to this spiritual disease. The denomination of my youth considered itself vastly superior to all others and much closer to God as a result of going to church *twice* on Sundays. Oncers were slackers. We were also distinctive in the harsh form of Calvinism we held to and our exclusion of moral failures.

Another form of competitive piety is heard among those who say, "You believe in one irrational belief, but I believe in three; my faith must be stronger than yours." In Lent some Christians engage in the competitive piety of "I have given up chocolate, alcohol *and* sex, but you have only given up cheese; surely I am closer to God. God must love me more." And that is where the spiritual disease becomes evident. Your sacrifice is less than mine. I am willing to sacrifice my life and indeed the lives of others for God; surely God will give me the greatest reward.

Any spirituality that hinges on a love that is conditional, and an acceptance that must be earned, is diseased and grounded in a defective understanding of God, of grace and of love. The conditionality of the love of the God central to competitive piety reflects the conditional love with which many were loved by their parents. Unconditional love and acceptance is hard enough to find and receive, let alone give.

The notion that we go about earning God's love and rewards is similarly flawed, yet key to those forms of competitive piety that lead to taking a hard line in rejecting certain groups, in vilifying others and in the extreme to acts of violence in the name of God.

I have even noticed a form of competitive piety among progressive Christians. "I believe in less than you do, and so the god of Reason must smile more beatifically upon me and smirk at you."

As a disease, competitive piety seems to me to be doing well. As experiential forms of spirituality become more central to twenty-first-century religions I expect to see and hear examples along the lines of the numbers and intensities of experiences racked up as notches on the belt of competitive experiential piety.

The challenge is, as it ever has been, to receive the unconditional love that is there, wallow in the acceptance that is there more fundamentally than all the rejection, and to sustain hope in self and other.

Further Reading
G. Bouma, *Being Faithful in Diversity.*

Healing

Jim Burklo

I worked in an agency that served hungry and homeless people.
One day a woman came to us for bread and milk, which we set out in our
lobby to give away with no questions asked.
I said hello, and we started to chat.

She revealed that she was a recovering alcoholic.
"What's your recovery process like?" I asked.
"For me," she said, "healing is like that of the lepers who came to Jesus
asking to be cured. He told them to go and show themselves to the priest.

"It wasn't until they turned away and went toward the priest that they were healed. It wasn't the priest who healed them, and Jesus didn't claim the credit, either.

"They were healed along the way to the priest.
The healing comes along the way to healing."

Creativity as God

Rex A. E. Hunt

Thinking about God as a supernatural or personal being, or primarily in personalistic or human-centred terms, has become increasingly problematic in our times for progressives. Such images and language do not fit the reality we see or experience.

Two contemporary theologians who faced this issue in their writings, have offered what could be helpful—be they similar—suggestions.

Karl Peters, a retired professor of Philosophy and Religion, has developed a model called 'naturalistic theism'. Peters specifically bases his model of God or the Sacred on the Darwinian idea of random variation and natural selection—God as the creative process rather than a being who creates the world. He writes:

> One aspect of this two-part [Darwinian] process is the emergence of new possibilities in nature, human history, and personal living. The other is the selection of some of these possibilities to continue.[1]

He suggests that part of the purpose of living is to engage in experimenting with new patterns of living—testing the boundaries.

> The creative process, which is the sacred centre of this evolving universe, continually brings new things into being even as it continues some traditional ways of living. This process is what we have understood as the divine.[2]

Another scholar to offer non-personal metaphors for God is Gordon Kaufman, the Harvard 'constructive' theologian. Arguing that the idea of God is an imaginative construct, he states what he sees as the problem with traditional religious language, as expressed in the biblical verse, John 3:16. Kaufman suggests that this much-loved sentence sums up beautifully a central theme of traditional Christianity. But for many thoughtful or progressive Christians today, sentences like this scarcely make sense.

Though they may be lovely poetry, whether they tell us anything about the real world with which we must come to terms every day may seem dubious.[3]

He boldly suggests an alternative 'language' beyond the images of biblical thinking:

> . . . I have for some years been developing and elaborating a conception of God as simply the *creativity* that has brought forth the world and all its contents, from the Big Bang all the way down to the present.[4]

Imagining God as *creativity*, he suggests, enables Christians to be much more attuned to what the modern sciences have been teaching us about our lives and the world in which we live. And makes it possible to bridge the divide often felt by progressives between religious faith and scientific knowledge.

Such non-personalistic ways of conceiving 'G-o-d', challenge the 'taken for granted' language and thought patterns of traditional Christianity. But then, theology has always warned of the dangers of religious language.

So where should a theological language for the twenty-first century begin? Not with 'G-o-d' as a personal Creator of the world and we humans as the climax of that creation, but as *Creativity* itself (or following Kaufman, as *serendipitous creativity*), manifest throughout the cosmos. That is, in shaping theology which uses the language and thought patterns of an alternative to the traditional human-centred language, which focuses on existential issues. In such language and theology the symbol 'G-o-d' designates "that creativity, that mystery, which undergirds our human existence in all its complexity and all its diversity".[5]

When the symbol 'G-o-d' is reconstructed in this way, perhaps progressive Christians can begin to feel more at home in this vast cosmos, with others, with all forms of life, with the sacred—awake to everything—living in harmony with the larger scheme of things as we know it.

Notes

1. K. E. Peters, *Dancing with the Sacred*, 1–2.
2. K. E. Peters, 82.
3. G. D. Kaufman, *Jesus and Creativity*, ix.
4. G. D. Kaufman, xi.
5. G. D. Kaufman, *God, Mystery, Diversity*, 109.

Further Reading

M. Benedikt, *God Is the Good We Do.*
G. D. Kaufman, *In the Beginning . . . Creativity.*

Dubious Doctrines and Suspicious Scriptures

Paul Alan Laughlin

As indicated in The Fundamentals (see entry below), progressive Christians tend to have serious doubts about such formal doctrines as the Trinity, the Fall and Original Sin, Hell and Eternal Damnation, Divine Inspiration and Inerrancy of the Bible, the Virgin Birth and Divinity of Jesus, the Atoning Death and Bodily Resurrection of Jesus, the Second Coming of Christ, and a shopping list of other end-time events: the Rapture, the Millennium, the General Resurrection, the Last Judgment, and the battle of Armageddon.

Progressives tend to question, as well, literal historicity of the alleged events and persons featured in the stories of the Hebrew Bible and New Testament, beginning with the act of Creation and ending perhaps with the portrait of God painted there and in the stories that follow. Nor are major human biblical players and events exempt from progressive Christians' rational scrutiny—including Noah and the Flood, Abraham and his Covenant, Moses and his Exodus, and Job and his travails.

In the New Testament, the attention of progressive Christians is mostly on Jesus and his sayings and deeds, while their reservations especially include his supposedly miraculous conception, the many miracles he reportedly performed, and his purported resurrection. The openness of progressive Christians to the principles and findings of modern science and its effects on historical thinking and biblical interpretation runs through all such doctrinal and biblical criticisms; and the usual result is either a radical reinterpretation or an outright rejection of the teachings and stories in question. Often added as matters of contention between traditionalist and progressive Christians—and occasionally grounds for charges of 'heresy'—are such practicalities as the proper role and status of women in the church, especially as regards ordination to clerical offices; homosexuality and gay marriage; and birth control and abortion—many of which issues transcend the otherwise seemingly clear Catholic-Protestant-Sectarian distinctions, and all of which reflect the diversity and disparity of beliefs that give progressive Christians still more to ponder.

Further Reading

P. A. Laughlin, *Remedial Christianity.*
J. S. Spong, *Why Christianity Must Change or Die.*

Earliest Christianities

Gregory C. Jenks

We tend to imagine our spiritual tradition as enjoying a golden era when it began, and to anticipate another golden era at some point in the future. Anything less at either end is disappointing—even underwhelming. Most of what we think we know about the early church comes from the Acts of the Apostles. Acts was written by an anonymous early Christian author, whom we call Luke, since he also wrote the Gospel of Luke. Acts presents the impression of a unified Christianity that slowly succumbed to divisions around personality, rituals and false teaching.

The letters of Paul provide a very different picture. These letters are the earliest writings in the New Testament (NT) and they show Paul engaged in acrimonious arguments with members of his own communities as well as with leaders of other factions in the early Jesus movement. Elsewhere in the NT we catch a glimpse of these other factions, including a group associated with the legacy of Peter, another that followed James, and at least one other major faction associated with John. Even the writings associated with Paul can be seen as coming from three different phases of early Christian history: the first generation in the time of Paul, another generation after the first leaders had died (Colossians, Ephesians, 2 Thessalonians), and a third generation early in the second century (1 & 2 Timothy, Titus).

Rather than beginning with a coherent set of beliefs and clear leadership structures, the earliest Jesus movement is better understood as a diverse and loose religious movement within Second Temple Judaism. As this informal association of communities addressed new challenges, there were intense disagreements over beliefs, practices, leadership, authority, and sacred texts.

The period between the death of Jesus in 30 CE and the first of Paul's letters around 50 CE is the least understood phase, and in some ways one of the most critical periods. Had those first followers of Jesus not kept alive the "dangerous memory of Jesus",[1] the legacy of Jesus may not have been much different from that of his mentor, John the Baptist.

When we look outside the New Testament, we see from the numerous non-canonical gospels, the apocryphal acts of various apostles, and the continuing controversies over doctrine, leadership and rituals, that early Christianity was highly diverse. The careful demarcation between orthodox and heretic is itself a marker of these divisions running deeply through the fabric of earliest Christianity. The victorious party chose to describe themselves as 'orthodox' and to dismiss their opponents as 'gnostics' and 'heretics'.

Luke-Acts celebrates the ascendency of the Pauline tradition over more conservative Jewish expressions of Christianity seen in Matthew, James and Peter, as well as over the more radical gnostic tendencies seen in the Johannine writings. Luke did his work so well that for most of the last two thousand years his account of Christian origins, written from the perspective of the second-century winners, has been mistaken for a description of what really happened.

Notes
1. E. A. Johnson, "The Word Was Made Flesh".

Further Reading
D. L. Duggan, *Constantine's Bible.*
B. D. Ehrman, *Lost Christianities.*
———, *The New Testament.*

Eco-Spirituality

Noel Preston

When theology and ethics are centred on the earth and its community of life, and belief in god is no longer theistic, what implications are there for personal prayer, public worship and communal expressions of faith? Moreover, how is 'the inner life' of practitioners of eco-theology nurtured? These are core questions for *eco-spirituality.*

In a theistic paradigm, prayer is dialogue with the divine being in the expectation that interventionist answers might follow which, for instance, alter the course of natural events like diseases. For pan-entheists, the idea of intercessory prayer is clearly problematic just as the idea of singing praises to one's god might be. Prayer is less about crying out to a god and more about seeking a state of union with the spirit of life and love. So understood, prayer is living in a way that seeks connectedness with all beings. The practice of meditation is likely to be an important component of this spirituality, especially as it nurtures compassion and insight.

Establishing suitable eco-spirituality rituals, (what I call 'celebrations of being'), may be a challenge, though rituals like grace at the family meal table can be a simple start, with a focus on the interdependence of all life forms. Different pathways will suit different people at different stages of their lives. Some might find practices built around communal activity more suitable while others are nurtured by solitude; some might be enriched more by an innovative use of symbols while others respond to the challenge of inspirational writings or music; some might be awakened to a sense of connectedness to nature by getting down and dirty in the garden while others are awakened by illness, which helps them discover how they are embodied and connected to all bodies.

Summing up . . . Eco-spirituality forms our identity and character in ways that connect us with what has been termed 'the Ground of our Being'. Arising from a fundamental reverence, awe and gratitude for life's unity, balance, difference and connectedness, eco-spirituality is centred on grace, the gift of unconditional, inclusive and empowering love, drawing on wellsprings of wisdom that are both contemplative and prophetic. It is a spirituality which challenges the illusions that easily capture us—for instance, that consumerism makes us happy, or even that there is a god out there who will save us; this spirituality enjoins us to pay attention to where we are, to tend our garden and care for our neighbourhood. In harmony with the Earth and the quest for life abundant, eco-spirituality calls us to act justly, love tenderly and walk humbly with our god (Mic 6:8), while, in the words of slogans popularised in the 1970s, we think globally, act locally and live simply so others may simply live.

In its practical, even political, expression, eco-spirituality works for eco-justice: the double-edged challenge of achieving environmental sustainability on the one hand and social justice in the human community on the other. It envisages a major re-orientation of human cultures to fairer and more sustainable cultures.

Further Reading

L. G. Geering, *Coming Back to Earth.*
N. Preston, *Beyond the Boundary.*

Faith

Jim Burklo

I want the faith of a madrone tree in a redwood forest.

Every day for a year, I walked along a certain path in the woods
of Northern California.
I entered an area where tall redwoods were replacing shorter hardwoods.
One day I looked up, and noticed something strange.
A mature, sinewy madrone tree
was growing next to a middle-aged redwood.

The madrone, angling out to reach for the sun,
leaned against the redwood that was starving it of light.
The madrone was shorter, but its wood was denser.
A thick branch of the madrone was cutting into the redwood trunk,
squeaking and making a little puff of fine sawdust
with each breath of the wind.
The redwood had formed blistering burls on either side
of the deepening wound in its trunk.
Every day, with each breeze, the madrone
sawed just a little bit deeper
into its redwood nemesis.

I could see that the madrone was going to prevail.
It was going to cut off the top of the redwood sooner than
the redwood could shadow it completely from the sunshine.
But I wasn't sure if it would happen in my lifetime.

I want the faith of a madrone tree in a redwood forest.

Ethics

Noel Preston

Before they were branded 'Christians' and before orthodoxy of belief
was dominant, first-century followers of Jesus were apparently known
as followers of 'the Way'—an ethic, if you like.

The best of religion always demands an ethical response. That is why the Golden Rule is found in the teachings of all major faiths and why the World Parliament of Religions has been able to articulate a global ethic. That said we need to note there is no necessary connection between ethics and religion or faith. It is also self-evident that good, moral people may not have religious beliefs, while believers are not necessarily morally good. Likewise, progressive Christians, who have moved beyond traditional theism, have no mortgage on what might be labelled 'a progressive ethic'. However, those who are attempting to move beyond their religious traditions are challenged to find a spirituality that supports them in confronting contemporary ethical challenges. Within this spirituality they emphasize living an ethical life—one that is consistent with the following account.

Christian or otherwise, ethics addresses the overarching questions: "How *ought* we live?" And, "What kind of person ought we *be*?" Others arise when we address these questions: "How do we journey through life with a maturing will and vision, despite the ambiguities and limitations of the human condition?" This question points to what some call 'grace', the inclusive and unconditional love that redeems our mistakes. When our ethical response is bracketed by (costly, not cheap) grace, it not only allows realism to modify idealism, it also rejects a harsh, legalistic, judgmental morality (too often characteristic of religious ethics) while emphasizing a compassionate ethic of new possibilities.

A progressive ethic is *situational or contextual,* responding to life's realities, rather than being based on abstract, prescribed moral rules. As well as being situational or contextual, a progressive ethic is *relational* and therefore compatible with the teaching of Jesus that law or morality rest on two commandments only: Love God and Love your neighbor. Such loving requires *right relating*—a term that has been used by progressives and their supporters in church debates about sexuality, because it puts the focus on the quality of relationships rather than the nature of acts.

Because all life is interconnected and inter-related, right relating is at the centre of all ethical responsibilities, personal and social, relating rightly to ourselves, our families, our communities, our god and to the Earth itself. So, an ethic responsive to contemporary challenges must be an *eco-centric ethic,* enhancing ecological systems and living communities, non-human as well as human.

This ethic is also *transformative,* guided by compassion expressed as social justice. That is, it is radically inclusive and committed to the common good, valuing the interests of all (not just those of ourselves and our kin), and especially the most vulnerable. Complex social policy questions are begged in all this. So, a transformative ethic presumes that when we sign up to this vision we must find ways to be politically active, working for the social and public good because the resources of Earth belong to all Earth's beings, including future generations. Indeed it becomes an ethic of eco-justice.

Further Reading

J. A. Hill, *Ethics in the Global Village.*
N. Preston, *Beyond the Boundary.*

The Problem of Evil

Lorraine Parkinson

Ground zero in progressive Christian thought is the elimination of belief in an interventionist God. Rejection of belief in a God who intervenes in human affairs and the affairs of nature has brought about profound changes in Christian understandings of the sacred, including the 'problem of evil'.

Traditionally, God the intervening omnipotent deity has been held directly responsible for every action of humanity, either bad or good:

> "God acts for the good through individuals, even if they don't know it."
>
> "Tragedies and catastrophes must have a purpose; nothing happens that is not part of 'God's plan'."
>
> "It's too bad that little Johnny died in the road accident, but God wanted another little flower in heaven's garden."
>
> "The people killed in the earthquake must have done something wrong."

Progressive theologians have distanced themselves from beliefs of those kinds about God. One understanding of the term progressive Christianity is that it embraces new knowledge of humanity, Planet Earth, and the whole cosmos. That knowledge informs the argument that the potential for evil is an essential element in the structure of the universe and in human moral development, involving choices between good and evil.

Not least in progressive thinking is the realisation that if God does not intervene physically in the world, then belief in Jesus as the divinely sent 'Christ' is standing on shaky ground. If God has not 'acted' to orchestrate the redemption of humanity from (God-inflicted) punishment for evil, belief in Jesus as the 'Christ' has neither credibility nor purpose. Out of this comes progressive rejection of the theology of original sin and the 'reward and punishment' concepts of heaven and hell. This development necessitates a profound rethinking of the significance of Easter, and of traditional symbols and metaphors associated with the Eucharist and Baptism. Repercussions for the future of the church are immeasurable.

In all of this there are unlimited opportunities for new and positive images of God. There is the potential to lift from God the mantle of unloving director of evil acts such as terrorist bombings or natural occurrences such as cyclones, as punishment for human sin. God is also freed from the role of whimsical answerer of prayer, where some requests are granted; others are not.

The problem of evil in a world created by a good God has confounded the best of christologically-constrained thinkers. A progressive restatement of Christianity which rejects christological dogma and embraces philosophical and scientific scholarship alongside Jesus' teaching, holds enormous potential. It offers the best hope for acknowledging the essential role of evil's potential in the freedom of both humanity and the natural world. It also offers hope for working *with* the God who created a world containing both good and evil, in developing the best possible world—what Jesus called the Kingdom of God. This transformed understanding of the 'problem of evil' is at the heart of the 'new reformation' of Christian thought called progressive Christianity.

Further Reading

M. McC. Adams and R. M. Adams, *The Problem of Evil.*
L. Parkinson, *The World According to Jesus.*
J. Polkinghorne, *Belief in God in an Age of Science.*

Faith

Rex A. E. Hunt

The comment caught my eye! Andrew Greeley is a poet, priest and sociologist. His writings are always interesting. In one such reflection he made when writing about faith, he said:

> There is no such thing as a little faith any more than there is a little pregnancy. Faith is an overwhelming power no matter how weak it may seem.[1]

It tickled my fancy, so to speak. So I thought I would check out some others and their 'faith' comments.

Australian Val Webb suggested: "Faith is the experience of the individual, not a system of dogmas to be accepted. It is a way of seeing, a consciousness of another dimension."[2] Gordon Kaufman in his book *In Face of Mystery*, agrees with W. C. Smith, Professor Emeritus of the Comparative History of Religion at Harvard, that up until the last two hundred years, both 'faith' and 'belief'

> were used primarily to express one's basic commitment in life, to acknowledge that one was giving oneself whole-heartedly to a particular cause or way of life or activity; they were virtually never used (as they usually are today) to suggest that the statement we are now making, though personally important to us, is perhaps somewhat doubtful.[3]

My theology mentor, Henry Nelson Wieman, meanwhile, seemed to sum them all up with:

> [Faith] is not a verbal statement. It is a way of life.[4]

They didn't say anything about a set of beliefs or affirmations even though honest theological thinking is important.

They didn't say anything about providing answers to a set of questions even though an intelligent religion is healthier than an unbelievable one.

They didn't say anything about shooting God into the hearts of others as we so often experience in the words of many evangelical or conservative Christians. Rather, their comments invite us to recognise and acknowledge the presentness of God already there!

Progressives suggest that Jesus recognised the presence of faith in the most unlikely of places. For, they generally suggest, faith is an *action*, a *commitment*, a *trust*, rather than a commodity or belief system. And in most cases it is an action, a launching out, a moving on against what appears to be overwhelming odds. For where there is radical questioning and doubt, there is also the possibility of new beginnings, of imagination, of hope.

We are always becoming. To be alive is to be becoming. Change is. Life refuses to be embalmed alive. And this is what faith is all about: a way of living, an attitude, a vision, that creates us daily.

The suggestion that we need to have faith *with* Jesus rather than faith *in* Jesus, makes sense to me.

Notes

1. A. Greeley, "Homilies" website.
2. V. Webb, *In Defense of Doubt*, 3.
3. G. D. Kaufman, *In Face of Mystery*, 346.
4. H. N. Wieman, *Intellectual Foundation of Faith*, 3.

Further Reading

C. H. Hedrick, *When Faith Meets Reason.*

V. Webb, *In Defense of Doubt.*

A 'Fallen' World?

John Shuck

I have heard it said quite often that we live in a fallen world. Some say this is the basis for the Christian religion. That assumption is rarely challenged. Two arguments are presented in favor of this assumption. One is theological and the other is experiential.

The theological argument comes from the story of Adam and Eve and their expulsion from the garden. This argument is rather weak as everyone (except for hard-core fundamentalists), knows that Adam and Eve are mythological. Not only is this story a myth, but as such, it has multiple meanings. One could read the story as the rise of consciousness rather than a 'Fall' into sin. Since it is a myth, why base our view of the world on it? One could choose any number of myths if myth is what we are after.

The experiential argument carries a bit more weight.

We experience death and suffering. If the world wasn't fallen there would be no death or suffering, so the argument goes. Let's look at death first. If there was no death there would be no life. Everything that lives, dies. Imagine how Earth would manage if there was no death. If some life-form were able to live indefinitely, it would take over, and then eventually it would die as there would be nothing left to eat. The moon is without death. Nothing dies on the moon. Nothing lives on it either.

To say that Earth is fallen because there is death is to disparage life and Earth itself. Life and death is what is. Any theology that is anti-death is therefore anti-Earth and anti-life. Classic Christian theology wants escape from death and therefore Earth. Earth is bad and fallen. Apparently, this view would have us live forever as bodiless spirits on the moon. It is Easter with plastic lilies. I would call that Hell.

The second part of the experiential argument is that Earth is fallen because we suffer. What is suffering?

Suffering is a subjective experience in response to the cycle of life and death. Suffering means we have feelings. My computer does not suffer. But I wouldn't want to be it. Certainly there are degrees of suffering. A critical part of our human quest is to be compassionate with those who suffer, including ourselves. As conscious human beings we try to alleviate excessive suffering. We also try not to cause suffering to others (that is, through violence). Like death, suffering is part of the package of life. Without suffering there would be no consciousness, no feeling, no passion. It would not be life as we know it. Death and suffering is what it means to be alive. Death is a biological necessity for life to occur, and suffering is what it means to be conscious of death. Without suffering we are not conscious, and without death we are not alive.

To say that Earth is fallen because there is suffering is to disparage consciousness. Some forms of theology argue that only human beings are fallen. The rest of creation is fine, but human beings are captured by sin. If humanity wasn't 'fallen' we would not do bad things or think bad thoughts. What is considered good and bad is subjective as well. What is considered good in one context is considered bad in another and vice versa. We have drives, most of them unconscious. Sometimes our decisions bring ourselves and others greater happiness and blessedness and sometimes not. At times we compete and at other times we cooperate.

To say that we are sinful and fallen is to disparage humanity. We are who we are. We are learning, often the hard way, about what can bring us more blessedness and what does not.

I do not think there is any advantage seeing the world or seeing human beings as fallen. We are evolving. Each day we increase individually and collectively in consciousness. I think if there is a task for us, it is to enjoy what is and to do what we can, so future generations can enjoy it as well. We experience bliss. We suffer. We live. We die. And I wouldn't wish it any different.

Further Reading

R. Holloway, *Between the Monster and the Saint.*
G. C. Jenks, *The Once and Future Bible.*
W. Loader, *Jesus and the Fundamentalism of His Day.*
E. Pagels, *Adam, Eve, and the Serpent.*

Feminist Theology

Val Webb

Feminist theology is an earlier progressive theology. From early times, Christian doctrine has been grounded in negativity towards, and even hatred of, women, claiming their subordinate role, natural inferiority and the source of evil, argued from biblical texts and patriarchal cultural myths. Any challenges to this over the centuries have been short-lived.

Current feminist theology dates from the late 1950's when enough women entered theological colleges, forming a collective voice confronting male cultural assumptions and biblical interpretation. In 1960, Valerie Saiving questioned the teaching that the human condition was anxiety brought on by the need for self-assertion in order to manipulate and organize the world for one's purposes (existentialism). 'Sin' was the addressing of this angst by magnifying one's power and making oneself like God. The remedy was total self-giving love, ignoring one's own interests and seeking only others' good. For Saiving, this 'sin' was not *her* experience as a self-giving woman without public power. She concluded that such theology was shaped by male experiences and that women's 'sin' was the opposite—constant self-surrendering rather than claiming their personhood and power as women "made in God's image".

Feminist scholars focus on women's experience, believing that the gospel must be good news for women as well as men. Feminist theological reflection begins with experience rather than male-created doctrines imposed on women, and identifies transformative ways of being in the world that reflect women's experiences.

Biblical scholar Marcus Borg calls feminist theology the most important development in theology in his lifetime, giving a fresh vantage point from which to do theology. Feminist biblical scholars have re-examined biblical texts long used against women, reinterpreting them or declaring them obsolete products of patriarchal culture rather than Divine Law. Texts like Gal 3:28—"There is no longer Jew or Greek, there is no longer slave or free, there is no longer male and female; you are all one in Christ Jesus"—are claimed against later pseudo-Pauline texts that returned women to subordination under Greco-Roman household codes. Women scholars also critique the use of the Adam and Eve story against women, as well as masculine metaphors such as the Trinity, replacing Father, Son and Holy Spirit with gender-neutral Creator, Sustainer and Redeemer. Feminine images for God and non-anthropomorphic images such as 'Spirit' further de-centre the male Father God image and its implications.

Women's experience is not homogenous, however, thus Feminist *theologies* emerged. Black women identified different types of oppression, giving birth to Womanist theology, followed by Mujerista (Latina), African, Asian, Indigenous, Post-Colonial, Queer and Eco Feminist theologies, and more. In each case (as for progressive theology), theology is seen as a human construction dependent on the context of those doing the theology, rather than eternal 'truths', and biblical texts from ancient patriarchal cultures are challenged when they no longer reflect contemporary worldviews.

Since feminist theology is about everyone having an equal voice in every conversation of life, it has provided a theological model for other experiences of religious and societal oppression and exclusion.

Further Reading

C. P. Christ, *She Who Changes*.
E. A. Johnson, *Quest for the Living God*.
E. Schüssler Fiorenza, *In Memory of Her*.
V. Webb, *Why We're Equal*.

The Fundamentals

Paul Alan Laughlin

Given their penchant for autonomy (see entry above) in matters of belief, progressive Christians have typically found many if not most of the traditional tenets of the faith, the so-called orthodox doctrines, to be problematic. The doctrines in question include those promulgated over the centuries by the Roman Catholic Church, and later, by the various Protestants bodies.

With respect to modern progressive Christianity, however, a good place to begin might be the 'Fundamentals', or essential beliefs of the faith often listed by fundamentalist Protestants, who themselves accept many of the Catholic and Protestant doctrines, but rework them and add to them. These Fundamentals were originally presented in the early twentieth century and named after a twelve-volume series of pamphlets, *The Fundamentals: A Testimony to the Truth*, which was published between 1910 and 1915 by the Bible Institute of Los Angeles for the purpose of bolstering Protestant orthodoxy against a host of perceived modern threats, not the least of which was progressivism's antecedent, liberalism.

The actual beliefs subsequently pegged as Fundamentals were at first five in number: (1) the divine inspiration and inerrancy of the Bible; (2) the Virgin Birth of Jesus Christ, which was taken to imply his divinity as well; (3) the death of Jesus as an act of atonement; (4) the bodily resurrection of Jesus; and (5) the historicity of Jesus' miracles. These staples have sometimes been revised or augmented by various fundamentalist groups to include other important beliefs, chief among them being the Second Coming of Christ and its attendant eschatological events (such as the Rapture, the Millennium, the Last Judgment, and the Battle of Armageddon). The divinity of Jesus implied in number three has sometimes been given a place in the list all its own, as have Hell and Eternal Damnation, the Trinity, and the Fall and Original Sin, to name but a few.

Progressive Christians, who are largely defined by their inquisitiveness and independence of thought (autonomy), naturally question traditional doctrines; and many if not most have found some or all of these troubling.

Further Reading

B. Bawer, *Stealing Jesus.*
J. S. Spong, *Rescuing the Bible from Fundamentalism.*

Who Made It?

Jim Burklo

At the children's museum, looking at a magnificent striped sea-shell,
Our four year old granddaughter asked my wife,
"Who made it?"
After a sigh and a pause, my self-described atheist wife answered,
"God."

When she told me this story, she asked me,
her ordained Christian pastor husband,
how I would have answered.

I responded by stretching my arms outward, upward,
downward, behind, beyond,
then gesturing inward, up and down my body with my hands,
then outward again.
"That's who made it," I said.

God

James Veitch

There is one broad way of thinking about God. It is the one familiar to all who have grown up in the Church.

God is the creator of all that is and who exists outside of us and our world. Over time, God has spoken to humans through special people and ultimately in and through the life of Jesus: a Jewish resident of the town of Nazareth who was executed by the Roman government of his day, but whom God raised from the dead as a special sign that God's presence is for real in our world.

God spoke in and through the words of the Bible and in and through the lives of women and men who have belonged to the Church—an institution he founded, that was led initially by his special friends—called disciples and apostles. God is thus known to have broken into our human world to tell us humans about our salvation and to establish a special relationship with people of all ages.

Jesus provides us humans with a human face of this God, and the words of the Bible help us to keep loyal to God, and the presence of God (in the words of the Bible and through the sacraments of the Church) nurtures the people who respond to this word and to the promise of salvation. Humans who are believers can keep in touch with God through prayer (speaking to and with God and listening to and for his voice), reading the Bible, and through sharing in the sacrament that commemorates the death and resurrection of Jesus—called variously the Mass, the Eucharist or Communion. At the end of their lives believers join God and Jesus in heaven—until then, their lives are nurtured and resourced by the spirit or presence of God.

This understanding of God was shaped and moulded by some of the best minds of their generation: Augustine, Anselm of Canterbury, Thomas Aquinas and John Calvin. From the end of the eighteenth century this way of thinking about God came under pressure. Philosophers such as Kant, Hegel, Nietzsche and Kierkegaard, paved the way for new ways of thinking to emerge.

Those who studied the Bible and who learned about the cultural contexts for the writings in the Bible, discovered a more ambiguous story than the one sketched above. As scientists studied the planet Earth and its context in its and other solar systems (starting with Copernicus and Galileo), a different understanding of creation emerged. Those who studied the history of the Church found a rather different story of human frailty along with successes and failures—hardly the stuff of divinely ordained efforts.

A major attempt to respond to the issues but still keep a revised understanding of God intact was made by the German theologian Friedrich Schleiermacher. Another German theologian, Karl Barth, tried to re-work the earlier understanding of God with a brilliant attempt, spread through thirteen volumes, and yet another German theologian, Paul Tillich, tried a much more radical approach. By the end of the 1960s, if the traditional understanding of God was not dead, then its integrity was severely undermined by biblical studies, church and general Western history, and science.

Since then, rather than a God 'out there' who can intervene and change the course of events, God has become for many progressives an 'inner voice', a 'presence within the human consciousness' that underpins life and enables humans to live well, justly and compassionately. Jesus puts a human face to such a divine presence but it is less certain and more in outline than a clear picture. Prayer is more like thinking things through with God in mind, (with the face of Jesus in mind), than addressing a God 'out there' with needs, worries, fears, and hopes.

A 'God within' puts humans clearly in possession of their own destiny and future. Belonging to the Church and participating in communion means more like identifying with the way of Jesus (who attempted to challenge the spiral of violence in his day with positive compassion for others, and by challenging the injustice), than it does celebrating the sacrifice of Jesus for our and others' failures and wrong doings. Recent decades have witnessed the idea of a 'God within' undergoing yet more change, as evident in the writings of Don Cupitt and Lloyd Geering.

Further Reading

K. Armstrong, *The Case for God.*
M. J. Borg, *The God We Never Knew.*
D. Cupitt, *Reforming Christianity.*
L. G. Geering, *Christianity without God.*

A 'Green' God?

Norman Habel

Is the God of the Bible 'green'?

In the history of Christian theology, the assumption has been that because God is a loving Creator, God must be green or whatever the theological equivalent may be. If, however, we read the Bible from the perspective of Earth or the Earth community, rather than from that of an anthropocentric theologian, we discover that the Bible includes not only green texts but also grey texts. Green texts include those where God is portrayed as valuing and sustaining creation. Grey texts include those where God is portrayed as de-valuing or destroying creation.

In Ps 104:27–30 for example, God is depicted as green. The breath of God gives life and renews—or in modern language—'greens' the face of the ground. In the Flood narrative, however, non-human creatures are devalued. In the first rationale for the Flood (Gen 6:5–9), humans are so evil God decides to send a flood. The flood, however, will not only wipe out humans, but will also eliminate all living creatures. These creatures are innocent. They are collateral damage. They are devalued. In such a tradition, from the perspective of nature, God is depicted as grey rather than green.

Most reading of the Bible or the Christian tradition has been so anthropocentric that we have not heard the voices of the non-human world, a world that has been devalued. God has been green for humans who have faith, but not necessarily for nature. Theology has even adopted the mandate to dominate living beings and to subdue Earth (Gen 1:26–28) as a fundamental expression of human relations with nature. And the God of the *imago dei* in this tradition is not green; humans represent God by dominating, not by valuing creation. The alternative mandate of Gen 1:15, to 'serve' and 'sustain' nature has largely been ignored.

The God of the Hebrew Bible is frequently depicted as grey. After the Flood, this grey God, however, seems to repent and have a green moment when the Creator makes a covenant not only with Noah, but also with the Earth creatures and with Earth herself. Earth is here a personal partner in a covenant with God. Rarely, however, do Hebrew Bible writers seem to connect with the green God of this covenant.

The question then remains whether the God of the New Testament is depicted as being interested only in humans, or whether the greening of creation is also a genuine concern of the Almighty. The tradition that God became incarnate as 'flesh', that is, as a piece of Earth, suggests a green direction. The tradition that creation, together with God's spirit, is groaning in hope of a new birth (Rom 8:18–27) also suggests a green impulse. If, however, heaven is really the better land we humans seek (Hebrews 11), then heaven is the place where God is really green. Does Jesus depict God as green? If humans are viewed as far more important than the lilies of the field, I wonder. If, however, humans are called to 'serve' nature rather than 'rule' it, as Mark 10:41–45 may well imply, Jesus may have been suggesting a green God in some of the sayings we have inherited.

Further Reading
L. G. Geering, *Coming Back to Earth.*
N. Habel, *An Inconvenient Text.*

The Historical Jesus

Gregory C. Jenks

History matters a great deal to contemporary Westerners. Jesus is one of the most significant figures in our cultural tradition, and he is absolutely central to Christianity. It is therefore no surprise that the quest for the historical Jesus has been one of the most controversial topics in biblical scholarship for more than two hundred years.

So what is the 'problem' of the historical Jesus? In brief, it is the tension between what a historian can say about Jesus and what Christianity says about Jesus. The gap between the 'Jesus of history' and the 'Christ of faith' has been at the centre of a major and continuing controversy. At the heart of this controversy is the question of truth; not simply what is true, but who determines what is true? Is the truth about Jesus settled by the church's traditional creeds, or is the truth about Jesus something that might yet be clarified by new research that is independent of—and not in any sense controlled by—the Church?

In post-Enlightenment cultural, tradition claims to authoritative knowledge based on revelation are discounted in favour of knowledge based on evidence, evaluated by human reason, and always subject to potential falsification if new evidence (or new assessments of existing evidence) becomes available. This constitutes a profound challenge to religious authorities and their claims to ultimate truth derived from revelation. It is this more than any specific finding about the historical Jesus that underlies the controversy.

Historical Jesus research proceeds by identifying the evidence available to the researcher, clarifying the methods to be applied to the evidence, and drawing reasonable conclusions that are subject to debate and correction in public discourse. Inevitably, such studies tend to emphasize the humanity of Jesus, his Jewish identity, and his reported actions and sayings. There can be no recourse to supernatural explanations in historical enquiry, and many aspects of the Jesus tradition will be identified as legend and myth. Religious claims about the nature and significance of Jesus are excluded from consideration by historians, in part, because such claims are not historical questions.

Scholars engaged in historical Jesus research come from a range of religious viewpoints, but as historians they are obliged to work within the realm of the natural and the probable. Whatever their religious perspective, such scholars will be seeking to answer a limited number of key questions about Jesus from which a larger profile of Jesus might be constructed. These will include questions such as: What did Jesus think he was doing? Why was Jesus killed? How do we account for the development of Christianity after Jesus' death? Any satisfying profile of the historical Jesus will need to be able to offer a persuasive and robust solution to such key questions.

Further Reading

J. D. Crossan, *Jesus.*
R. W. Funk and R. W. Hoover, *The Five Gospels.*
R. W. Hoover, *Profiles of Jesus.*
L. Parkinson, *The World according to Jesus.*

Holy Communion
(Lord's Supper/Last Supper)

Rex A. E. Hunt

Many meals. Many forms and interpretations. This seems to be the result of even just a brief exploration of the biblical traditions surrounding the Christian eucharistic meal called the Lord's Supper, or Holy Communion.

Church statements that claim the words said and gestures done around a holy table were determined by an original Lord's Supper (or "the Lord's style of supper"[1]) by Jesus, are neither helpful nor accurate. There is not one Lord's Supper in the New Testament, but various, and these various Lord's Suppers cannot be harmonised into such a thing as "*the* New Testament witness about the Lord's Supper".[2]

Progressives will be interested to know that in its reflection on this matter, the Jesus Seminar concluded:

> The last supper . . . was not a historical event. Nevertheless, the Fellows were clear that Jesus often ate meals with his disciples and others and that these meals had symbolic value. . . . Since Jesus ate frequently with his followers, there must have been a last meal with them.[3]

Meanwhile, European scholar Willi Marxsen was quite direct:

> Jesus did not at all institute the Lord's Supper which we celebrate today. . . . [But] at the same time we must add that none of these forms is fully without a tie to Jesus—even if this tie can only be demonstrated through a much-involved tradition-history.[4]

One thing does seem certain, however: from the beginning there was a clear social context for these meals. Those who shared in them saw themselves as being part of a group, part of the social bonding of the community, connected.

On the surface, it can be a fearful task to undertake a re-expression or reconstruction of the Lord's Supper/Holy Communion because of the centrality it has within Christianity. But that shouldn't stop anyone from attempting that task.

Therefore, reconstructing the practise of the Lord's Supper in line with modern biblical scholarship, it is best to describe the celebration as an event. That is, the bread and the wine "are the occasion and not the embodiment"[5] of the historical Jesus' presence. Take. Bless. Break. Give. The fourfold pattern of the meal's action—all verbs—is *celebrated*, rather than *embodied* in so-called substances 'for the forgiveness of sins'.

Expressing this understanding, it is important that one's language and actions be also carefully considered. The suggestion offered here is instead of saying the traditional words—'Body of Christ', 'Blood of Christ'—when the bread and wine is served, that other words—such as 'Bread broken for you', 'Wine poured out for you'—be used, while the spirit of the liturgy be a celebration of the whole of life—a banquet—rather than a wake—a sacrifice.

Notes

1. J. D. Crossan, *The Greatest Prayer*, 136.
2. W. Marxsen, *The Beginnings of Christology*, 119.
3. R. W. Funk, *The Acts of Jesus*, 141–42.
4. W. Marxsen, *The Beginnings of Christology*, 117.
5. J. B. Cobb, Jr., "The Presence of the Past and the Eucharist", 229.

Further Reading

D. E. Smith and H. E. Taussig, *Many Tables*.

H. E. Taussig, *In the Beginning Was the Meal*.

Interfaith Dialogue

Val Webb

Christian attitudes to other religions have been described as exclusivist, inclusivist and pluralist. Exclusivism sees Jesus as the only way to God with no salvation outside the Church. Inclusivists allow for a Divine encounter in other religions but salvation only through Jesus Christ. Pluralism sees many paths to the Divine.

When progressives move beyond exclusivist claims about Jesus and salvation, the barriers between religions begin to break down. Similarly, when the Divine is imaged as Energy, Life, Spirit within the universe, or the universe as God "in which we live and move and have our being" (Acts 17:28), the Sacred we share must necessarily be present in other religions and their followers. Interfaith dialogue does not, therefore, seek to convert the other, but urges each to learn from the other and, through discussion, become more enlightened whatever-they-were-before. We share the experience of being human and the questions and concerns this humanity brings. However, our solutions will not all be the same, or be expressed in the same language and forms—they differ with different contexts and needs.

Interfaith dialogue is no longer an optional exercise in our global society since religions play a significant role in the world's politics, ethics, social organization and global conflicts. Today we are inevitably interconnected and we need to understand the religious beliefs of others if we are to live together in peace and community. This does not mean there are no differences between religions or that we need to accept everything done in the name of religion everywhere. Just as we are different from our friends and don't agree with everything they say and do, we can talk together across religions and recognize their uniqueness while celebrating our common search.

What is "common ground" in such dialogue? Christians cannot simply assume that their explanation of, and solution to, the human condition—sin, forgiveness, salvation—is the same for other religions. For traditions arising out of India, liberation (salvation) means moving from our present existence that is unreal to the underlying real. Chinese religions talk of the need to move from disharmony to harmony with self, community and the universe. Many indigenous traditions seek to bond with the earth/land, their Mother. Compassion is at the root of most faith traditions, however: "do to others what you would have them do to you"—words found in teachings as far back Confucius and the traditions of Zoroastrianism. This and other *human* life experiences give us places to start the dialogue.

Further Reading

D. Eck, *Encountering God.*
H. Smith, *The Illustrated World Religions.*
V. Webb, *Stepping Out with the Sacred.*

Oddservation

Jim Burklo

On my night hike,
a coyote stared at me.
Dinner? her eyes asked.
God? asked mine.

John and Jesus

Rex A. E. Hunt

One of the long-term debates within theological thinking is between those who argue Jesus of Nazareth shared a similar vision of the expected 'kingdom of God' to that of John the Baptiser, or 'dipper'—a vision shaped by Jewish eschatological expectation of imminent divine intervention. And those who want to claim Jesus' "ordering vision" concentrated not on the future—whether near or distant—but on "God's present but collaborative kingdom".[1]

Scholarship on this remains divided. It was a controversial enough issue to divide some of the early decision-making processes of the Westar Institute/Jesus Seminar—that Jesus was not an apocalyptic figure.

Who was John the Baptiser? From all that we know (and do not know), scholars suggest John was a highly visible and influential

Jewish folk hero "whose charismatic reputation almost certainly preceded and overshadowed the public career of Jesus".[2] He seems to have spent most of his youth living in the desert wilderness, along the Jordan River. That he offered "baptism as a cleansing from sin in that location", writes Roy Hoover, which "seems to imply that he regarded the Temple establishment in Jerusalem as religiously bankrupt . . .".[3]

Storytellers and poets, both modern and biblical, have always presented him in colourful terms. The storyteller we call Matthew describes him, and in a detail never given to Jesus. According to tradition his language and preaching were controlled by the themes of crisis, judgment and renewal.

> It was also an anti-temple movement, replacing the temple's mediation of the forgiveness of sins with the mediation of forgiveness through baptism.[4]

Some scholars, reflecting on the stories, have suggested Jesus started out as a follower or disciple of John. But, they conclude, John was seen by Jesus as too much of an alarmist. So he, Jesus, left John's reform movement when he chose to follow a different dream.

It is poet and theologian John Shea who captures this feeling well in his poem about John: "The Man Who Was a Lamp":

> John expected an ax to the root of the tree
>   and instead he found a gardener hoeing around it.
> He dreamt of a man with a winnowing fan and a fire
>   and along came a singing seed scatterer.
> He welcomed wrathful verdicts,
>   then found a bridegroom on the bench.[5]

Other ideas our tradition suggests (although serious scholars regard as historically dubious), is that John and Jesus were related—cousins. Meanwhile the synoptic tradition suggests the arrest of John the Baptizer by Herod Antipas was the trigger event that spurred Jesus on to commence his own public activity—lasting anything from one to three years.

While the debate continues in some quarters, primarily with those who would call themselves conservatives or evangelicals, many progressives claim in John and in Jesus we are faced with two different ordering visions. Imminent apocalyptic doom preaching verses present kingdom of God wisdom teaching.

Notes

1. J. D. Crossan, *The Greatest Prayer*, 93.
2. M. H. Smith, "Israel's Prodigal Son", 109.

3. R. W. Hoover, "The Jesus of History", 49.
4. M. J. Borg, "Jesus Before and After Easter", 3.
5. J. Shea, "The Man Who Was a Lamp", 177.

Further Reading

M. J. Borg and N. T. Wright, *The Meaning of Jesus*
The Jesus Seminar, *The Once and Future Jesus.*
R. J. Miller, *The Jesus Seminar and Its Critics.*
B. B. Scott, *Jesus Reconsidered.*
B. Wilson, *How Jesus Became Christian.*

Leadership

Peter Catt

There is no executive control centre in the brain. No centre of command. Cooperative interactions among the various components of the brain produce an ordered and imaginative response to the world. Reflexive responses do not use the brain at all. For the sake of the body the spinal cord gets on with the task of reacting rapidly to the changing world.

Quantum physics suggests that the relational form of organization and control we encounter in the body is a reflection of the way the universe itself is organized and structured. It would seem that the universe is a set of relationships.

As I see it, this invites us to recognize a number of things.

First, that the Western concept of the individual is a nonsense. We are persons who are products of our relationships; our relationships with others and with the planet as a system.

Second, that control and order are not interdependent concepts. Order can be the product of relational activity; it is not just an effect of centralized, controlling power.

These two insights speak to our understanding of leadership. For church people it speaks to the way oversight and ministerial and lay leadership are exercised. A universe that has relationships at its heart challenges the legitimacy of any hierarchy that is based on distant or naked power. Such structures sideline most of the available talent and, while manufacturing a form of order based on control, rob the body of the processes that create dynamic life.

Leadership that understands the relational nature of the universe enables the development of structures, which encourage participation in decision-making and in the working out of those decisions. It uses processes that uncover synergies and imagines the future as a creative field. It needs to be noted this is not just about the democratization of the church. For under the current paradigm, democracy is often little more than an exercise of tyranny by the majority.

Quantum physics may help us rediscover with renewed appreciation some aspects of the early church: convocation as a *calling together*, authority as *giving life*, and obedience as the capacity to *listen and hear well*. It may even lead us to rediscover what it means to say that a bishop is the *Pastor Pastorum*, the pastor to the pastors, and remind us that we are called to a covenantal life.

Further Reading

M. J. Wheatley, *Leadership and the New Science.*

Liturgy
Making Meaning in Community
Margaret Mayman

Liturgy is a communal response to the sacred through language and ritual.

Progressive people of faith have been encouraged to learn that 'liturgy' derives from a Greek word, *leitourgia*, which roughly translates as "work of the people". For those who have felt disenfranchised from the creation of words and acts that create religious meaning, this seems to suggest its origin was less priestly and more participatory than we have come to experience it. However for centuries, the work of the people in liturgy has been limited to verbal responses made to the priests' leading. Progressive Christians expect much more from liturgy.

'Liturgical' has also been used to describe the branches of Christianity that have followed a fixed pattern of worship, some using repetition each week from a prayer book, others using a common framework in which the congregation is led through gathering, naming the reality of human life, engaging the texts and the world, responding, sending out and blessing. This structure continues to be meaningful for many. The rhythm of the service is known, and within it we find our shared meaning and our very selves. The rhythm of authentically progressive weekly liturgy, enacted and shared in community, nourishes and sustains.

In parallel with the rethinking of progressive theology, progressives are re-imagining the content of liturgy. Understandings of the sacred that are non-theistic require a reframing of worship that is focused on the human search for meaning in community. Prayers are not addressed to an "out there" deity but instead express our sense of gratitude for all that is good in creation and relationship, and lament and hope that our world is still so lacking in justice and peace. Rather than being imaged as supernatural, the sacred is deeply natural. Language for the sacred and for humanity is inclusive.

Environmental awareness is vital. Musical styles connect with twenty-first-century sensibilities and the language of song shares the insights of progressive theology in sorrow and in joy. Though we must avoid exploitative appropriation of other religious traditions, we may learn from them, dialogue with them, and accept from them gifts of understanding and practice that enrich our own. Above all, progressive liturgy expresses connection and interdependence, and with that comes a profound appreciation of diversity.

Liturgy is an art form. The role of progressive liturgist is of one who draws together the threads of the tradition and weaves them into the realities of the contemporary world. The liturgy must be an aesthetic experience crafted from beautiful words, images and music that nourish the human spirit. The minister becomes, if not an artist, at least a curator, enabling the spiritual and theological work of the people. And like any estimable art experience, progressive liturgy must allow for participation and response. Progressive theology has nourished our minds. Progressive liturgy engages our bodily senses, emotions and spirits. It draws back the veil between visible and invisible reality.

Human beings are shaped by stories. I believe the power of story is central to our re-imagination of liturgy. Liturgy has liberating and resistant potential. In the liturgy, we tell biblical stories and other stories from the poets, philosophers and prophets of our own time. Engaging in a progressive Christian liturgy enables us to tell a story in profound opposition to the individualism, consumerism and militarism that marks our world. It invites participants to be aware of the other 'liturgies' that operate, usually unnamed, in our society. These are the economic and political liturgies we usually sleepwalk through, that tell us there is no alternative to the lack of justice and peace we now experience. The practice of liturgy reminds us another world is possible and that we are not alone.

Liturgy cannot be separated from community. The spiritual journey, the human hunger and thirst for mystery and meaning, are motifs still redolent in Western cultures but, like so much of our life, they have been individualised, commoditized, and marketed for a price.

Progressive faith communities provide an experience of ritual and meaning-seeking that is offered freely without expectation of payment. The power of all this cannot be underestimated. Experiencing liturgy in the context of a caring community provides a powerful antidote to the loneliness that haunts modern humans. So many people live vacillating between maddening busyness and depressive inactivity. Practising liturgy invites us to live differently, to face the void and to create new meaning. So we may live grateful for life, and compassionate toward other beings, open to mystery.

Further Reading

M. J. Borg, *The Heart of Christianity*.

M. MacLean, "Worship: Pilgrims in the Faith".

M. Pierson, *The Art of Curating Worship* ('emergent' rather than progressive, but useful).

H. Taussig, *A New Spiritual Home*.

G. Vosper, *With or Without God*.

A Mystical Lord's Prayer

Paul Alan Laughlin

The first and perhaps most important thing that sets off this version of the Lord's Prayer from the others is its theology, which dispenses entirely with the personal, parental Father-Sky-God of the original, and replaces 'Him' with a non-personal, immanent power-presence (or source-force), an infinite one (or One) that is none other (or non-Other) than the spiritual core of the person or persons reciting or singing the prayer. The implicit theology of this prayer, then, is not monotheism but monism. . . .

The second distinctive feature . . . follows from the first; for having eliminated a personal divine Other above, this Lord's Prayer . . . has no petitions for any intercessory acts on behalf of a human indi-

---

Author's note: This 'Lord's Prayer' is obviously not a new version of the traditional one, but an alternative to it spawned out of specifically mystical progressive Christian spirituality. It is all the more suitable for use in worship by the fact that I tailored it to fit the well-known and widely used 1935 musical setting for the original King James wording by composer Albert Hay Malotte. —PAL

vidual or group. In their stead are strong affirmations of how we are already emboldened from within ourselves to become better persons and to accomplish ever-greater things. This 'Lord's Prayer', then, can properly be regarded as a daily reminder of our full human potential—miraculous and praiseworthy in its own right—to be good and do good.

Thus, my Lord's Prayer is not an invocative device, but an *evocative* exercise in self-realization—or perhaps Self-realization, if the ego-self is to be distinguished from one's deepest and truest identity, as it is in most mystical traditions. For humanists, this 'within' may be seen differently: as our rational and empirical faculties, perhaps after the fashion of Plato, who equated the human 'soul' *(psyche)* with the intellect. In either case, what we have here is an acknowledgement of a mysterious and *in some sense* divine Immanence (versus Eminence)—a reference to the indwelling mysterious Presence and Power that (at least for mystics) permeates or infuses the cosmos, and that (for humanists as well, though probably *sans* the capitals) abides in nature, human nature, and therefore ourselves.

> O presence and pow'r within us,
> Being and Life of all.
> How we are filled, how we o'erflow
> with infinite love and gladness!
>
> We shall this day sow grace and peace,
> and show mercy to all,
> and gentle loving-kindness.
>
> And we shall be not so self-serving,
> but a constant source of giving.
>
> For ours is the essence,
> and the wholeness,
> and the fullness forever.
> Amen.

The Nag Hammadi Library

Rex A. E. Hunt

The Nag Hammadi Library is forty-five texts in thirteen papyrus books or codices. It was found in 1945 at ancient Chenobaskian, now Nag Hammadi, some 370 miles south of Cairo, Egypt. The stories around this find say a man named Muhammad Ali was looking for fertilizer for fuel and stumbled upon a clay jar containing several codices of manuscripts.

Included in this find were a complete copy of the Gospel of Thomas, plus the Secret Book of John, the Gospel of Truth, the Letter of Peter to Philip, the Treatise on the Resurrection, the Gospel of Philip, two texts on Baptism and two on the Eucharist, one called the Thunder: Perfect Mind, which raises important issues related to gender, and many others (including a version of Plato's *Republic*), almost all of which were previously unknown. These fourth century texts, in Coptic, are sometimes dialogues with Jesus, or texts about Jesus. Some seem to 'echo' parts of New Testament texts, but others are quite different. They were initially classed as being part of the religious movement called Gnosticism, even though that term itself is never used.

As a result, this 'accidental' archaeological find has changed the way many scholars now look at early Christianities—yes, plural! Indeed, some claim this library will turn out to be more important than the Dead Sea Scrolls (found three years later, in 1948) because "it offers new perspectives of Christian beginnings outside the canon".

An often overlooked fact in some Christian origins scholarship is: there was not one unified group or vision called 'Christianity'. There were several, separate groups, often not knowing of the others' existence. And when these different visions met, it was often a clash! Harvard scholar Karen King explains:

> Early Christians intensely debated such basic issues as the content and meaning of Jesus' teachings, the nature of salvation, the value of prophetic authority, the roles of women and slaves, and competing visions of ideal community. After all, these first Christians had no New Testament, no Nicene Creed or Apostles' Creed, no community established church order or chain of authority, no church buildings, and indeed no single understanding of Jesus.[1]

However, as history is usually written by the winners, "the viewpoints of the losers were largely lost since their ideas survived only in documents denouncing them. Until now."[2]

There are two major consequences for our knowledge of Christian origins as a result of this discovery: It gives us (1) a more nuanced understanding of Gnosticism, with access to key authors in their own writings, and (2) a complete copy of the Gospel of Thomas, in Coptic translation.

Progressive Christians study the Nag Hammadi Library because it offers this alternative voice in ancient debate, a voice the winners declared as 'heresy' as they sought to marginalise their opposition's impact—and then enacted their decisions through force—even death. Progressive Christians study these writings because much in Christian belief and practice rests upon historical claims, and "an accurate view of history is crucial".[3]

Notes

1. K. L. King, "Letting Mary Magdalene Speak", 1.
2. K. L. King, 1.
3. K. L. King, 1.

Further Reading

K. L. King, *The Gospel of Mary of Magdala*.
E. Pagels, *The Gnostic Gospels*.
J. M. Robinson, *The Nag Hammadi Library in English*.

The New Testament
(in Chronological Order)
James Veitch

James Moffatt (1870–1944) was the first person to translate the New Testament (NT) from Greek and place the literature into a chronological order. He undertook this project while a minister of the Free Church of Scotland.

It was his intention to use the Revised King James Version and to re-arrange the text into a chronological order but was prevented from doing so by the holders of the copyright. He was left with no option but to undertake his own translation.

The Historical New Testament, published in 1901, ruffled the feathers of leading British NT scholars to the point where Moffatt would no longer refer to this work and seems to have abandoned it. The problem: in the course of explaining why he produced his own translation in historical and chronological order, he had suggested that NT scholars erred in failing to share the results of their scholarship with 'people in the pews' at a time when knowledge of how the Church (and Christianity) had begun and developed in its early years was critical to keeping them 'in the pews'. His fellow NT scholars were not amused and to his dying day it was said Moffatt regretted making this criticism. His book, though, is an outstanding compendium of information, knowledge, and scholarship, that would have marked him out as one of the most promising scholars of his time.

His order of the books reflects the results of critical NT scholarship in the last quarter of the nineteenth century—the letters of Paul come first; Mark precedes Matthew; and the order finishes with 2 Peter. Moffatt believed it was absolutely critical for each writing in the NT to be placed in its own historical context so that its contents could be understood in the twentieth century. But this was a lone voice.

The *Twentieth Century New Testament* published throughout 1895, 1900 and 1901, with a one-volume edition published in 1904, was more noted for the quality of its translation than for the order of the NT books. Thirty-five 'anonymous' people (almost all were social radicals) were involved in preparing the translation, over half were ministers of various mainline churches and the rest were laity of different backgrounds, including two women. None were recognised NT scholars. Mark as the first gospel is the only innovation.

A publication in the tradition of Moffatt was the work of G. W. Wade, a biblical scholar, at the time a Canon of St. Asaph Cathedral in Wales, and was entitled, *The Documents of the New Testament: Translated and Historically Arranged with Critical Introductions* (1934). The reason this publication was not controversial is it had the support of the Archbishop of Wales, and its title suggests a less confrontational approach to a critical understanding of the NT text. Well-intentional and not as radical as Moffatt, the book did not catch the imagination of the Church. The economic depression and growing disturbances in Europe diverted any attention it might have received.

The Jewish scholar Hugh Schonfield produced *The Original New Testament* in 1985. The translation reflects a Jewish understanding of the NT but the order is only marginally re-arranged with the Corinthian correspondence set out chronologically. Mark appears as the first gospel.

A translation and rearrangement of the NT in the critical tradition of Moffat by James Veitch was produced in four parts between 1993 and 1995. The chronological order is benchmarked against Duling/Perrin, *The New Testament* (1982/1994), and the translation is aimed at conveying the sense of the Greek text into modern English. Volume one rearranges the internal chronological order of the seven letters of Paul. Volume two begins with Mark—a novel dated post 75 CE—and includes second-generation 'Pauline' writings and Matthew (circulating around 80 CE). Volume three is about the 'church' of the nineties through the eyes of James, Hebrews, 1 Peter, Revelation, followed by Luke and Acts (circulating around 95–100 CE). Volume four contains the literature of 100–150 CE: the Johanine writings (129–125 CE), some Pauline family writings, and finally Jude and 2 Peter (ca. 150 CE). Veitch's edition of the Gospels (1994), *Jesus of Galilee: Myth and Reality*, begins with Q (based on Luke) followed by Mark, Matthew, Luke and John (the text of the latter is rearranged).

The most thoroughgoing reconstruction of the chronology of the NT since Moffatt is the work of the Jesus Seminar, and was the inspiration and vision of the distinguished American NT scholar, Robert Funk, working with other NT scholars in the Westar Institute and publishing through Polebridge Press. This has resulted in the publication of *The Five Gospels* (1993); *The Acts of Jesus* (1998); *The Complete Gospels* (2010), and most importantly, *The Authentic Letters of Paul* (2010)—in which the seven letters of Paul are rearranged chronologically.

The restructuring of Christian faith and its truth for a progressive church must begin with the literature of the New Testament placed in historical context and rearranged chronologically. This foundation has been more than a hundred years in the making.

Further Reading:

J. Veitch, *Jesus of Galilee*.

Jesus and Non-Violence

John Shuck

Jesus was non-violent. Except for his demonstration in the temple, when Jesus turned over tables, there is no evidence the Jesus movement was a violent or a destructive one. The turning of the tables was more of a symbolic act. It was the event that likely got him killed.

It was subversive to be sure. He meant to overturn Empire. His political, economic, and social vision was counter to that of Empire and of his own religious leaders. He advocated for economic justice, social justice and peace among ethnic groups.

But his method was non-violent as best as I can tell. That is the key. The seeds of violence and destruction grow. They produce bitter, poisonous fruit. It doesn't matter how just the ideal, violence poisons everything for many generations. That is the case if it is done by radicals or by armies.

The way of Jesus was a new way of living and being. It was an intense movement. Jesus was singly-focused. He meant it when he told his followers that life with him would be dangerous, without comforts, and without contact with family. Obviously, Jesus didn't think everyone would follow him.

It is anachronistic after two thousand years when Jesus has become a mythological figure, the Cosmic Christ, the second person of the Trinity, to say that to be a Christian or a follower today means to become a homeless wanderer as the historical person was. Although, for some that might be what it means.

Further Reading

R. W. Funk, *A Credible Jesus.*
R. W. Hoover, *Profiles of Jesus.*

Oral Tradition

Rex A. E. Hunt

What is now known as the printed biblical Gospels were originally shaped by an oral storytelling tradition. Spoken. Sounded. In a culture where the majority of people—maybe 90–95 percent of the population—were non-literate.

The primary form of communication in an oral-aural culture is the human voice. The spoken word is something that happens, a moment in time. Indeed, in an oral sound-dominated culture, spoken words can have a harmonising tendency rather than analytic, dissecting tendencies. So the storyteller (or communicator) needs to adopt the attitude of being 'an awakener' rather than a 'depositor'.

The 'imprint' of orality is shaped by several characteristics:

- performed orally
- audience participation during the telling
- techniques are employed: short sentences, provocative and memorable words/core, oft-repeated phrases
- social context of the particular storytelling event
- evoke another story in response

Oral storytellers do not ordinarily remember exact wording. Knowledge is shaped by memory, in pre-textual, oral form. But neither is it just memory mindlessly regurgitated. It is memory rethought rather than memory as mere transmission. As Brandon Scott says: "in oral communities purveyors of the tradition freely omitted, invented, modified, enlarged"[1] their stories, layering and stitching them together to conserve tradition in an episodic manner. When stories were written down—that is, oral and writing became 'blended'—it seems the act of writing was primarily to aid memory and the telling, rather than to keep a permanent record. In these instances the oral tradition did not come to an end with writing. Oral performance and aural hearing continued. A story gained its 'authority' in its telling, not in it being written down.

Oral tradition is not a fixed thing as it is in cultures shaped by writing or print. It is very fluid, passed on as talk, from generation to generation. Likewise, oral cultures have no dictionaries.

An oral culture simply does not deal in such items as geometrical figures, abstract categorisation, formal logical reasoning processes, definitions, or even comprehensive descriptions. All of these are shaped by text-formed thought.[2]

The cultures and communities in which the Jesus movements arose were essentially oral. Jesus was a Galilean, travelling, secular sage— more in tune with the Wisdom tradition than the Priestly tradition— who wrote nothing. He spoke Aramaic and, according to some modern scholars, very possibly some Greek. We do not know if he could speak Hebrew. His words have been preserved only in the Greek. He taught his followers orally.

> The gospels portray Jesus as one who speaks, not as one who writes. Jesus' disciples also responded to his teaching orally; they repeated his most memorable words to one another and to outsiders.[3]

No fully shaped or connected narrative of either Jesus' life or teachings is preserved in oral tradition. Neither is there any systematic record of relationships, if any, among the various Jesus movements which formed in Galilee and southern Syrian villages, and what later became known as Christianity. "Peasant movements generally leave no records."[4] That 'recording' came with the bishops, official teachers, and church councils of the fourth and fifth centuries.

Notes

1. B. B. Scott, "What Did Jesus Really Say?", 3.
2. W. J. Ong, *Orality and Literacy.*

3. R. W. Funk and R. W. Hoover, *The Five Gospels*, 27.

4. R. A. Horsley, *Jesus in Context*, 54.

Further Reading

R. Alves, *The Poet, the Warrior, the Prophet.*

T. E. Boomershine, *Story Journey.*

D. Cupitt, *What Is a Story?*

M. E. Lee and B. B. Scott, *Sound Mapping the New Testament.*

Sign for a Tree

Jim Burklo

As I rounded the bend on the trail up Sonoma Mountain in northern
California,
I read the sign:
"TRAIL CLOSED AHEAD DUE TO TREE FAILURE."

I stood and meditated on its implications.

By its logic, the gracefully shaped brown nuts scattered on the trail
must have resulted from acorn stem failure.
The lovely medallions of yellow and orange on the ground
were the result of leaf atrophy.
The blue feather of a Stellar's Jay, lying on a bed
of fallen redwood needles,
was the consequence of plumage dislocation.

The bleached bones of the opossum lying in the dry grass of the meadow
were the result of insufficient coyote evasion.
And the mountain upon whose flanks I walked
was the result of a fault.

It seemed to me that the tree's passing merited a different sign:
"At the kink in the trail ahead, you will circumambulate the remains
of a tall tanbark oak which from a pretty acorn grew,
many decades ago.

"For years of seasons, wet and dry, it lifted branches
and serrated leaves skyward, communing with sun and wind.

"Old and full of days, it died with flourish,
dropping in one grand whoosh to the ground.

"Walk around it and wonder.
May your footsteps be prayers of thanksgiving for its life.
And may this kink in the trail remain as a memorial to it,
long after its trunk crumbles into rich forest soil."

Parable

Rex A. E. Hunt

The parable is a prime genre of biblical storytelling, and certainly the central form of Jesus' teaching. However, despite the force and often simplicity of the parables, they have been listened to in a variety of ways at different times. Generally speaking, there are four different ways parables have been heard:

1. allegorical
2. ethical
3. existential
4. literary/cultural

Current progressive scholarship tends to see the parable as 'extended metaphor', which fits within the literary/cultural category.

What then is a 'parable'? In general terms a parable is a short, fictional, oral narrative, which upsets or shatters a dominant worldview. Following the suggestion of biblical scholar J. Dominic Crossan, they are stories that shatter the deep structure of our accepted world and thereby render clear and evident to us the relativity of the story itself.

Parables concern themselves with the concrete, the everyday. That is, the ordinary—people and events—is the context or matrix for understanding the extraordinary or the strange. They are not about abstract thought. Their function is not to instruct but to haunt.[1]

The world of Jesus' parables is the fabric of daily life in a Galilean village or family rather than an urban setting. The subjects of his parables were robbery on an isolated road, coins, a vineyard, day labourers, sheep, and wayward children. His parables do not speak about God; neither does he develop a doctrine of God, predict his passion and death, depict a last judgment, or commission the disciples to establish a church.

The focus of Jesus' parables is what he calls the kingdom or realm of God. And the reason for this focus in Jesus' parables? Not special, abstract listening, but listening that may open other possibilities for the listener, possibilities in this world which have not yet been experienced or which need to be recalled and re-experienced.

This was the story nature of Jesus' 'revolution'. Jesus revolts in parable, suggests Brandon Scott, and

> the parables create a counter-world, a hoped-for world that redresses the world as it is and surely makes sense, regardless of how it turns out—even if it results in crucifixion.[2]

Many scholars have held that the parables of Jesus are the bedrock of tradition. Accepting that understanding, one group of scholars who have worked extensively on parables is The Jesus Seminar. As a result of their deliberations they concluded a total of thirty-three parables could be classified as:

Red   Jesus most likely said something like this (and should be included unequivocally in the data base for determining who Jesus was);

Pink   Jesus may have said something like it (and should be included with reservations/modifications in the data base for determining who Jesus was);

Grey   Jesus probably didn't say it, but it contains some similar ideas (and should not be included in the primary date base, but some of the content might be used in determining who Jesus was);

Black   Jesus didn't say it. It belongs to a later or different tradition (and should not be included in the primary data base in determining who Jesus was).[3]

From those thirty-five, five parables in six versions received a 'red' vote, while twenty-one parables in twenty-eight versions received a 'pink' vote. These were classified as 'authentic parables'.

Notes

1. E. F. Beutner, "The Haunt of Parable", 1.
2. B. B. Scott, *Re-Imagine the World*, 140.
3. R. W. Funk, B. B. Scott, and J. R. Butts, *The Parables of Jesus*, 21.

Further Reading

C. W. Hedrick, *Many Things in Parables*.
W. R. Herzog II, *Parables as Subversive Speech*.
B. B. Scott, *Re-Imagine the World*.

Paul

James Veitch

A quick look at the contents page of a copy of the New Testament shows the name of Paul is connected with thirteen of twenty-one Letters: this in itself indicates his importance. However, Paul's name and a tale of his exploits appears in another book entitled the Acts of the Apostles, which at first glance appears to be a historical account of the beginnings of the organization known as the Church and the beginnings of the world religion known as Christianity.

The traditional story is that Saul of Tarsus (to use his earliest known name) started out as an opponent of the fledging movement that sprang up following the death of Jesus spearheaded by the latter's close friend Peter. But at a critical point some three years after Jesus had been killed, Saul was converted to the way of Jesus and became Paul.

From the accounts in Acts, Paul was a dominant personality. He was quick-witted, a brilliant thinker and strategist, and a persuasive public speaker. He was fearless and courageous and what made him special was his Roman citizenship. In the eyes of the compiler of Acts he was an insider, so to speak, and as a follower of Jesus this connection gave him extra protection when he spoke. Paul was not one to join others, other than on his own terms, so the relationship with Peter and the close friends of Jesus is depicted as fragile. So he turned his immense energy into travelling through the Roman Empire, founding new faith communities wherever he went.

The Letters tell the story of where he travelled and what he said and how he organized the groups of people he attracted into the Way of Jesus (an early name for the church). Originally a Jew by faith, he came to found religious communities that were Jesus-centred, and as more non-Jews joined, the character of these communities changed. Rather than reforming or transforming the Judaism of his day—his original intention—he founded more and more non-Jewish communities of Jesus followers who, in time, gave his movements their special character.

Was Paul the real founder of the church (and not Jesus or Peter), and did Christianity—a non-Jewish religious movement—become in his hands the beginning of a new and different religion? Was Paul at the centre of the parting of the ways between Judaism and the Christianity he created?

From the nineteenth century onward the life and influence of this man has been at the centre of much attention. F. C. Baur, a German theologian, asked the hard questions in 1831 and 1845: what did Paul really know about Jesus; what was the nature of the relationship between Paul and others like Peter, who were his opponents when he was writing his letters; what kind of Jew was he, and what was the core of his thinking? Baur answered some but not all of his own questions and one of the conclusions he arrived at was the historical Paul, as distinct from the Paul of Church history and Christian imagination, was the author of only Galatians, the Corinthians letters, and Romans. The others connected with his name were written in his honour by others.

Today, with the advent of historical and literary criticism, and a better knowledge of ancient communities through the work of archaeologists, anthropologists, and classical historians, and, with the help of Jewish New Testament scholars, a new and fresh picture of Paul is emerging. There is every possibility the Letter of Acts was not a historical document written by Luke, the legendary author of the gospel that bears his name, but storytelling about Peter and Paul (with Paul as the model follower of Jesus), influenced by the writing style and technique of the Jewish writer, Josephus, and compiled sometime between 125 and 150 CE, probably with the so called 'heretical' writings of Marcion of Sinope (85–160 CE) in mind.

This means the historical Paul is known only to us in his letters, and the letters he wrote number not thirteen, as in the contents page of the New Testament, perhaps not four as F. C. Baur concluded, and maybe not the seven (1 Thessalonians, Galatians, 1 and 2 Corinthians, Philippians, Romans and Philemon) that New Testament scholars have discussed since the mid-1930s, but fourteen or fifteen. For what scholars have discovered is that in 1 and 2 Corinthians, seven separate letters can be identified, and the edited final version has not placed these in chronological order. Philippians contains three letters, and the final version is not in chronological order, and Romans had a cover sheet (the final chapter) that does not belong to the letter as a whole. If 1 Thessalonians, Galatians and Philemon are added to this new list, then Paul, it seems, wrote quite a lot we did not know about. Reading Paul's letters, chronologically and contextually, will also change how the modern reader understands the writings of Paul in the New Testament.

If finding the 'historical Jesus' has had a major impact on the interpretation of the Gospels, then finding the 'historical Paul' will have an even greater impact on our understanding of how the church really began and how we read the New Testament.

Further Reading

J. D. Crossan and J. Read, *In Search of Paul*.
A. Dewey, et al., *The Authentic Letters of Paul*.
J. Veitch, *The Origins of Christianity and the Letters of St Paul*.
_____, "Spotlight on Saint Paul".

Pluralism

Paul Alan Laughlin

Religious pluralism, the belief that religious truth is not found in any single faith, is an attitude typical of progressive Christians. It lies toward the left side of a spectrum of religious attitudes that ranges from exclusivism, or absolutism, on the right, to relativism on the left.

Exclusivism maintains either that there is one true religion or that there is one truth about religion. Exclusivists invariably assume they have or represent that true religion or truth stance. In other words, no one of this mindset has ever said, "There is one true religion or religious truth, and—damn!—it's hers, not mine." Occupying this far right side of the spectrum are, of course, fundamentalist Christians, but ironically, doctrinaire atheists as well. For their part, Fundamentalists know their religion alone is right, while confirmed atheists are convinced that only their take on religion—namely, that it's baseless and perhaps harmful—is right.

At the far left on this spectrum is relativism, which holds that all religions or religious beliefs are merely opinions that, however long they've been held and promulgated, are finally just one person's or group's viewpoint over against a lot of equally or more or less plausible alternatives. Relativism is the position of most skeptics and cynics. Just to the right of relativists, but still to the left on the spectrum of religious attitudes, is pluralism, which maintains that all of the enduring religions of the world contain truth, but none perfectly, and each is valid and valuable in its own way, especially for those who follow it. This was the faith stance of Gandhi, as reflected in this famous quotation:

> I came to the conclusion long ago . . . that all religions were true and also that all had some error in them, and whilst I hold by my own, I should hold others as dear as Hinduism. So we can only pray, if we are Hindus, not that a Christian should become a Hindu . . . [b]ut our innermost prayer should be a Hindu should be a

better Hindu, a Muslim a better Muslim, a Christian a better Christian.

Pluralism is also reflected in mythologist Joseph Campbell's claim: "All religions are true, but none literal." Progressive Christians have historically been inclined toward such an open-minded, tolerant and ecumenical attitude and to avoid or reject especially the rigid certainty of exclusivism.

Further Reading

D. R. Griffin, *Deep Religious Pluralism.*
J. H. Hick and P.F. Knitter, *The Myth of Christian Uniqueness.*

Prayer

Michael Morwood

Prayer is sometimes described as "the raising of the mind and heart to God". This description is likely to stand the test of time because it allows for wide interpretation and understanding. It also allows for many variations in practice. It invites—and always will invite—reflection on 'God' and where and how 'God' is to be found or experienced.

This description of prayer allows for metaphor, and in this vein has been a source of rich spiritual experience for many people who pray *as if* God actually listens and thinks about things, or *as if* God needs to hear from us (and even demands we tune in frequently to keep in touch). Prayer is 'like' talking to a listening God who even talks back occasionally. This form of "raising the mind and heart to God" is valuable—so long as we realize we are immersed in metaphor and in religious images which help us to give expression to the deepest longings and desires of our minds and hearts, mindful of a mystery—call it Divine Presence, Ground of all Being, Spirit, Breath, the One, God—whatever you like, that is ultimately beyond anything we can imagine.

Most Christian liturgical and vocal prayers use this form of prayer. Unfortunately it is rarely recognized as metaphor. Instead, this form of prayer has been understood as the "raising of the mind" to an elsewhere-listening deity. This common practice has cemented in the minds of many, if not most Christians, that this is what prayer is really about: trying to contact and converse with a 'God-person' who communicates the way we humans do.

Let us 'talk to God' by all means, but let us recognize the '*as if* nature of what we are doing and know this form of prayer is not for God's sake, but ours. The mystery of God cannot be adequately honoured, expressed, or understood, by imagining we are addressing or communicating with a deity who listens in from the heavens.

So, to whom or to what are we 'raising' our minds and hearts, if not to an elsewhere, listening-in deity? And, what is the point of prayer?

We are raising minds and hearts to 'God' understood as the source and sustainer of all that exists, but understood, in fidelity to Christian tradition, as an everywhere presence. There is no 'outside of' God. So we want to raise minds and hearts to an all-pervasive Presence holding everything that exists in connection and relationship. We want to raise minds and hearts to awareness that we exist *in* this Presence and that being human is a wonderful way to give expression to this reality.

Understood in this context, prayer covers a wide field. It is about deepening awareness of a Mystery ever present to us. It is about deepening awareness that we give human expression to this Mystery, we call 'God'. It is about deepening awareness of how this Presence is expressed in patterns of development operating throughout the universe and how we are connected with all that exists within those patterns of operation. It is about knowing ourselves, and yearning to give the best possible human expression we can be of this Mystery. It is about awareness, affirmation and challenge. It is about changing us (not God) and making this Presence evident in our personal lives, in our social lives, and in our political, justice and economic systems.

Further Reading

M. Morwood, *Children Praying a New Story.*
———. *Praying a New Story.*

Process Theology

Val Webb

Philosopher mathematician Alfred North Whitehead (1861–1947) developed a cosmology and language that could incorporate all knowledge and experience, including science and religion, within the same scheme of thought.

Western philosophy traditionally spoke of static, discrete beings, enduring substances and essences—which is why early Church Fathers had problems arguing that Jesus was both God and man. Since science in Whitehead's time had moved from mechanistic explanations to viewing the universe as an interconnected organism, with every event affecting everything else, Whitehead's Process philosophy moved from a 'substance' to an 'event' oriented universe with the God-idea described *within* this framework, nor separate from it.

Whitehead argued that everything in the universe is composed of a series of events or "actual occasions of experience", not a continuous flow but discrete events following each other, the previous event having causal efficacy for the next. Each emerging event 'feels' the preceding event, selecting what it wishes to incorporate in the present event. Human beings, animals, plants and rocks are not single series of events but a multiplicity of series in the brain, digestive system, photosynthesis etc., not all experienced consciously but all contributing to what is becoming in any moment. While the process is the same in frogs and wheat, different levels of complexity lead to different levels of consciousness. Each emerging event has a 'subjective aim' that determines how the new event will become and the 'initial aim' of this organizing principle is what Process theologians call Divine activity. This 'aim' (God) suggests the maximum possibility (which we can choose or reject) for each new event and as any event perishes, it becomes part of the ever-growing Divine memory, available to be 'felt' by others for further events. As we choose optimal Divine 'aims,' we move to richer experiences, becoming more 'like God' or in tune with the Sacred.

The Process God is therefore not an external Being but part of the interconnected universe where God is both in everything yet more than the sum of its parts (panentheism), working in us and the world, affecting and affected by the events of the universe. Thus our actions are not determined by God but rather this 'initial aim' of every event urges us and the universe towards novelty and wholeness—immanent persuasive Spirit rather than all-powerful external Being.

While Process thought is much more complex than this description, it allows a God-space within its philosophy—Divine Urge/Energy/Life of the universe—which better suits a contemporary scientific worldview.

Further Reading

C. Christ, *She Who Changes.*
J. B. Cobb, Jr., and D. R. Griffin, *Process Theology.*
B. Epperly, *Process Theology.*
C. R. Mesle, *Process Theology.*
A. N. Whitehead, *Process and Reality* (a difficult technical read).

Queer Spirituality

Margaret Mayman

Queer Spirituality is the name given to the rise of a powerful and healing expression of religiosity among lesbian, gay, bisexual, transgendered and intersex persons (LGBTI).

While a great deal of mainstream religion has focused on homosexuality as an ethical problem, queer spirituality is the positive, life-affirming practice of spirituality among queer people. It assumes the goodness of LGBTI sexual orientation and gender expression, and names the ethical problems of homophobia and compulsory heterosexism. Rather than operating from a deficit scenario, queer spirituality recognizes the particular spiritual gifts and insights of LGBTI people.

Queer is a word that has been reclaimed from its original negative connotation of 'odd' or 'atypical'. The subversive power of self-naming is recognised by queer individuals and faith communities, challenging the negative meanings that have been used to describe queer experience and shape queer reality. Queer is an open, inclusive word that in itself challenges rigid dominant definitions and allows for fluidity and change. Associated with the adjective queer, is the verb queering, LGBTI people are queering religion, spirituality and theology by uncovering the lives of queer people who have been hidden by the dominant discourse. As a form of liberation theology, queer theology, reflects theologically from the perspective of the queer person in ways that both nurture the spiritual life of queer people and challenge the negative homophobic biases of mainstream religion and theology. Justice-making is an essential spiritual practice for queer people of spirit and this includes making connections in analysis and advocacy between multiple forms of oppression and diverse communities of resistance.

Many queer people refuse to give up on living life as a journey of faith just because we are queer. Searching for the deepest meaning of life, living in ways that create justice, compassion, love, and peace, are essential parts of who we are and what we believe. Spirituality is our relationship with the sacredness of life, nature and the universe. This relationship is no longer confined to formal devotional practices and institutional places of worship. For some people spirituality is best expressed in a community in connection with a historic tradition. Spirituality is the way of living life that is sometimes developed into religion but not always.

While many LGBTI people have left religious communities and rejected religion as essentially homophobic, others are finding progressive, welcoming faith communities in which they can find a new spiritual home. Inclusion of LGBTI persons and openness to queer spirituality are often marks of progressive faith communities. In opposition to the homophobia of many denominations, progressive faith communities have celebrated the relationships of LGBTI persons and welcomed us into the full life of faith communities through the recognition of gifts of leadership in ordination. There is also an international LGBTI denomination, the Metropolitan Community Church, which has made significant contributions to the development of a queer spiritual tradition.

Queer theology pays particular attention to queer life and as such has some unique contributions to make to the wider theological corpus. Unlike other minority groups who are identified by physical appearance, queer people face a life-long practice of coming out, of challenging the dominant paradigm of sexual and gender expression. It is life-long, because it involves the integration of queer identity into every aspect of our lives, throughout our life journey. Coming out involves rejecting hetero-normativity by being clear about what we are not; it involves a process of self-knowing and self-acceptance that enables us to be our authentic selves; and through this process a coming to know oneself as participating in the Sacred.

Another area of significant contribution to theology generally is in the sphere of theological reflection on the body. Much of religion has denied the body but if we and our planet are to survive this is a failure we must overcome. We need a spiritualty grounded in embodied existence. Queer people's stories invite us to take embodied experience very seriously as a resource for spiritual truth.

Queer people who have journeyed to a place of peace and understanding with our bodies have much to share with those who think that spiritual experience means denial of the body. The insight that our bodies are important cannot be ignored if we are to live healthy, whole and joyful lives. Body and spirit need each. Healing and loving touch have religious significance, whether that touch is sexual or otherwise.

Queer people have contributed to dangerous and powerful new movements in western Christianity, to a sex and body positive spirituality that understands the revolution for love and justice must be sexual as well as spiritual. We glimpse the Queerness of God and we have the courage to do theology aware of our embodied, sexual, gender differentiated selves and that sort of theology is theology that the world sorely needs.

Further Reading:

L. W. Countryman and M. R. Ritley, *Gifted by Otherness*.

M. M. Ellison, *Erotic Justice*.

E. Stuart, et al., *Religion is a Queer Thing*.

Prayer
Jim Burklo

Dear One,
I feel . . . (What am I feeling in my body and in my heart?)
I want . . . (What do I desire, whether it seems worthy or not?)
I release . . . (What and whom do I need to forgive, for what or whom do
I want to stop grasping?)
I accept . . . (What am I willing to receive, to affirm, in this moment?)
I thank . . . (For whom and what am I grateful?)

So it is, Amen!

Reading the Bible
Gregory C. Jenks

Reading the Bible is a practice that has been an integral part of Christianity from the start. Since that time the definition of 'Bible' has changed significantly, as for the first followers of Jesus the collection of sacred writings was more or less what we know as the 'Old Testament'.

The Bible was read then—and continues to be read now—in the hope of discerning a message from God. The shorthand label for this message is the 'word of God'. The prophets of ancient Israel proclaimed the word of the Lord, and in many churches around the world readings from the Bible finish with the acclamation, 'The word of the Lord.' This doesn't mean "these words were written by God" (although it may often seem that is how people are thinking), but rather: "Take this to heart and you will discern what God wants you to know."

Privately in their individual devotional practices, and collectively in classes and worship, Christians read the Bible in a quest for holy wisdom relevant to their everyday life here and now. The purpose of reading the Bible is not to acquire information about the past, or even to settle arguments between Christians over beliefs and practices, but to discern who we are and how we should act.

This engagement in spiritual discernment using the discipline of Bible reading requires us to take the Bible seriously, but that does not mean we must take the Bible literally. We might take very seriously the idea that all life comes from God, without taking literally any of the creation stories found in the Bible. In fact, to take everything in the Bible literally could mean we cannot take it seriously.

As with any book that we choose to read, the Bible invites us to engage in a process of creating meaning as we read the stories, poems, lists and regulations. Without a reader the words are mute shapes on a page, like notes on a musical score. With a reader the tune starts to come to life, and with a skilled reader some wonderful performances may be anticipated.

Reading the Bible is an inherently social act. Even when done by an individual privately, it involves the convergence of multiple human cultural achievements. The Bible was made possible by the invention of the alphabet in ancient Canaan. It requires a society with sufficient wealth and complexity to support an educated elite to produce, preserve, and transmit the texts, as well as generations of scribes and scholars. I need to have the language skills to read the text, and the text in my hands is the product of advanced technologies. My reading of the Bible will most likely be life-giving when exercised in the company of other people who are sharing my journey, and whose insights act as correctives and stimulants to my own glimpses of that holy wisdom we call the 'word of the Lord'.

Further Reading

M. J. Borg, *Reading the Bible Again for the First Time*.
G. C. Jenks, *The Once and Future Bible*.
S. L. McKenzie, *How to Read the Bible*.

Religious Naturalism

Rex A. E. Hunt

Progressive theologian Val Webb asks in her latest book:

> Is the Divine within us, within nature, within everything, or is everything within the Sacred? Or, is GOD somewhere else, separate from us, perhaps in the heavens?[1]

Religious naturalism seeks to offer a response to these questions. It does so by exploring and encouraging religious ways of responding to the world on a completely naturalistic basis, without a supernatural, omnipotent being which is 'other than' the natural world.

Religious naturalism is a set of beliefs and attitudes (the metaphor 'Big Tent' is now often used to describe its broad and inclusive range of beliefs, principles, and backgrounds) that affirm there are religious aspects which focus on this world. It recognizes that nature is constitutive of who and what we are as human beings. And wonder and awareness (and mystery) need to infuse our experiences of life if we are to live full and valuable lives. Indeed, we are 'interrelated beings' — both to the past and the present, and to nature itself. We are rooted in an imperfect, unfinished, and evolving 'web' of natural processes. Novelty rather than order is the nature of the 'divine'.

Those who have embraced this thinking, in a variety of ways, make for an interesting who's who: Henry Nelson Wieman, Ralph Wendell Burhoe, Karl E. Peters, Ursula Goodenough, Philip Hefner, Charley Hardwick, Chet Raymo, Loyal Rue, Sheila Greeve Davaney, Brian Swimme, Marvin C. Shaw, Michael Dowd, Jerome A. Stone.

In his book *Religious Naturalism Today. The Rebirth of a Forgotten Alternative*, Jerome Stone suggests that religious naturalism could prove very helpful to those casting about for a credible religious outlook [and] realize that here is a tradition with immense religious and conceptual resources . . . a new major dialogue partner in the chorus of religious and theological voices.[2]

While Hardwick finds four basic features within naturalistic theology:

1. that only the world of nature is real,
2. that nature is necessary in the sense of requiring no sufficient reason beyond itself to account for its origin,
3. that nature as a whole may be understood without appeal to any kind of intelligence or purposive agent,
4. that all causes are natural causes, products of other natural events.[3]

So, what are some of the issues being faced by 'religious naturalists' which may inspire those 'progressives' 'casting about'? Stone makes these suggestions:

1. whether the object of religious orientation is the whole universe, or part of it—such as a creative process,
2. whether the idea of 'God' can be reconceived within a naturalistic framework,
3. whether the object of religious orientation has the quality of power or goodness, is morally ambiguous or determinate, and
4. what sources of religious insight does religious naturalism explore: the world as understood scientifically or by an appreciative perception?[4]

Religious naturalism suggests there is no personal god 'out there', external to human beings and the material world/universe. To offer a metaphor from Stone's writing: it is more like the caffeine in the coffee than like a cherry on top of a sundae.

Notes

1. V. Webb, *Stepping Out with the Sacred*, 10–11.
2. J. Stone, *Religious Naturalism Today*, xii.
3. C. D. Hardwick, *Events of Grace*, 5–8.
4. J. Stone, *Religious Naturalism Today*, 225–29.

Further Reading

U. Goodenough, *The Sacred Depths of Nature*.
K. Peters, *Dancing with the Sacred*.
J. Stone, *Religious Naturalism Today*.

Religion and Terrorism

James Veitch

Religion 'used to empower and or to authorize acts of violence in order to strike fear in the innocent to achieve significant political outcomes' has had a long history.

One of the most famous incidents from ancient times is the story of Jericho and the massacre of its inhabitants in the name of God. Another ancient group were the *Sicarii*—the 'dagger men'—a first century movement who fought in the years leading up to the Jewish Roman war of 66–73 CE.

The subsequent two thousand years is full of similar stories across cultures, with human violence in the Western world reaching a high point in what is called *la Grande Terreur*—the 'great terror'—of the French Revolution. (The English words *terror*, meaning "to shake with fear", and *terrorist*, meaning "the person who is the cause of this fear", are derived from this period of European history).

A hundred and seventy-two years later the bombing of Hiroshima and Nagasaki, 7–9 August 1945, caused the deaths of around two hundred thousand Japanese. Nearly a year later (22 July 1946) terrorism had a new beginning driven by religious concerns. The King David Hotel in Jerusalem, was attacked by the right wing Zionist underground movement, Irgun. Ninety-one people were killed and forty-six injured. Subsequently, in Palestine/Israel and across the Middle East, religion has driven and empowered the terrorism.

The 1979 Revolution in Iran and the defeat of the Soviet military in Afghanistan in 1989 acted as catalysts inspiring the emergence of

Muslim movements that resorted to acts of violence to further their political objectives. One of the most important of these objectives was the restoration of the caliphate, a form of rule, instituted at the time of the death of the Prophet Muhammad in 632 CE. It ended on 4 March 1924 when the 101st Caliph, Abdul Mejeed, was deposed by the Turkish parliament. The caliphate had as its 'mission' 'one nation under Allah' stretching from Indonesia to Russia, made up of Muslims from different ethnic origins and numbering today around 1.5 billion people; a third of the population of the world.

The caliphate had an impressive cultural, social, political, scientific and religious history, for six hundred years, but following the fall of Bagdad in 1258 CE, it increasingly lost its way caught by the rising tide of international economic and military forces, and Governments with policies alien to its own. In the twentieth century the Caliphate was reduced by the effects of colonization to become a shadow of its former influence, but even so the unexpected exile of the 101st Caliph stunned the Muslim world. With the energy needs of many nations driving them to seek oil and gas from Muslim countries, who are mostly the guardians of these natural resources, the opportunity to restore the influence of Islam has come to the fore.

Al Qaeda, (along with the many movements it has created) advocates the restoration of the Caliphate and the rejuvenation of Islam worldwide. They took their struggle to New York on 11 September 2001. The attack on the Twin Towers was an event that stunned the world but it also began an unprecedented period of conflict in the Middle East leading to war in Afghanistan, Iraq, instability for Pakistan and retaliatory terrorist attacks in South East Asia, the Middle East, North Africa and parts of Europe. More than one and half million people died in the conflicts.

The assassination, on 2 May 2010, of Osama bin Laden, the leader of Al Qaeda, occurred at the same time as an Arab Uprising (2010–2011) was spreading across parts of the Muslim world, leaving the world guessing as to what will ultimately happen. More troublesome than this is the reality that for many terrorists religion is what empowers them to do what they believe they must—and this seems to turn religious faith upside down. There are troubling times ahead.

Further Reading

M. Duffy Toft, et al., *God's Century*.

R. A. Horsley, "The *Sicarii*: Ancient Jewish 'Terrorists'".

P. Taylor, *Talking to Terrorists*.

J. Veitch and J. Martin, *The Death of Osama bin Laden and the Future of Al-Qaeda*.

D. P. Wright-Neville, *Dictionary of Terrorism*.

The Resurrection
(and Jesus)

James Veitch

John Bowden who edited the SCM *Dictionary of Theology*, began the Conclusion to his article on "Jesus" with these words. "There is a good deal that we probably do know about Jesus; the trouble is that we cannot always be sure precisely what it is."[1]

The reason for this scepticism lies in the character of the gospels and the literature of the New Testament. The New Testament is not concerned about historical details. Its writers are concerned with recording the belief that Jesus the historical man was and is the Christ. And they do this in different ways.

The first gospel (the Gospel of Q and the later Gospel of Thomas) recorded sayings that marked Jesus out as a special storyteller: there was no narrative about his birth or his death. It was his words, and the words of others who had understood his mind, that offered encouragement and hope for his friends and followers who lived in rather grim Roman colonial times.

The Gospel of Mark, circulating about the year 75 CE as a text possibly concluding at 15:41, told the story of Jesus in the form of a novel. Mark is not a historical novel but a story made up by the author with possibly the example of Josephus and other Greek writers in mind. But again there is no reference to his birth or to his resurrection. What grabbed the attention of the writer was the execution of Jesus (the only historical note in the Gospel)—Jesus was a good man who had died a bad death. But in the story of his life, made up by the author, all that he did and said pointed towards his death and therefore his vindication as one of God's finest spokespersons.

The Gospel of Matthew, circulating in the early 80s, and which includes Q, continues Mark's story line, adds a story about his birth, enlarges the story of his death, and for the first time adds stories about the discovery of an empty tomb; and in two verses refers to a resuscitated Jesus (28:9–10).

The Gospel of Luke, circulating in the late 90s CE, and which includes Q, enlarges on Mark's main story line, on Matthew's birth stories and on the stories of his death. It also adds stories about the activities of a post resurrection Jesus: a perfect fit for a gospel circulating in the Greek religious world.

The Gospel of John, circulating around 120 CE, adds to the stories of his death, and adds resurrection stories, two of which provide the clearest indication of any writer of how the reader was to understand the resurrection. The meeting between Mary Magdalene and Jesus (20:11–18) has all the hallmarks of being a human grief story. So does the meeting between Jesus and Thomas (20:24–29).

Deeply grieved and hurt by the death of Jesus, Mary 'sees' and 'talks' with Jesus and then feels the relief of knowing he has survived a terrible death and is no longer confined to an unknown grave where he cannot be revered as a martyr. Mary's and Thomas's grief give rise to the Jesus of faith. What is an inner grief experience in which Jesus appears is extrapolated into an objective appearance outside of grief into human time and space—but the latter is the work of the storyteller. Without an appearance of the deceased in dreams or daytime visions those closest who grieve the death can never be assured that the person has survived death. Grief, the deepest of human emotions, provides the origin of the metaphor of 'bodily' resurrection. It is another way of vindicating the Jesus of *Q* and of his closeness to God, and of acknowledging Mark's storytelling tradition that gave the words of Jesus their potency and their life.

Notes

1. J. Bowden, *Dictionary of Theology*, 312.

Further Reading

S. J. Patterson, "Was the Resurrection Christianity's Big Bang?"
B. B. Scott, *The Resurrection of Jesus.*
_____, *The Trouble with Resurrection.*
G. Vermes, *The Resurrection.*

Revelation and Reason

James Veitch

How do we know that what they believe about God and about Jesus is for 'real'? Many claims made about God and about Jesus depend on the answer.

At the first Council of Nicaea that met between 20 May and the 25 July 325 CE an answer was given. It was drawn up then revised and promulgated at the second Council that met in 381 CE at Constantinople. The answer or creed is still used today. The Council was called to resolve a conflict in the Church at Alexandria.

Arius, a presbyter in the Church at Alexandria, believed Jesus was a human being, though created by God and born of the Virgin Mary. The Bishop, Alexander of Alexandria, and most of the Bishops and clergy present believed Jesus, though born of the Virgin Mary as a human, was the Son of God and was of the same 'substance' as God his Father and was co-eternal with him. Both claimed the support of verses in the Gospel of John. Arius said of Jesus: "The Father is greater than me" (14:28) and the Bishop quoted Jesus, saying, "I and the Father are one" (10:30 and 17:21). With only two dissensions the position of the Bishop was adopted by the Council. Arius was declared a heretic and exiled.

This declaration of the divinity of Jesus was the most important decision ever made by the Church: it laid the basis for Christian doctrine and the development of liturgies. It cleared the way for the civil roles assigned to bishops by the Emperor Constantine. The decisions were later re-affirmed in the Chalcedonian formula of 451 CE.

The Council also settled the date for Easter, the 'Christian Passover', revised by Dionysus Exiguus (470–544 CE) and still later by Pope Gregory in 1582. This decision replaced Passover with Easter. Nicaea decided the question of the divinity of Jesus however, before there was a New Testament (NT). The contents and the order of the NT were agreed by another Council in 397 CE and by the translation of the NT into Latin by Jerome (347–420 CE) sometime after 380 CE. The NT and the OT combined became the Bible after 400 CE. What the disciples were thought to believe about Jesus according to Nicaea is now in writing in the Gospels and the letters of Paul. The questions about belief were settled as the creed and were later confirmed in the festival of Easter and by the emergence of the NT. Belief is now founded on revelation. Augustine (354–430 CE) and later St Anselm (1033–1109) expressed it in this way: *do not seek to understand in order to believe but believe that you may understand.* Aquinas (1225–1274) built on this formula. So did Luther (1483–1546) and Calvin (1509–1535).

Late in the eighteenth century the divinity of Jesus came under the microscope. Hermann Reimarus (1694–1768) questioned the bodily resurrection of Jesus and attacked the concept of revelation. Although his critique was muted, the question of how Christians know that what they believe about God and about Jesus is for 'Real' had become a central theological problem.

Nicaea would be stoutly defended by Karl Barth (1886–1968) and more recently by N. T. Wright. On the other hand, following the lead of the German theologian Fredrich Schleiermacher (1768–1834), Robert Funk (1926–2005), influenced by the thinking of Bultmann (1884–1976) and Tillich (1886–1965), founded the Jesus Seminar (1985) to rigorously engage the question of how we know that what we believe about God and Jesus is for 'real'.

Funk wrote: "I do not want my faith to be in Jesus but in . . . some version of whatever it was that Jesus believed." In order to know that what we believe about God and Jesus is for 'real', we should first re-discover what it was that Jesus said and did, and therefore what he believed about God. This is to turn the Nicea-Constantinople creed on its head, and displaces revelation with reason.

Further Reading

R. W. Funk, *A Credible Jesus*.

J. A. T. Robinson, *Honest to God*.

J. A. Veitch, "Revelation and Religion in the Theology of Karl Barth".

Rites of Passage

John Bodycomb

In *Les Rites de Passage* (1909) French anthropologist Arnold Van Gennep (1873–1957) found all cultures mark transitions from one stage to another. Ceremonies were associated with birth, initiation, marriage, and death, etc. Progressives are challenged by baptisms, weddings and funerals. In these one meets a motley mix of humans, many of whom will not be seen again until the next one. Some have residual Christian memory. . . .

"Hi, is that the reverend?"

"How can I help?"

"We want to get Michael Jackson done. We all got done as kids, and Mum says we should organise it for him."

"Sounds like a lovely thing to do for Michael. You're Mrs Jackson?"

"No, that's his first names."

"I didn't get your name."

"You want mine or his dad's. We're not married yet."

"Yours is fine."

"Gloria-Jean. Call me Gee-Jay; everyone else does."

Should one bend over backwards to show Gee-Jay & Co. that God's love is indiscriminate, or consider how this erodes the given gospel? How does one mediate the tension between gospel inclusiveness and 'cheap grace', as Bonhoeffer called it? Even if there's a deep-and-meaningful with the young parents, what sort of wording won't be gobbledegook to grandparents, godparents, uncles, aunts, et al.?

Another call. "You won't know me, but I went to Sunday school at your church. My name is Agnes Day. My husband and I were wondering if you would do a wedding for our Holly." "I don't see why not. Tell me a little more, though."

Holly and partner have been cohabiting for two years, saving to pay off a house, sleeping and socialising on week-ends. They're in church for the occasional wedding, funeral or 'christening', as Mrs Day calls it. Neither is hostile to organised religion; they're just not interested. When Holly's parents say a church wedding would be 'nice', they say, "You find a church and we'll look at it."

If the minister is a progressive, what should go into the ceremony? One option is elegant 'prayer book' language, which some love because it sounds archaic! Another is a form for marriage that is not inelegant, but is contemporary and congruent with progressive thought.

Another call: Sunday evening! "Jim here from Tranquillity Funerals, Alan. I have the family of George Ternipp in the next room. Mr Ternipp passed away yesterday. Did you know him?" "I don't think so. Was he associated with this parish?" "The family say he was married there, and always said he wanted his funeral there." "Right. And Mrs Ternipp?" "Alive, but in care. Could you do it on Wednesday?" "Must it be Wednesday?" "They want it over quickly. Not a big occasion." "The reason?" "It takes some of the pain out of things. They don't want grandchildren getting upset with a coffin out front."

Alan knows a funeral is better prepared, and those close to the deceased in better shape, if there is breathing space between the death and the funeral. He also knows there should not have to be a choice between jubilant celebration and mournful misery. The fact is, someone is no longer with us, and death is final. But there are resources other than 'denial'.

At many funerals, 15 percent will be churchgoers; 85 percent may range from those with a residue of affection for the religious content, to those who feel totally out of place! In a religiously pluralist society, there may be members of other faiths. Given that a funeral is to help people deal with loss and grief and say their 'good-byes', sensitivity is at a premium. Rites of passage? Phew!

Further Reading

W. Carr, *Brief Encounters.*

Science and Religion

Michael Zimmerman

As University of Wisconsin historian of science Ronald Numbers shows in his fascinating book *Galileo Goes to Jail and other Myths about Science and Religion*, the battle between science and religion that everyone *knows* has been raging for centuries, in fact, isn't nearly as real as it might appear. Consider how clearly he sets forth his surprising thesis: "The greatest myth in the history of science and religion holds that they have been in a state of constant conflict."[1]

Numbers goes on to argue that the belief that these two fields have been at war forever largely arose from two books published in the nineteenth century. In 1874 John William Draper published *History of the Conflict between Religion and Science*, which built on work of Cornell University president Andrew Dickson White. A bit later, in 1896, White himself produced his massive, two-volume opus entitled *A History of the Warfare of Science with Theology in Christendom*.

As with most myths, there is a kernel of truth in Draper's and White's accounts. But, as Numbers says, "Historians of science have known for years that White's and Draper's accounts are more propaganda than history."[2] Both, as Numbers explains, were promoting personal anti-religious agendas and both were engaging in hyperbolic, but very persuasive, rhetoric.

If the Herculean struggle between religion and science is a myth, what is the reality? In 1997 Stephen Jay Gould, in a widely cited essay, attempted to demarcate the boundaries of both science and religion by defining "non-overlapping magisteria" for the two. While some have called his efforts naïve and simplistic, there is great value in recognizing, as he did, that religion and science use different methodologies to ask and answer different questions.

The two come directly into conflict when some religious adherents make specific truth claims about the world that science has shown to be false. Typically, such conflict arises when a sacred text is interpreted literally rather than metaphorically. That this conflict is unnecessary is evidenced by the fact that thousands upon thousands of religious leaders have joined an organization called The Clergy Letter Project and have signed a statement that says, in part, "Religious truth is of a different order from scientific truth. Its purpose is not to convey scientific information but to transform hearts." The statement goes on to promote science, making it clear that religion is not threatened but enriched by scientific knowledge: "We urge school board members to preserve the integrity of the science curriculum by affirming the teaching of the theory of evolution as a core component of human knowledge. We ask that science remain science and that religion remain religion, two very different, but complementary, forms of truth."

The U.S. National Academy of Sciences has endorsed just this perspective on the relationship between religion and science in their book entitled *Science, Evolution, and Creationism*. "Science and religion are based on different aspects of human experience. . . . Attempts to pit science and religion against each other create controversy where none needs to exist."[3]

Notes

1. Numbers, *Galileo Goes to Jail*, 1.
2. Numbers, 6.
3. National Academy of Sciences, *Science, Evolution, and Creationism*, 8.

Further Reading

The Clergy Letter Project website.
S. J. Gould, "Nonoverlapping Magisteria".
National Academy of Sciences, *Science, Evolution, and Creationism*.
R. L. Numbers, *Galileo Goes to Jail and Other Myths about Science and Religion*.

Social Justice

Noel Preston

Historically, religious institutions have been ambivalent in their commitment to social justice. There have been extensive periods in the history of Christendom when the church has been an instrument of gross injustice.

During the twentieth century a range of factors combined to renew focus on matters of social justice. For instance, international conflicts led to *The Universal Declaration of Human Rights*. Within Christian theology, influential movements of Liberation Theology and Feminist Theology emerged. These theological revisions connect directly to the emergence of progressive Christianity. They support an endeavour to go beyond social welfare measures toward social change. They employ social analysis to transform unjust structures, the economy, social policies and laws—an ongoing process continually refined through action and reflection.

The recovery of social justice as a constitutive element of Christian mission was aided by rediscovering the prophetic biblical emphasis on justice for the marginalised, expressed in Jesus' vision of the Kin(g) dom of God. Central to the gospel is the injunction to love God and neighbour. In complex social, racial and international relations, love translates into the struggle for social justice. That is, justice is love distributed.

The idea of 'distribution' is suggestive of the practical content in social justice (sometimes termed 'distributive justice'). A just society is one that practises *fairness*, redressing inequalities by redistributing resources. Along with *equality*, *freedom* is another principle underpinning social justice. The tension between 'freedom' and 'equality' led to competing philosophies and political platforms in the modern era. This is expressed in the rival claims of *socialism* and *capitalism*. That said, a progressive religious position is not simply aligned with any political philosophy or party or social justice program.

There are other principles central to a progressive approach to social justice. At the top of this list is *a commitment to the most disadvantaged, the poor, the powerless in any society.* That is why progressive religious activists take up issues like poverty, indigenous minorities, sexual discrimination and the treatment of prisoners. In a nutshell, social justice requires us to reflect and act ethically, about economic issues, from the standpoint of the poorest, not the rich; or environmental questions from the standpoint of the most threatened species, and so on. At the personal level, this involves care and compassion giving priority to the vulnerable and the vulnerability in us all. Other guiding principles widely accepted as necessary for social justice are: *inclusiveness, access, equity and commitment to the common good.* This latter idea suggests the further principle of *sustainability* which emphasizes the interests of all (human and non-human) in developing a global society and environment, which aims for the good of all, for present and future generations. In a sense, *eco-justice* embraces social justice.

Eco-justice is premised on the view that the human degradation of nature is fundamentally linked to the social patterns and social institutions that oppress human beings. We cannot address one without the other. Poverty is an ecological problem, just as violations of nature's bio-diversity and the biosphere have exacerbated the extent of global poverty.

Further Reading

N. Preston, *Beyond the Boundary.*

Ode to Cleanser

Jim Burklo

I try to forget you, hide you under the sink
Till the ring in the toilet brings you back to mind.

You are the dirt I enlist to fight dirt,
The janissary I send to fight your own kind,
The homeopathic remedy for grime.
Desert in a can, a little dune of you
Is all it takes to make a bathtub shine.
A short sandstorm of you
Is all it takes to make a faucet gleam.

Though you clot like the Sahara
When rare rain turns its dust to mud,
You never rot.
With a shake or a poke, you are at my service,
A faithful servant that sleeps till I need you.
Oh, if only I could stroke your container
With an ungloved hand, and drive all filth away!

Genie in a cardboard bottle, Three wishes I make of you:
Clean my kitchen,
Clean my bathroom,
And do both without me.

Spirituality

Fred Plumer

Every major religious movement in history has started with an individual who had a profound, transformative, 'spiritual' experience.

This experience or series of experiences transformed his or her perspective on reality and of self. Some may have called it enlightenment, others awakening, and others 'born again'. As other people noticed differences in these individuals, they asked what had changed. I believe these 'changed individuals', probably with some reluctance, became teachers of a path. What is important to note, for purposes of this cameo, is how many things these teachers had in common when they attempted to describe what they had experienced and what had changed in them. In spite of different cultures, different settings, the most common characteristic these new teachers described was a profound experience of a sense of Unity or Oneness with all Creation, Life, God, or possibly the 'Father'. Jesus was no exception.

When Jesus tried to explain his experience of the Realm or Kingdom of God, he talked about what he experienced using metaphors and images of his times. Over the centuries, much has been lost in translations, and because of the contemporary ignorance of what these images were meant to portray. I believe we find the best insight of this phenomenon in the Book of Thomas, since this book does not appear to have been redacted as heavily as other Gospels.

Thomas' Jesus states:

> . . . the Kingdom is inside you and it is outside you. When you come to know yourselves, then you will be known, and you will see that you are children of the living father. . . ." (v. 22)

He also declares:

> . . . When you make the two into one, and when you make the inner like the outer and the outer like the inner, and the upper like the lower, and when you make male and female into a single one, so that the male will not be male nor the female be female, when you make eyes in place of an eye, a hand in place of a hand, a foot in place of a foot, an image in place of an image, then you will enter the kingdom. (v. 84)

In other words Thomas' Jesus was not teaching people how they must behave or think so they might end up in some wonderful place when they die, but rather a path which could enable the follower to experience something profound and transforming—something that will change one's way to view and relate to reality in the present moment. It was his assumption that what he experienced, we, the followers, might experience as well.

What is this 'place', this experience? It is the experience of Oneness—Oneness with all Creation, with God, with the Father. It is the experience that according to Neil Douglas-Klotz, Jesus referred to as "Sacred Unity".

So how do we have this experience? How do we gain this perspective of our reality according to the Jesus path? Some of those teachings are obvious. We must learn to trust the Universe. We must learn to take responsibility for our actions that have harmed others or ourselves and commit to changing our ways. We must learn to forgive, even our enemies. We must learn to love without conditions.

These are the lessons we can garner in the classroom. But they only work when we practice them.

However, Jesus the Teacher was very clear that if we really wanted to experience that Sacred Unity, we would have to come out of our 'classrooms', our homes and our hiding places of comfort, and meet people in need wherever they are in order to offer true compassion to those who suffer, and those in need. He suggested that we do this no matter how much different than us they might be, even our tribal enemies. Real compassion means a willingness to share with others. It may mean self-sacrifice. It might even prove to be costly.

Let me be clear. This is not an 'ought' or even some 'Kantian categorical imperative'. This is an opportunity to discover and experience Sacred Unity. It is a 'state of being' where all divisions, all separations, all boundaries disappear. It can be the place where Oneness is experiential and transformative at the same time. We can be confident that Jesus lived in that 'state of being', in that reality. However we must not forget what he repeatedly told his students and followers: "Go and do likewise."

Further Reading

C. Bourgeault, *The Wisdom Jesus.*
M. Fox, *A New Reformation.*
E. Pagels, *Beyond Belief.*

Wesleyan Quadrilateral

Paul Alan Laughlin

'Wesleyan Quadrilateral' is a phrase coined by twentieth-century American Methodist scholar Albert C. Outler to identify the four sources of authority that he discerned in the collected theological musings of the founder of Methodism, John Wesley (1703–1791):

1. scripture (the Bible)
2. tradition (the history of Christian thought and doctrine)
3. reason (one's own and that of other intelligent people)
4. experience (both personal and communal)

Although Wesley almost certainly gave primacy to the first of these, scripture, and saw the other three as interpretative aids in determining its theoretical meaning and practical implications, his quadrilateral was and remains inherently progressive in its identification of two internal and therefore liberal sources of authority (reason and experience) over against two external and inherently conservative ones (scripture and tradition).

These four criteria, therefore, not only clearly set Wesley apart from both the Catholic claim of a bilateral source of authority (scripture and tradition) and Luther's unilateral *sola scriptura* (scripture alone), but also strongly suggest that both of these positions were naïve in ignoring the inevitable role of the individual in discerning the meaning of any scriptural passage, as well as in drawing practical implications from it. Wesley's quadrilateral thus opened the way for his successors, both within and beyond Methodism, to elevate reason and experience in importance, and with them to reinforce any individual's right to claim autonomy (see entry above) in determining religious and theological truth.

Further Reading

T. A. Campbell, et al., *Wesley and the Quadrilateral.*
A. C. Outler, *John Wesley.*
D. A. D. Thorsen, *The Wesleyan Quadrilateral.*

World Religions

Val Webb

Who are we? Why are we here? Is there Something greater than us? Can we contact that which is ultimately real? How? These human questions have been asked down the centuries and various answers have formed the world's religions.

"Religion" comes from the Latin *religio*, "to bind" — binding humans with the Sacred. While no one can prove an Ultimate Reality as an objective fact, we are surrounded by people in different cultures and times who have been convinced about, or had faith in, a Sacred dimension to life, whether called God, Brahman, Mother Earth, Mystery or Emptiness.

Religions address the 'human condition' — that awareness that something is wrong with the world; where do we want to be; how do we get there and how this involves (or not) the Sacred? Generally, in religions of Middle Eastern origin (Judaism, Christianity and Islam), the human problem is sin or disobedience and the solution is forgiveness and restoration of right relationship with Abraham's God (monotheism), as described in their Sacred texts. In religions arising in India (Hinduism and Buddhism), the human condition is ignorance of our true nature and our grasping at external things and the solution is discovering our true nature. Hindus discover that their individual self, *atman*, is actually the Universal Self *Brahman*. Buddhists realize their *no-self* and become 'buddhas', or enlightened ones. In Chinese religions (Confucianism and Daoism), the human condition is disharmony with self, society and the world and the solution is restoration of this natural balance—by education and a structured society in Confucianism; and through *Dao* (*Tao*) in Daoism, the mysterious way of nature and power that maintains harmony. Indigenous religious traditions sense the presence of the Sacred with/around them in nature and bind their communal life to this through story and ritual. Separation from land/ earth/nature results in alienation and 'lostness'.

By recognizing the contextually specific origins of religions as the human desire to bond with Something More, however described, we can move beyond truth claims and doctrines as the foci of religion and share the common search for human transformation, whether called salvation, liberation, enlightenment, healing or perfection. Traditional Christianity's insistence on Jesus as Divine and salvation residing only in the church has long created a stumbling block for serious engagement across religions, but in today's multicultural, multi-faith communities, knowledge of, and dialogue with, other religions is no longer an option but essential for human understanding and harmony. By learning how the Divine appears in religions other than our own, we enlarge our own possibilities for transformation.

Further Reading

T. M. Ludwig, *The Sacred Paths.*
H. Smith, *The Illustrated World's Religions.*
V. Webb, *Like Catching Water in a Net.*
V. Webb, *Stepping Out with the Sacred.*

Reclaiming the Faith's Freethinkers

Heretics or Heroes?

Paul Laughlin

Introduction: What Is 'Heresy'?

Heresy is any belief, opinion, doctrine or theory that is held by one or more proponents of a particular religion, but that is at variance with the beliefs or doctrines deemed as correct (or orthodox) by an established authority within that faith. Its adjective form is *heretical*, and one adjudged to hold such a belief is called a *heretic*.

Heresy is synonymous with two other words used in the history of Christianity. The first is *anathema*, an ancient Greek word that originally connoted a gift to a deity, but which is used in the New Testament to mean "excluded", "condemned", or "accursed". That word was employed from early on in official ecclesial circles to condemn both a heresy and its perpetrator, and upon conviction usually entailed the excommunication—and eventually the possible execution—of the offending party and the eradication of his or her writings. A second, less loaded, and more descriptive synonym for heresy is *heterodoxy* (from the Greek *heterodoxos*, literally "of other opinion"). This synonym suggests a rather more neutral sense of the term heresy than the more sinister, pejorative connotation it has had for most of Christian history and still in common parlance today.

The whole idea of heresy in this negative sense gained real momentum in the writings of the first important Christian apologist, which is to say 'defender' of the faith. He was Irenaeus (d. *ca.* 202 CE), a native of Asia Minor who became the bishop of what is now Lyons, France. In the late second century he authored a book entitled *Against Heresies*, a vigorous attack upon the perceived threat of Gnosticism to what he regarded as *orthodoxy*—that is, "right belief". His main target was Valentinus (treated below), whom Irenaeus opposed on the basis of scripture, tradition, and—not surprisingly—episcopal authority. His book was so influential it virtually defined heresy not only among Irenaeus' contemporary defenders of orthodoxy, but among Catholic, Eastern Orthodox, and some Protestant Christians well into modern times. Heresy, after all, is what the many Christian councils and synods, and eventually the Inquisition, were created to oppose and eliminate. Thanks in large part to Irenaeus, therefore, throughout Christian history the term heresy has been a pejorative: a source of accusation, an indictable charge, and an occasion for censure or some other dire punishment, in many cases including torture and death.

As already suggested, however, the word heresy has a much more benign origin than its later usage might suggest. It derives ultimately from the Greek verb *hairein*, which means "to choose". It therefore connotes a freedom of choice in matters of belief on the part of an individual or group over against an authoritative system that would deny such latitude in favour of a set of doctrines or dogmas that must be assented to and accepted as necessarily true or orthodox. Heresy, then, is always an act or expression of *autonomy*, which is to say self-determination, self-regulation, and independence of the intellect over any sort of *heteronomy*—the authority of another, be that 'other' an ecclesiastical institution, specific authority figure, religious tradition or fixed creed. The ecclesiastical powers in any given age and place have a vested interest in defining, opposing and, if possible, eliminating beliefs that have been chosen or even invented by wilful individuals or groups rather than merely accepted as revealed truth; and they have frequently found such parties to be in error, offensive, or downright dangerous. From a progressive Christian perspective, however, autonomy and freedom of choice in matters of belief and practice are essential. To put it another way, progressivism highly values internal authority—be it reason or experience—over any external authority, and thus makes heresy not only a positive option, but as Peter Berger nicely puts it, an *imperative.*

It is in this spirit that we shall take a quick and admittedly selective look backward to identify the fifteen most influential individual heretics in the history of Christianity, avoiding for the sake of brevity such heretical groups as the Cathars (also known as the Albigensians). We shall examine these individuals precisely for the purpose of appreciating and reclaiming them for their inadvertent contribution to the modern progressive Christian perspective, which they could not have anticipated and might even have rejected, freethinkers as they were. Indeed, we shall see each was progressive in his or her own way and on one or another issue, sharing only a determination to use their minds and to believe only what was rationally sound. After our survey, we shall close with some examples of modern figures who, for a variety of reasons, either have been publicly accused or formally charged of being heretics, or who would otherwise probably qualify as *bona fide* heretics in the minds of many, had that label not fallen into general disuse in the past century or so, even in Roman Catholic circles, where the term was first coined and embraced. We shall proceed in approximate chronological order.

A Survey of Christian Free-Thinkers (a.k.a. 'Heretics')

1. Marcion, a Radical Rationalist

Marcion (85–160 CE) was a cleric and theologian who became the first significant heretic of Christianity. He was a native of a coastal city on the Black Sea in what is today northeastern Turkey. The heart of his alleged error was his refusal to acknowledge the God of the Hebrew Bible as the same deity represented by Jesus, and his consequent rejection of Judaism as incompatible with Christianity.

The God of what most Christians now regard as their 'Old Testament' he called the Demiurge, the creator of the universe all right, but still a petty, jealous, and angry tribal deity who demanded obedience to laws and severely punished those who refused to conform to them. Marcion recognized the God of Jesus Christ, by contrast, as a universal deity whose primary attributes were love, benevolence, compassion, and mercy. Jesus he identified as the Son of this heavenly Father, but also as a purely spiritual being only appearing or pretending to be a material human being—an idea that would come to be known as Docetism (from the Greek word meaning "to seem") and pronounced a heresy in its own right. As if his dualistic (two-God) theology and his Docetist view of Jesus were not enough to draw the ire and opposition of the mainstream, Marcion proposed a scriptural canon for the emerging religion. It amounts to Christianity's very first Bible, though it excluded not only specifically Jewish writings—the Hebrew Bible—but most of the Christian writings in circulation and use among his contemporary churches, some of which would much later become staples of the New Testament.

Marcion's canon comprised only eleven books: a single gospel, Luke's, but abridged to remove Jewish references and any mention of the childhood of Jesus; and ten letters of the Apostle Paul, whom Marcion believed to be the only true interpreter of Jesus and his mission. During the 140s CE, Marcion moved to Rome and there perfected his theology and gathered a following, but was eventually officially ex-communicated for his heresy—a term first used in Christian circles to refer to him. He returned to Asia Minor, where he continued to promote his ideas and drew there an even larger following, one that competed with Catholicism in that region for centuries. For its part, the Roman Catholic Church responded to the perceived threat of Marcion by establishing orthodox doctrines, forging a system of canon law, and beginning the process of establishing a Christian canon of scripture, all to protect itself from the likes of him.

For the history of progressive Christianity, however, Marcion stands as a positive model for his use of reason over against scripture and the loose consensus of belief among his contemporary fellow Christians, as well as for basing his own views on what for him was intellectually obvious: that the God of the Jews and the God of Jesus were incompatible.

Further Reading

E. C. Blackman, *Marcion and His Influence.*

J. B. Tyson, *Marcion and Luke-Acts.*

2. Montanus, an Exponent of Experience

Montanus, whose birth and death dates are uncertain, was a second-century native of ancient Phrygia in west central Anatolia (modern-day Turkey), not far from Marcion's home town, and, like this probably older contemporary, was one of the first important Christian heretics. Exact dates for him are difficult to discern, but he seems to have come to prominence sometime around the mid-point of the second century CE.

The heart of his heresy was ecstatic prophecy: he claimed to represent and spoke in the name of the second *Paraclete* (Comforter, or Advocate) promised by God to the early Christians in John 14:16, the first presumably having been Jesus and the second, the Holy Spirit. (Some followers of Montanus interpreted the implications of this sequence in such a way that they became Christianity's first Modalists, that is, deniers that the Father, Son, and Spirit are co-eternal persons but amount instead to successive modes or phases that a single God has gone through over time.) Among his many revelations, Montanus advocated a strict, celibate asceticism and a harsh system of penance, and predicted an imminent second coming of Christ and the establishment of a New Jerusalem in his native Phrygia. He was accompanied by two equally charismatic women, Priscilla and Maximilla, and with them attracted a substantial following, especially in Asia Minor.

He was soundly denounced by numerous Christian leaders and synods convened to counteract the threat posed by one purporting to have a direct pipeline, as it were, to God—one that would render the emerging ecclesial hierarchy unnecessary. Montanus and his followers (called Montanists) responded by separating themselves from the Rome-based Church. Their most prominent convert was Tertullian, a north African Christian theologian responsible for coining the important orthodox term 'Trinity', and was himself an avid heretic fighter—especially against Marcion (see above)—but who nevertheless was eventually denounced himself as a heretic because of his adherence to Montanism.

The fate of Montanus himself is unclear; according to one almost certainly spurious account, he and his companion Maximilla hanged themselves on separate occasions, but both in a similar state of ecstatic intoxication. The movement lived on for several centuries, concentrating eventually around the North African city of Carthage, and something of its spirit, at least, lives on among modern-day Pentecostals, who have sometimes been labelled neo-Montanists. As for Montanus' connection to modern progressive Christianity, he stands as an early example of one who responded autonomously, not to reason, as Marcion had done, but to his own experiences over against a powerful, emergent orthodoxy and its supporting magisterium—in other words, for autonomy against heteronomy in matters of belief and practice.

Further Reading

W. Tabbernee, *Prophets and Gravestones.*
C. Trevett, *Montanism.*

3. Valentinus, an Unorthodox Unitist

Valentinus (*ca.* 100–*ca.* 160 CE) was an Egyptian Christian philosopher of the mid-second century CE and one of the earliest and most notorious among early Christian heretics. He was born near and educated in the city of Alexandria, which was not only an important Christian centre at the time but also a hotbed of Middle-Platonic philosophy, whose leading light then and there was the Jewish philosopher Philo Judaeus. Exactly whom Valentinus may have heard or studied under is unclear; he only claimed to have had one teacher, Theudas, whom he identified as a disciple of St. Paul and a recipient of that apostle's most esoteric teachings.

Only fragments of his writings remain, preserved—as is often and ironically the case—as quotations in the refutations authored by his opponents and suppressors. What is certain is he was a gnostic, which means he believed in a kind of esoteric spiritual knowledge (*gnosis*) that alone had the power to save at least some segment of humanity, and that could only be obtained through a divine emissary. While most gnostics of that era were dualists, pitting good and evil, spirit and flesh, and so forth in opposing dyads, Valentinus was a monist, that is, a believer that all was finally One, the universe a kind of closed system with spiritual depth. This One, which he called the *Bythos* (Depth), did not create the material world so much as emanate or radiate it through three intermediate zones, gradations, or levels of existence. The highest of these was the *Pleroma* (Fullness), a purely spiritual realm where the eternal divine powers called 'Aeons', mediated between the spiritual and material world. Next was the *Kenoma* (Emptiness), where Wisdom dwelled. Finally, there was the *Kosmos*, the material world created by the Demiruge, the same subordinate creator deity that Marcon had posited.

Human beings occupied the very top level of this lower world, and were divided into three groups: the pneumatic (spiritual), who were capable of returning to the *Pleroma* through *gnosis;* the psychical, ordinary Christians who had souls rather than spirits, and therefore could achieve only a lesser, celestial home; and the somatic (bodily), mainly Jews and pagans, who were human only in a physical sense, and therefore spiritless, soulless, and unsalvageable. Valentinus also devised a three-fold method of scriptural interpretation that used allegory to capture the highest (pneumatic) sense of the most spiritual texts. Though his specific philosophical system is now dated and no doubt unacceptable to most modern progressive Christians, Valentinus nevertheless stands out as an early Christian who used rationality to determine his own belief system over against the prevailing orthodoxy, and who in the process struck a blow against literalism in the reading of scripture.

Further Reading

B. Aretius, *A Short History of Valentinus Gentilix.*
I. Dunderberg, *Beyond Gnosticism.*

4. Arius, a Debunker of Doctrines

Arius (256–336 CE) is perhaps the most famous (or infamous) heretic in Christian history. He was born in Libya and died in Constantinople, but his ecclesiastical career was as a *presbyter* (priest) in the Church of Alexandria, Egypt.

Arius lived at a time in which there was probably a general consensus among Christians that Jesus had been—and due to the resurrection, still was—divine in some sense, but his precise relationship as Son to the Father, much less to the Holy Spirit, had not yet been officially established. Arius, no doubt inadvertently, helped to trigger what would later be known at the Trinitarian Controversy when, around 318

CE, he denied both the eternality of the deity of Jesus as Son-Christ and his equality with the Father. Arius maintained the Son and the Father were not of the same being or substance (*homo-ousios* being the technical philosophical Greek term), but merely of similar being or substance (*homoi-ousios*)—a verbal difference of one Greek letter. He further held the Son had been created (or begotten) by the Father, and before that had not existed; and indeed had been called the Son as a recognition of his divine role rather than of any actual divine lineage. These views effectively subordinated the Son-Christ-Jesus to God the Father; and indeed Arius' position came to be known as Subordinationism.

His view gained great popularity throughout the Christian world and became so controversial that the Christian Emperor, Constantine, convened the Council of Nicea in 325 CE to settle the matter. It did— against Arius and the emergent Arianism: it asserted that the Son had been eternally begotten by the Father and therefore was co-eternal with him; and that the Son was of the same substance as the Father, and therefore co-equal to him. Arius and his followers and their views were pronounced *anathema*, which by that time meant not only heretical but dangerous. That official finding left the status of the Holy Spirit to be defined at a later date, but for all intents and purposes set the stage for an official Trinitarian doctrine with one Godhead but three co-eternal and co-equal Persons that are *substantially* (that is, *in being* or *essentially*) the same, and yet distinct.

Many Christians, of course, have struggled over the centuries with the strained logic of the Trinity—for example, how a Father and a Son can be the same age (namely, eternal); and most modern progressive Christians have probably shared in their puzzlement, with many concluding with Arius that equating, in effect, Jesus with God makes no rational sense. That leaves them, like Arius, in the minority among Christians as a whole and at odds with official doctrine, not only that of the Catholic Church but of many Protestant denominations as well. Arius' appeal to reason in matters of faith, then, has not been totally suppressed by external authorities, and to that extent, at least, his spirit survives, especially among progressive adherents of the faith.

Further Reading
T. McCall, *Which Trinity? Whose Monotheism?*
R. Williams, *Arius.*

5. Origen, an Eccentric Exegete
Origen (*ca.* 185–254 CE) was an early Christian theologian and scholar of scripture. Like Valentinus, he lived in Egypt and was based in the city of Alexandria, which, as mentioned above, was an important centre of

early Christianity and a hotbed of Greek philosophy; and he brought these two traditions together in his theological and biblical endeavours. As there was not yet a New Testament, but only various competing collections of early Christian writings, the 'Bible' for him was the Hebrew canon, which he interpreted in a variety of ways, including allegorically. His theology, not surprisingly, was quite similar to that of Valentinus in many ways, including his view of God and Christ in non-personal terms: as First Principle and Word (*Logos*), respectively.

What really earned him the reputation as a heretic, however, was his belief, first, that the Son was subordinate to the First Principle ('Father'), which suggested a hierarchy in the Trinity; and, second, that souls were pre-existent *and* subject to reincarnation in a process that would eventually reunite them and all spiritual entities, including even the damned and demons, with the God-Principle, not just in a communion, but an actual union—and, in effect, a universal salvation. (The fancy Greek term for this process of universal restoration is *apocatastasis*.)

Despite his pre-eminence as Christianity's first systematic theologian and the fact he eventually died as a martyr for the faith, such views, deviating as they did from those set forth at the Councils of Nicea (325 CE) and Chalcedon (451 CE), were declared heretical in the sixth century, and helped to keep him from elevation to sainthood by the Roman Catholic Church. The fact that, despite his appreciation for allegorical interpretation of scripture, he reportedly had taken the 'Eunuch Passage' (Matt 19:12) literally and castrated himself, did not help his case.

Another count against him was his having agreed to be ordained a priest while on a trip to Greece by way of Palestine, against the wishes of his own bishop back in Egypt. As questionable as these choices may have been, however, progressive Christians can at least embrace Origen as a forerunner and model in his drawing his own conclusions on the basis of his intellect, and his willingness to endure criticism and censure from his more mainstream, orthodox contemporaries and successors.

It should be recognized, however, that Origen's view of reason was not the 'pure reason' touted by many modern Western philosophers but one illuminated by the divine Logos, which alone was Pure Reason and which revealed knowledge of the God-Principle to the individual through its extension, the human intellect. It is for that reason that Origen is often described as a mystic, which is to say, one who searches for the Ultimate Reality within him or herself—in one's own spirit, or mind, or (as in Origen's case) both.

Further Reading

R. A. Greer, *Origen*.
F. Prat, "Origen and Origenism".

6. Pelagius, a Defender of Divine Decency

Pelagius (*ca.* 354 CE–*ca.* 420 or 440 CE) was a Celtic and perhaps British monk, ascetic, and theologian best known for his opposition to key teachings of his contemporary, Augustine of Hippo, whose later promotion to sainthood indicates who officially won their controversy. Pelagius spent most of his career in Rome, where he was well known for his extreme asceticism and articulateness. Even Augustine early on regarded him as 'saintly'. But Pelagius was unable, on rational grounds, to accept Augustine's doctrine of original sin and denial of freedom of the will.

Against his popular rival, Pelagius argued that the so-called 'Fall' of Adam and Eve did not leave their descendants totally helpless and hopeless in their quest for salvation through some genetic flaw the primordial couple had passed on, but only hampered them by their bad example. Therefore human beings had retained enough free will to be able to choose to be and do good—to be sinless, in fact—with or without God's grace, if only they tried hard enough. Also, death was not, as Augustine held, the result of Adam's and Eve's disobedience, but a natural phenomenon; and babies who died before being baptized were not damned to hell. This view came to be known—and usually denounced—as Pelagianism. Indeed, Pelagius blamed Augustine's contention that people were utterly sinful and dependent on divine grace for the rampant immorality that he found in Rome and elsewhere.

Pelagius was a prolific writer on theological issues, but most of his writings were denounced and destroyed, so we can only reconstruct what he believed from literary fragments and quotations preserved, again ironically, by those wishing to refute them. His stance, however, seems to boil down to this phrase: "If I ought, I can." God's very provision of commandments, he reasoned, suggests on the part of human beings, their ability to obey; for only an ogre would make demands of people he knew to be—as Augustine would have it—completely powerless to comply. Therefore, original sin (the condition passed down to humanity from a disobedient Adam and Eve) must not be as debilitating, or freedom of will as hampered, as Augustine maintained.

For his efforts, Pelagius was declared a heretic in 418 CE at the Council of Carthage, a meeting called by Augustine himself for the purpose of condemning his arch-nemesis—a year after none other than

Pope Zosimus had declared him innocent. Pelagius is still regarded by many as the worst heretic in all of Christian history, precisely because his views so directly affect the central issue of salvation.

Progressive Christians, however, tend to have a more positive view of human nature than do the official teachings of the Roman Catholic Church and many if not most Protestant churches, and might well regard Pelagius as a hero defending both formal logic and common sense in theological matters. They would also applaud his bold defence of autonomy (internal authority) over the heteronomy (external authority), the latter represented by Augustine's ecclesial status and power.

Further Reading

R. F. Evans, *Pelagius.*
R. C. Sproul, *Willing to Believe.*

7. Meister Eckhart, a Model Mystic

Meister Eckhart von Hochheim (*ca.* 1260–1328) was a German Dominican priest, preacher, theologian, and mystic. He is often dubbed Johan or Johannes, though his actual first name is unknown.

The *Meister* (Master) in his name is an academic title, indicating he had obtained an advanced degree in theology; and as a scholar he produced an impressive body of theological writings, all steeped in Greek philosophy. But he also held prominent clerical offices all over Germany, and was a very popular preacher, widely known for his folksy, accessible oratory and the practical applicability of his sermons. Very late in life, however, he found himself on trial for heresy; he died before his conviction and papal censure in 1329. What most upset his detractors was his blurring of the clear distinction between God and humanity that monotheism demands.

For Eckhart, God was not the anthropomorphic Father-figure of the Bible, but the Absolute Principle or Unity or Pure Intellect, though he also referred to God as Being—not a Being, mind you, but something closer to the quality of Being or Being Itself. Eckhart's God had no attributes beyond perfection, and thus was incomprehensible, yet not unknowable. Eckhart saw human beings as fundamentally intellects, which, as 'sparks' of the Pure Intellect, implied an essential unity with the Absolute. In Eckhart's own words: "God is in all things, but . . . nowhere so fully as in the soul—in the deepest recesses of the soul."

So it was that Eckhart could declare: "My ground is God's ground, and God's ground is mine," and, "The knower and the known are one." Such language is that of a mystic—that is, one who searches for the Ultimate or Absolute within oneself and ideally experiences a profound sense of unity with the cosmic All and a corresponding loss of individual identity. Such an experience, whether real or imagined, is profoundly threatening in monotheistic religions like Christianity, perhaps because the main purpose of religious institutions and their officials is to mediate between a transcendent (Other) Creator God and that deity's creation and creatures. But Eckhart's God was neither a Creator nor a transcendent Other. What is commonly called Creation was for him the result of *emanation*, that is, an outpouring of the Fullness that is God. The result was a God present within all things in such a way that they are themselves essentially divine. Most of Eckhart's contemporaries rightly regarded such thinking as pantheistic, and they further objected to his apparent relativisation of Jesus as the unique Incarnate Word in assertions like this: "Every creature is a word of God."

Here again, a heretic offers a model and inspiration for progressive Christians, including those with no mystical disposition or orientation, in that Eckhart relied on internal authority (autonomy)—in his case, intuitive-experiential *and* intellectual—over against the external ecclesial establishment (heteronomy).

Further Reading

O. Davies, *Meister Eckhart.*

B. McGinn, *The Mystical Thought of Meister Eckhart.*

8. Melchior Hoffmann, a Rebellious Re-Baptizer

Melchior Hoffmann (*ca.* 1495–1543) was one of the early German pioneers of the radical Anabaptist wing of the Protestant Reformation. He was not a scholar but a traveling businessman with a passion for the study of the Bible and other religious and especially mystical writings. He eventually embraced the teachings of Martin Luther and became a lay preacher on his behalf.

Luther at first endorsed Hoffmann and his preaching, but gradually distanced himself from him because of the latter's increasingly radical views, eventually denouncing him and warning religious and civil authorities that he was dangerous. Hoffmann's business trips took him through Scandinavia, and he seemed to stir up trouble wherever he went there, especially among Luther's followers—for example, by speaking of the magical elements that the great reformer had retained in the Lord's Supper with his subtle doctrine of the objectively real (but not physical) presence of Christ in the bread and wine.

Under the influence of proto-Anabaptist Kaspar Schenkfelder (1489–1561), Hoffmann preferred a more spiritualized, subjective view of the ritual, claiming that the participants partook of the spiritual body (or heavenly flesh) of Christ, which was the only body that Jesus had ever had—an unorthodox view of the Incarnation to say the least. Hoffmann also appears to have adopted Schwenkfeld's rejection of oaths, pacifism, and infant baptism, and to have espoused freedom of conscience in religion and the necessity of visible sainthood—all of which eventually became staples of Anabaptism.

Thus, Hoffmann was gradually drawn further and further to the left of Luther in the emerging Protestant spectrum, and specifically to the emerging Anabaptist teachings, which denied the effectiveness of infant baptism and encouraged its followers to become, as the very name of their movement suggests, re-baptized. Hoffmann was himself re-baptized in 1530. Thereafter, he began to found churches and to perform re-baptisms. He also began to claim the role of prophet and predict on the basis of scripture the Second Coming of Jesus for the year 1533 in his own city of Strasbourg, which thenceforth would be the New Jerusalem. That prophecy was not fulfilled, of course, but its revolutionary dimension contributed to the disastrous Münster Rebellion of 1533–34, which had actually been fomented by two of his Dutch followers. For his comparatively passive part in the uprising, Hoffman was imprisoned in 1533 and died in custody ten years later.

What is most instructive for progressive Christians in the case of Hoffmann is the fact that the heresy is relative: Luther, who had himself been declared a heretic by the Roman Catholic church because of his own autonomy, was soon chagrined to see himself being left behind, in a sense, by a disciple doing the very same thing, and reaching even more radical conclusions than his early hero. There is, then, a word of caution for progressive Christians: the appeal to internal authority may well open a can of worms, taking one beyond not just others' comfort zones, but one's own as well.

Further Reading

K. Deppermann, "Melchior Hoffman and Strasbourg Anabaptism".
C. Neff and W. O. Packull, "Hoffman, Melchior (*ca.* 1495–1544?)".

9. Michael Servetus, Troubled by the Trinity

Michael Servetus (1511–1553) is the Latinized form of the name Miguel Servet, or Serveto. He was a Spanish Renaissance man both literally and figuratively, being first and foremost a physician and theologian, but also a linguist, biblical scholar, lawyer, geographer-cartologist, meteorologist, astronomer, anatomist, pharmacologist, and—last but not least—a Christian martyr. He appears to have been drawn toward Reformed (Calvinist) Protestantism quite early in his life, but was perhaps more influenced by the example and work of the great humanist scholar Erasmus, who himself was no stranger to theological contro-versy and at least informal charges of heresy.

Servetus travelled extensively in Europe, particularly Italy, France, Switzerland, Germany and Austria, supporting himself with odd jobs and doing his scholarly work in his spare time. In mid-1531, Servetus began to publish a series of works on the doctrine of the Trinity, re-jecting the whole notion as unbiblical, illogical, and a stumbling block in Christianity's relationship to the other two—and more thorough-going—monotheisms of the world, Judaism and Islam, both of which saw their sister Abrahamic faith as tri-theistic. At the same time, he espoused a very high role for Jesus Christ, insisting that he was none other than the incarnate divine Word (*Logos*) of God, and denying only that this Christ-Word was co-eternal with God the Father, as the ortho-dox ancient Creeds would have it. Yet he rejected the subordination-ism of Arius (see above), but in favour perhaps of the kind of Docetism that Valentinus promoted.

Along the way and almost as an afterthought, Servetus denied the idea of predestination, but it was his position against the Trinity and, to a lesser extent, against infant baptism that caught the attention of John Calvin, the Reformed Protestant theocrat of Geneva, Switzerland. After some contentious correspondence with this powerful figure, Ser-vetus made the mistake of traveling through his city, where he was rec-ognized, jailed, tried, convicted, and burned at the stake—despite the fact they had no authority but only the power to do so. In this way, the French Catholic Inquisition, which had only recently condemned Ser-vetus for heresy, was thus denied the privilege of meting out the same 'justice', only legally. Though strictly speaking not a Unitarian himself, since the term had not yet been coined, Servetus has been adopted by Unitarians and Unitarian-Universalists as their first martyr-saint.

For progressive Christians in general, he serves as an exemplar in the application of reason even to major doctrines of the faith, as well as a warning against underestimating the lengths that some traditional-ists will go to in defence of their fear-based religion, including murder.

Further Reading

L. Goldstone and N. Goldstone, *Out of the Flames*.
M. Hillar and C. Allen, *Michael Servetus*.

10. Giordano Bruno, a Tireless Truth-Seeker

Giordano Bruno (1548–1600) was an Italian priest, astronomer, math-ematician, philosopher, and withal a freethinker and gadfly of the first rank. He was born near and educated in Naples, and in his adolescence became a monk in the Dominican order. In his twenties, he was ordained a priest, a position he later would reject, reclaim, then renounce again.

His earliest fascination with an emergent modern science appears to have focused on the function of memory, and he is said to have developed geometrically-based mnemonic techniques and extraordinary retention skills. But his attention soon turned as well to astronomy, and specifically to cosmology. His researches in that field led him to reject on scientific grounds Copernicus' version of heliocentrism, which placed the sun at the centre of the entire universe. Bruno maintained instead that it was merely one among many such heavenly bodies in what was essentially an infinite universe.

It was not his scientific theories that initially got him into trouble with church authorities, however, but his willingness to study the ideas of controversial schools of thought (like Hermeticism) and free-thinking individuals (such as Erasmus), and to accept positions long deemed heresies (for example, Arianism). Learning that ecclesiastic authorities in Naples were planning to raise heresy charges against him, he fled what was essentially his home town and began a series of travels and sojourns around Europe, during which he managed to alienate the Catholics of France and Spain, the Calvinists of Geneva, the Anglicans of England, and the Lutherans of Germany. This pattern only continued when he returned to Italy in 1591 and became a university lecturer and private tutor.

His controversial teachings again led even his supporters to initiate a heresy trial in Venice on an amalgam of charges, ranging from scientific cosmology to theological dogma. After several months, he was transferred (early in 1793) to the authority of the Inquisition in Rome, where he remained imprisoned for seven years while defending himself against charges of blasphemy, heresy, and—for good measure—immorality and sorcery. Among the doctrines he was accused of questioning, rejecting, or distorting were: the Trinity, the Incarnation, the divinity of Christ, the Virgin Birth; and of advocating such controversial ideas as the infinity and eternality of the universe and the plurality of worlds within it. Beyond the science of his cosmology, however, Bruno maintained the eternality and infinity of the universe was coextensive with God's own, the latter being immanent within nature and, presumably, human nature—a thoroughly pantheistic view. He was convicted of heresy in 1600 and turned over to civil authorities, who soon after burned him at the stake for crimes against the state.

Progressive Christians today would do well to honour Bruno for his intellectual curiosity, his dedication to scientific endeavours, and his determination at all costs to apply the results of his researches to even the most fundamental doctrines of the Christian faith.

Further Reading
H. Gatti, *Giordano Bruno and Renaissance Science.*
I. D. Rowland, *Giordano Bruno.*

11. Jacobus Arminius, a Guardian of Grace

Jacobus Arminius (1560–1609) is the Latin version of the name of Dutch pastor and theologian Jakob Harmenszoon, who was active a generation or so after the death of John Calvin (1509–1564) as an opponent of most of the major themes of that Swiss theologian's Reformed Protestant theology. The one point of agreement between the two was their belief in the total depravity of humanity because of Original Sin, the congenital universal human condition caused by the primordial disobedience of Adam and Eve, which both agreed had rendered human beings utterly incapable of achieving salvation on their own.

But Calvin had further concluded:

1. that the only divine grace effective in salvation was that conferred in Jesus' redemptive death
2. that God had predestined only some people to receive this gift, the so-called 'Elect'
3. that this gift of grace was irresistible to these fortunate ones
4. that once received, it and its saving effects could in no way be surrendered or otherwise lost

In glaring contrast to these four points, Arminius held that God had conferred on humankind a 'prevenient' grace—a kind of natural, universal, pre-emptive ability that precedes any bestowal of the special divine grace attributable to Jesus' atoning death and that actually makes it possible for its recipients to choose to embrace the salutary effects of Jesus' atoning and redemptive death, something that they could not do if *totally* depraved. These effects, therefore, were not limited to the Elect alone, but were available to everyone, who—according to him—had the power to both choose and lose salvation.

Thus, while Arminius could hardly be described as a humanist (that is, as one having a thoroughly positive view of human nature), his beliefs were clearly a giant step away from Calvin in that direction. Indeed, some of Arminius' followers, who were called Remonstrants, later moved still further: in the direction of Pelagianism, the belief that human beings effect their own salvation, or at least Semipelagianism, which held that people start the salvation process via their own faith, with God finishing the process by reciprocating with grace. Arminius' view, which only after his death was systematically formulated over against Calvinist orthodoxy and called Arminianism, made him a heretic among the decidedly non-humanistic Reformed Protestants who were quite influential in Holland at the time, and its adherents were expelled from Holland for a time. Arminianism was later deliberately adopted by John Wesley, the eighteenth-century British Anglican cleric and founder of Methodism, and many of the early Baptists were also either explicitly or implicitly Arminians in their championing of the 'soul liberty' of any individual to choose what her or his conscience dictates, a decidedly progressive view not much in evidence among their evangelical successors today.

Arminius' appeal to reason and positive view of human nature, at least in comparison to Calvinism, are hallmarks of the progressive wing of Christianity, which he—however inadvertently—helped to forge against an entrenched orthodoxy.

Further Reading

T. M. van Leeuwen, *Arminius, Arminianism, and Europe.*
R. E. Picirilli, *Grace, Faith, Free Will.*

12. Galileo Galilei, Vilified Then Vindicated

Like Michael Servetus (see above), Galileo (1564–1642) was another true Renaissance man: astronomer, physicist, mathematician, philosopher, designer, inventor, and one of the early founders not only of modern physics, but of modern science and the modern scientific worldview that prevails as the dominant shared understanding of reality in the developed countries of the world today.

Not a theologian or even someone concerned with church doctrine, Galileo stands as the first significant example of a person being accused of heresy not because of his doctrines, but *purely* on the basis of his scientific findings. The issue was his public endorsement in 1610 of the Copernican notion of heliocentrism, that is, the view the sun is the centre of the universe. Both he and Copernicus were wrong on this score, for we now know the sun is the centre of our solar system, which is nowhere near the centre of the universe (if the universe even has one).

But they were more correct than the majority of thinkers in their day, including the Roman Catholic hierarchy and most contemporary Protestants, who were geocentrists; that is, believers in the earth's centrality of the universe. Their main argument—beyond not being able to feel the earth moving through space—was biblical. The first chapter of Genesis, for example, puts earth centre stage, as it were, with the sun, moon, and stars created after it in order to give it light. Several Hebrew Bible passages, including three Psalms, present the earth as firmly placed and immovable; and another has a prophet ordering the sun and moon to stand still in the heavens, thereby implying it is not the earth but those heavenly bodies that are moving. So, in 1615, Galileo's views were examined by the Roman Inquisition, which cleared him; but a few months later, his heliocentrism was condemned as unbiblical and heretical, and he was forced to promise to stop promulgating it. He did so, but in 1632 published a work that very publicly embraced heliocentrism. He was therefore tried again by the Inquisition for heresy and forced to recant under penalty of death. He did so, but nevertheless spent his remaining dozen years under house arrest.

Galileo was finally vindicated by the Catholic Church in 1992 in the form of a declaration by Pope John Paul II that the scientist's condemnation had been in error, the result of a "mutual misunderstanding". A possible lesson here for a progressive Christian is it may take some time for traditionalists to see the wisdom of your thinking on religious and theological issues, and to appreciate the value of reason in questions of faith in general.

Further Reading

J. Reston, *Galileo.*
J. L. Heilbron, *Galileo.*

13. Anne Hutchinson, Unorthodox and Unruly

Anne Hutchinson (1591–1643) was an early resident of the Massachusetts Bay Colony, arriving there from her native England in 1634, some four years after its founding, and expelled as a heretic some four years after that.

Anne was the home-schooled but well-read daughter of one dissident Puritan minister and an avid follower of another, John Cotton, whom she followed to America after he was forced to leave his native land by bishops of the Church of England because of his heterodoxy. The Massachusetts colony, however, was no haven of religious freedom; it was instead a theocracy in which the clergy wielded both religious and civil authority in matters great and small, doctrinal and otherwise. It was also a bastion of Calvinist orthodoxy.

Anne challenged both the church-state connection and some finer points of Calvinist (or Reformed) doctrine, and for good measure claimed the freedom to interpret scripture under her own God-given authority and, perhaps worse, the right to teach biblical studies to men as well as women. This stance was in apparent contradiction of the scriptural dictum—contained in 1 Tim 2:11–12 and often misattributed to Paul, who was not the actual author of that book—that women were to be subservient and not presume to have any authority over men. To make matters worse, she was very popular and attracted a sizeable, and therefore threatening, following. On top of everything else, she was an advocate for the rights of Native Americans.

All of these activities and views led to the charge of *antinomianism* (literally, "lawlessness", but really "incorrigibility"), and eventually, in 1637, to a heresy trial before none other than John Winthrop, who was not only a Puritan cleric but the first Governor of Massachusetts. Despite a brilliant, articulate, and unflinching self-defence, she was found guilty not so much for her doctrinal deviations, but for 'slandering' the ministers—that is, bucking their authority. She was placed under house arrest pending her next trial, which took place the following year in Boston and focused more on her 'blasphemy'. She was again found guilty and exiled. She then migrated first to Rhode Island, which had recently been founded as a haven of religious freedom by Freethinker Roger Williams, and later to New Netherlands, where she and most of her family were ambushed and murdered by some of the Native Americans she had defended. She was eventually (in 1987) pardoned and her order of banishment was revoked by then Massachusetts Governor, Michael Dukakis.

Hutchinson, often identified as the first American feminist, may serve as a lesson to progressive Christians that in the end their labours in the promotion of free thought may be most severely punished by those poised to benefit most from them.

Further Reading

E. LaPlante, *American Jezebel.*
M. Winship, *The Times and Trials of Anne Hutchinson.*

14. George Fox, a Quaking Quietist

George Fox (1624–1691) was an English Separatist Puritan or Dissenter—that is, a Protestant who had broken from the established Church of England (aka the Anglican state church) over issues of belief, practice, or both—who pushed the boundaries of even that radical movement with his mysticism.

Fox was reared and home-schooled in rural England, and from childhood had a strong disposition toward religion, moral purity, contemplation and the simple life. Never completely comfortable with cities, in his early twenties Fox began to travel from town to town in the vicinity of London, frequently seeking the advice of clergy, who were often alarmed by his spiritual introversion and increasingly radical ideas.

Fox himself was a gifted lay preacher, especially in countryside and market place settings, and by age twenty-three was quickly drawing a considerable following that eventually took on the name 'Friends of the Truth' or simply 'Friends'. They were often mocked and corporally punished by mobs because of their views and style. From his mid-twenties on, Fox himself was frequently incarcerated, usually on charges of blasphemy, which in a state-church context is a civil crime. The real reasons for his imprisonment, however, were probably his pacifism, refusal to swear oaths, and advocacy of social equality, including women's rights, roles, and status.

Throughout his early adulthood, Fox further added to suspicion about him by expressing his aversion to rituals, church buildings, ecclesial authority, and both the ordained ministry and the formal study required for it. In the end, though an avid student and citer of the Bible, he rejected the necessity of it—along with the other Christian conventions he found lacking—as having been eclipsed in importance by true (by which he meant *inward*, which is to say *mystical*) spiritual experience. Though he apparently had no intention of founding a new sect or denomination of Christianity, at least early on, his so-called 'Society of Friends'—dubbed 'Quakers' by an early detractor—came to be just that. Its members were persecuted, prosecuted and jailed by the hundreds, even during the period of the Puritan Protectorate under Cromwell, and only freed from this hardship with the Toleration Act of 1689. Meanwhile, between bouts of illness and a depression that had plagued him from childhood, Fox himself travelled to the American colonies and the Netherlands, where Quakerism was taking root, and wrote extensively. He died of natural causes in 1691.

What progressive Christians can most learn from Fox is perhaps the strength of his conviction and fearlessness in the face of a daunting establishment bent on suppressing his radical ideas by any means necessary; and the truth that being a mystic and a pacifist does not necessitate withdrawal from society or passivity, but indeed demands social engagement and activism in the cause of what is right, fair and just.

Further Reading

R. Bailey, *New Light on George Fox and Early Quakerism.*
J. Yolin and L. Ingle, *Friend.*

15. William Ellery Channing, a Rational Religionist

William Ellery Channing (1780–1842) was the virtual inventor of Unitarianism, which may well be regarded as the very first institutional expression of modern progressive Christianity. A highly-educated theologian in his own right, Channing was also an articulate, dynamic, and widely known preacher. In fact, the defining moment for Unitarianism was an ordination sermon he preached in 1819 for a young man graduating from Channing's alma mater, Harvard College and Divinity School.

The sermon was titled "Unitarian Christianity", and in it he laid out his extreme anti-Calvinist views of God and humanity. In opposition to the dreadful, despotic deity promoted by the Calvinists, Channing presented a loving one. Along the way, he denounced the notion of the Trinity, and that one tenet gave his brand of Christianity its name. But his views of humanity were just as troubling to Calvinists: contrary to their insistence that humanity is fundamentally depraved (which is to say, utterly sinful), he argued the God-likeness of our species. He further developed this second important unorthodox theme nine years later in yet another ordination sermon, "Likeness to God", in which he argued human beings had the potential to be like God, a view diametrically opposed to Calvinism. In all of this deviation from the mainstream New England Protestant view of the Christian faith, which was revelation-based, it was clear Channing valued the role of reason (as opposed to scriptural revelation) in shaping beliefs and theologies.

The one troubling aspect of Channing is he apparently shared in the racist views of his day in regarding African slaves as inferior to whites, with the result that for most of his long career as the pastor of a prominent New England church, he did not support the abolitionism that was so prominent among his fellow liberal thinkers. He did, however, come to abolitionism rather late in his life and career, no doubt in part because his beloved reason dictated a change of mind and heart. By then, and despite his long-held opposition to abolitionism, Channing was widely regarded as one of the shapers of Transcendentalism, despite the fact he not only affiliated himself with the leading lights of that movement but actually regarded them as extreme in their views and style of advocacy with respect to their views.

Latter-Day 'Heretics', Relatively Speaking

Some seven years after Channing preached his famous sermon, the Roman Catholic Church executed its last heretic—at least to date—under the auspices of the Spanish Inquisition. He was CAYETANO RIPOLL and he met his end by garrotting in Spain in 1826, convicted of deism—the view of God as creator of the cosmos, but not a responsive or interactive maintainer thereof. Ever since, however, the term heresy has been tossed around by a variety of Christian religious authorities, often as charges directed toward one another.

Such free usage nicely reflects the post-Reformation institutional fragmentation of the faith into countless pockets of authority. These range from Catholic to Eastern Orthodox to Protestant to Sectarian— the latter category referring to relatively new non-Catholic, non-Eastern Orthodox Christian groups not traceable to Continental Reformation roots. Such Christian sects would include Latter-day Saints (LDS), Adventists, Jehovah's Witnesses, Christian Scientists, Theosophists and several varieties of New Thought groups (for example, Unity), all founded in the nineteenth century and made in America, as it were. The various denominations comprising this latter group have routinely been accused of propagating heresy—or of being a 'cult' in the relatively recent pejorative sense of that word—by the older and more established churches. These newer forms of Christianity have especially been disparaged by the Catholics and Evangelical Protestants of the United States, where the sects are more prominent. Indeed, it could be said these sects and their idiosyncratic scriptures, beliefs and practices have served to make mainstream Protestants appear almost orthodox in the eyes of Catholics, thereby underscoring just how relativistic the whole concept of heresy has become!

Charges of heresy in the past two centuries or so have also been directed, mostly informally and sometimes only rhetorically, and primarily against three sorts of thinkers: scientists, biblical scholars and theologians. As far as the first group is concerned, public enemy number one is still CHARLES DARWIN (1809–1882), who in 1859 published his *The Origin of Species*, which touted a theory of evolution via the mechanism of natural selection. That view would be given theological expression nearly a century later, quite ironically, by a French Roman Catholic priest named PIERRE TEILHARD DE CHARDIN (1881–1955), whose *The Phenomenon of Man* (*Le Phénomène Humain*, 1955) presented a God within rather than above the natural order and evolving together with it. He, too, has been charged with heresy over the last half century or so by a number of self-styled (and sometimes self-appointed) guardians of the Christian faith, including many of his fellow Catholics.

Close behind such evolutionary thinkers in receiving the scorn of Christian traditionalists would be the various framers and defenders of the Big Bang theory of the origin of the universe, which—again, ironically—was first promulgated by GEORGES LEMAÎTRE (1894–1966), a Belgian Roman Catholic priest, physicist and astronomer, whose ground-breaking idea has become something approaching orthodoxy among scientists.

As for modern heretics closer to home, so to speak, the first important figure in modern biblical scholarship was DAVID FRIEDRICH STRAUSS (1808–1874), author of *The Life of Jesus* (*Das Leben Jesu*, 1835), whose focus on the historical Jesus to the explicit exclusion of his divinity rocked the European Christian establishment, Catholic and Protestant alike, even as it laid the foundation for the modern historical-critical study of the Bible. Among his early Australian heirs would be CHARLES STRONG (1844–1942; see below) and SAMUEL ANGUS (1881–1943). Meanwhile, on the international scene there would be RUDOLF BULTMANN (1884–1976), ROBERT W. FUNK (1926–2005), JAMES M. ROBINSON (b. 1924), JOHN DOMINIC CROSSAN (b. 1934), and ELISABETH SCHÜSSLER FIORENZA (b. 1938)—all regarded by a host of conservative Christians as heretics, but by their followers and fans, as progressive Christians. In many ways, Fiorenza's successful career as a biblical scholar is a kind of homage to the remarkable ELIZABETH CADY STANTON (1815–1902), who, in addition to laying the groundwork for mid-to-late twentieth-century feminism with her insistence on the natural rights of women, including suffrage, spearheaded the production of *The Women's Bible* (1895), which boldly challenged the prevailing view of Christian scriptures. Indeed, it was so radical that even free-thinking women's rights activists opposed its publication on the grounds it might undermine the case for women's suffrage. What it did, in fact, was lay the foundation for some first-rate feminist biblical scholarship that emerged half a century later among the likes of LETTY RUSSELL (1929–2007) and PHYLLIS TRIBLE (b. 1932).

Often identified as "The Father of Modern Liberal Theology," FRIEDRICH SCHLEIERMACHER (1768–1834) in effect shifted the focus of theology from God to the believer in his *Speeches on Religions* (*Reden über die Religion*, 1799), which located the basis of religion not in divine revelation, but in a universal human intuitive sense he called a "feeling of absolute dependence". To paraphrase a claim of philosopher Alfred North Whitehead about Plato, the history of modern progressive Christian theology has been but a series of footnotes on Schleiermacher's work: PAUL J. TILLICH (1886–1965) and existentialist theology; THOMAS J. J. ALTIZER (b. 1927) and "Death of God" theology; HANS KÜNG (b. 1928) and global theology; MATTHEW FOX (b. 1940) and creation spirituality; and a variety of feminist and womanist theologians (ROSEMARY RADFORD REUTHER, MARY DALY, JACQUELYN GRANT); Black theologians (JAMES CONE, J. DEOTIS ROBERTS, CORNEL WEST); Latin American liberation theologians (GUSTAVO GUTIÉRREZ, LEONARDO BOFF, JUAN LUIS SEGUNDO); process theologians (CHARLES HARTSHORNE, JOHN B. COBB JR, MARJORIE HEWITT SUCHOCKI); and realist, or secular, theologians (GERD LÜDEMANN, DON CUPITT, LLOYD G. GEERING)—to name but a few of the most prominent. Many of these were threatened with, and some actually experienced, excommunication from their traditionalist churches. Some of the most recent persons to be dismissed from their position or accused of heresy are the first woman in the world to hold a chair of Catholic theology, UTA RANKE-HEINEMANN (charged 1987), Scottish born (Australian resident at the time) theologian PETER CAMERON (charged 1992), English Anglican priest ANTHONY FREEMAN (charged 1994) and the former Dean of Clonmacnoise within the Church of Ireland, ANDREW FURLONG (charged 2002). Not mentioned are the many Roman Catholic priests and brothers who have 'resigned' due to pressure from Archbishops or the Pope, because of their progressive views. In Australia in recent times these include MICHAEL MORWOOD and PETER KENNEDY.

In addition to the scientists, biblical scholars and theologians who have attracted the label of 'heretic' from some circles of the Christian faith and 'hero' among progressives in modern times, one would be remiss in overlooking a tradition of popularisers who have advanced a progressive Christianity, many of them not scholars of religion or professional theologians, and have thus drawn charges of heresy. We might start with American statesman THOMAS JEFFERSON, his open deism, and his *Jefferson Bible*, the real title of which was *The Life and Morals of Jesus of Nazareth* (completed around 1820, but not published during his lifetime). Ironically, Jefferson died of natural causes the same year his fellow deist, the aforementioned Ripoll, was executed for his belief by the Spanish Inquisition. Also among these modern popularisers of alleged heresies was RALPH WALDO EMERSON (1802–1883), whose misnamed Transcendentalism challenged the traditionalist Christians of his day with what was actually an immanentalist view of God—that is, a belief that God is profoundly within nature rather than above it. Twentieth-century popularisers of a heretical-progressive Christian view would include J. B. PHILLIPS (*Your God is Too Small*, 1961), JOHN A. T. ROBINSON (*Honest to God*, 1963), BISHOP JAMES A. PIKE, (*A Time for Christian Candor*, 1964), LESLIE WEATHERHEAD (*The Christian Agnostic*, 1965), JAMES M. KAVANAUGH (*A Modern Priest Looks at His Outdated Church*, 1967), BISHOP JOHN SHELBY SPONG (*Rescuing the Bible from Fundamentalism*, 1992), and MARCUS J. BORG, (*The God We Never Knew*, 1998). All of these books were written by prominent clergy; most were bestsellers in their publishing niche; and some remain in print and quite popular among present-day readers. The success and popularity of such books may well constitute a kind of modest triumph of heresy *and* progressivism in the twentieth century.

Also not to be forgotten is the small but increasingly prominent group of progressive Evangelical Christians like JIM WALLIS (b. 1948), whose half-century of commitment to issues of social justice, peace, care for the poor and oppressed, and—most recently—environmental stewardship, places him firmly in the tradition of that earlier Evangelical Christian rebel, WALTER RAUSCHENBUSCH (1861–1918). Rauschenbusch was a Baptist minister and theologian whose embracing of modern historical-critical biblical scholarship led him to become one of the principal forgers of the so-called 'Social Gospel'—the appearance of which outraged traditionalist, conservative Christians and drew from them charges of heresy. It is still remembered and roundly denounced today, but thanks in large part to Wallis and his visibility as a 'media darling', advisor to President Obama, and best-selling author, even Evangelical progressivism appears to have gained considerable momentum.

Reclaiming the Heretics for Progressive Purposes

As already suggested, both the term heresy and the concept it represents have been used relatively infrequently and mostly rhetorically among Christians over the last two centuries. Formal heresy trials have been rare and, more importantly, non-lethal among Protestants since the Puritans of the Colonial era, and even in Roman Catholic circles, where in the past heresy proceedings were frequent and often fatal— evidence the infamous Inquisition—the idea of heresy has been downplayed for over a century. Catholic attention to heresy has especially waned since the Second Vatican Council in the early 1960s. Prior to that, Protestantism as a whole was routinely and publicly denounced by Roman Church officials and apologists as one giant heresy. Since Vatican II, however, Catholics have tended to refer to Protestants more euphemistically and ecumenically as "our separated brethren", thereby calling the whole notion of heresy into serious question. What has deflated what was formerly the terror of heresy more than anything was the end of any semblance of the intact and authoritative Christendom the Roman Church had maintained even after the rise of Eastern Orthodoxy in the eleventh century.

The real blow to the notion of heresy was the Protestant Reformation of the sixteenth century, which resulted in an ongoing proliferation of competing schools, sects, churches and denominations in Western Christianity, which in turn yielded a plethora of authorities, each claiming to have the authentic version of the faith and its tenets. That situation effectively rendered heresy in the negative sense problematic in both principle and practice. For what was and is orthodox in one branch of the faith may be heretical in another.

Nevertheless, progressive Christians have often been either informally or officially labelled as heretics, especially by the more clerically-controlled and hierarchical branches of their religion, and always because of their commitment to freedom of conscience and choice in matters of faith. Fortunately for those so charged, there are now plenty of safe havens within institutional Christianity, especially in branches where ecclesial power and authority are more widely shared and differences of opinion more tolerated or even highly valued.

Now that allegations of heresies and heretics appear to be waning, it may be high time for those of us Christians who value progressive thought and action to resurrect, so to speak, the many condemned as heretics in the past, and to acknowledge them for what they really are: heroes of the Christian faith, and some of them actual martyrs for it. Under different circumstances, their free-thinking might well have enriched Christianity in their own day; and it may do so for us today, as we appreciate and celebrate what they modelled: not only the positive role of the intellect, of doubt, of freedom of thought, and of differences of opinion about doctrines, theologies, creeds, and other components, but the specific questions they raised and wrestled with as well. In their honour, we may want to embrace for ourselves the label 'heretic' and its root connotation of freedom of choice, especially in matters of belief, and to take up its banner, not in subversion of the faith, but in support of it.

Further Reading

D. W. Bercot, *Will the Real Heretics Please Stand Up.*

P. Berger, *The Heretical Imperative.*

J. L. González and C. G. González, *Heretics for Armchair Theologians.*

Charles Strong

An Early Australian 'Heretic'

Norman Habel

With the rise of progressive Christianity and the Common Dreams conferences held in Australia—Sydney (2007) and Melbourne (2010)—it might be assumed such a movement is relatively recent in Australia. One might well argue, however, that the voice of Charles Strong at the end of the nineteenth century anticipates much of the current thinking.

The Australian Church based on Strong's approach may have closed in 1955, but the radical thinking of Charles Strong has been said by some to pre-date the voice of Bishop Spong toward the end of the twentieth century.

As Strong says:

> Thus Christianity re-interpreted escapes from 'carnal' theologies, traditions, questions about dogmas, infallible books, infallible churches, and presents itself as a Spiritual Life which is its own witness, and to which perhaps such things are felt to be a hindrance often rather than a help.[1]

The Australian Church

Charles Strong was born in 1844 in Scotland, began university at fifteen, was ordained in 1868 and became a minister of Scots Presbyterian Church in Melbourne in 1875. Due to an anonymous pamphlet accusing him of heresy relating to the doctrine of atonement, he was removed from his church in 1883 and returned to Scotland.

Upon his return to Victoria in October 1884, Strong was approached by a group of friends and supporters who asked him to preach for them during the next twelve months in a hall which they would hire. In November 1885, a new church was constituted and Strong was asked to be its first minister. Although involved in the formulation of its aims and objectives, Strong made it clear he was not the founder of the 'Australian Church'.

The Australian Church in Melbourne defined itself as "a comprehensive church whose bond of union is the spiritual and the practical rather than creeds or ecclesiastical forms".[2]

Strong had a disdain for religion that focussed on preparation for life after death, salvation and damnation, services and sacraments, the Bible and vestments. The task of the church, he claimed, is to preach "freedom, justice, peace, compassion and reconciliation".

Membership of the church required "sympathy with the general spirit and aims of the society, the honest effort to carry into modern life and thought the religion of Reason and Love and contribution to the funds of the society according to ability".[3] The notion of a church that was non-dogmatic, inclusive and tolerant was, however, not new. It was one of the important ideas of the liberal religious movement of nineteenth-century Scotland and England.

Progressive Hermeneutics

The hermeneutical task, according to Strong, is to

> re-interpret Christianity in the light of modern knowledge, the principles of development, and the spirit of religion as distinguished from the letter; to re-interpret Christianity just as Copernicus and Galileo re-interpreted astronomy.[4]

In the light of his writings, this re-interpretation of Christianity might well be understood as follows:

- Embracing modern knowledge—science, cosmology, psychology and nature. Nature is not an alien power—it enters us, we enter it—it draws out our secret mental forces and we draw into it. We are nature.
- Following the Spirit not the letter—Jesus did not ask the woman who anointed his feet whether she believed in a creed, but if she had faith in him.
- Knowing the Spirit—as the 'universal all-animating Spirit', an eternal and deep dimension of reality. The Trinity is re-interpreted in terms of this deep Spirit in the universe.
- Reading via the Spirit—with a clear mind that is part of the eternal Mind led by the universal Spirit/Word to follow the Gospel of trust in God as Light and Love.
- Reading Nature—embedded within deep mysteries of life.
- Understanding the Gospel—as the message that God is Spirit, that God is love and that God so loved the world as to send his Son to draw us into sonship and make us partakers in a divine life.

For Strong, the Gospel of John was the canon within the canon. The themes of John, such as life, light and word, were central to his reinterpretation of the Gospels. In his own words, "Salvation is no longer accepting an offer of deliverance from hell, but being saved from ourselves and lifted into Christ's life and God's life."[5]

Spiritual Christianity

Strong also speaks of a 'spiritual Christianity', a movement that links us with the spirit deep in all things and the spirit deep in each human. Spiritual Christianity ought to be an expression of who we are, expressing the spirit/divine within. When we discern the Spirit of Christ in the text, rather than search for doctrine or theology, we facilitate this process.

An extraordinary feature of Strong's spirituality is its distinctive incarnational base. This base is read in line with the approach of Clement of Alexandria. So "the Word of God became man, so that thou mayest become God".[6] In other words, the incarnation is not an *ephhapaz* ("once and for all") event, but an expression of an eternal present reality. The word or spirit becomes/is incarnate in every human. Every human is an expression of the incarnation of God's presence. As Strong writes:

> The essential idea of Christianity in such writers as Justin, Clement and Athenagoras, is the revelation of God in man, that man may be drawn into God through the Logos or Word. God in man and man in God, is indeed the very keynote of spiritual Christianity in the early church, the Middle Ages and modern times.[7]

According to Strong, Christianity must be reborn. It must change with the times, knowledge and the evolution of humanity in society. Christianity must reflect the kingdom/spirit of God within each of us and ultimately be connected with the cosmic spirit. Christianity must shed the book and letter worship of the past and adopt a new cosmology—no more heaven and hell! And finally, Christianity must be part of the moral force for social change.

For Strong, what is true of the way people live life is also true of the way interpreters have read the text. The task is to explore the depths and discover that a Spirit/spiritual connection with Christ means a profound connection with the Centre, with the Divine, with Life itself. Christ is the 'way' to that Life. The Gospel for Strong is therefore essentially Life with all its deep divine dimensions! Or in the words of Strong,

> . . . the gospel is that God is Spirit, that God is Love, and that 'God so loved the world' as to send his Son to draw us into sonship and make us partakers in a divine life; glimpses of a world at length inspired with a 'spirit of life in Christ Jesus'.[8]

Social Justice

Social justice was central to Strong's re-interpreting of Christianity. He saw this dimension associated with both evolution and Scripture. He believed there has been and continues to be an evolution of human knowledge. Christians need to take this reality into account when reading the Bible, re-reading theology, re-interpreting Christianity and living social justice.

Spiritual Christianity Has a Crucial Moral and Social Dimension

God is not the God of the individual only or of the physical universe, but also the God of the Social Order. God's nature cannot be interpreted apart from the laws of that Order manifested in social nature. The fundamental principle of social justice is: Live by the law of Love!

Strong organized the social work of the Australian Church. It included aid for children, a crèche for the children of working mothers (led by Mrs. Strong) and a Working Men's Club. He set up societies for the discussion of literature and music, and the Religious Science Club. He strongly supported women's right to vote and was heavily involved in prison reform. He also maintained a strong interest in the value and significance of religions other than Christianity.

Strong was vehemently opposed to any wars. "I cannot reconcile war and democracy, war and the Christianity of Christ." He preached fiercely against the Boer War, declaring it to be rampant militarism and morally wrong. As a result, many of his followers no longer attended his church.

Strong's interest in world peace and his views on peaceful means of settling international problems made him unpopular during the 1914–1918 War and resulted in the resignation of many members of his congregation. His opposition to war and to a proposal by the Australian Government in 1917 to conscript Australians for service in overseas countries aroused the disapproval of friends and supporters. The press in Melbourne also attacked him for the first time in his career.

The Kingdom Of God

Strong interpreted the Kingdom of God in line with this re-reading of the Gospel. According to Strong the Kingdom includes:

- the rational ethical divine meaning that permeates the universe
- the evolutionary unfolding of that divine purpose in human experience
- the justice of God expressed in goodwill, love and brotherhood to all
- a willingness to suffer until this great 'law of our being' is realised in society

Conclusion

Strong rarely functioned as a modern preacher, taking a particular text and doing a detailed exegesis as the basis for his sermons. Rather he functioned with a progressive theology which may be summarised as spiritual, evolutionary and moral. Yet, these three are all expressions of a divine unity. There is an underlying interconnectedness of the physical, the spiritual and the ethical. And that unity is not in some distant realm, but within each of us. Nor is it a distant concept; rather it is an energising force—that divine Love which moves all things to live, to love and to realise the Kingdom of God in creation. Our task is to discern that Love in the text and be agents of that Love in society.

Notes

1. C. Strong, *Christianity Re-Interpreted and Other Sermons,* 15–16.
2. C. Badger, *The Reverend Charles Strong and the Australian Church,* 104.
3. C. Badger, 104.
4. C. Strong, 9.
5. C. Strong, 14.
6. C. Badger, 104.
7. C. Strong, 116.
8. C. Strong, 17.

Further Reading

C. Badger, *The Reverend Charles Strong and the Australian Church.*
Lectures from the Charles Strong Symposium on the Strong Trust website: www.charlesstrongtrust.org.au

'progressive'
Christianity Alive

Some encouragement . . .
because we are not alone!

COLLATED BY REX A. E. HUNT

Being a 'progressive' Christian

Keith Rowe

Until recently I simply described myself as Christian, without any qualifier. I now describe myself as progressive Christian, not because my basic views have changed (though they have developed, hopefully matured) but because the views I have held in over forty years of Christian ministry contrast dramatically with the more conservative theologies and understandings of the Christian role in society that dominate the church scene in our time. What are some of the emphases that characterise us?

Progressive Christianity is a contemporary form of Christian existence that has deep roots in the Christian tradition. We seek to contribute to the renewal of the Christian way and the human adventure through rethinking Christian belief in the light of insights and understandings not available to earlier generations and to the renewal of Christian living through recapturing the radical social implications of the way of life embodied in Jesus. There is no single creed that binds progressive Christians together though there are emphases that bind them together as a renewal movement within the Christian Church. It's a loose, cross-denominational network rather than an organised entity.

Many are seeking an escape from the coercive and heavily creedal and structural uniformity traditionally demanded by churches. Every person must do their own believing yet within the supportive and critical environment of a community of fellow pilgrims. There are common emphases and attitudes that define progressive Christianity.

Progressive Christians recognise that truth is larger than what the Christian church believes and does. God is understood to be active in all areas of life, bringing new insight, new appreciations of the wonder of creation to birth. Truth is larger than can be held within the formulations or theologies of any tradition, any religion, any scientific conclusion, any political or economic system, any philosophy, ancient tradition or holy book. So progressive Christians seek to live in conversation with all areas of human knowing, experience and exploration—philosophical formulations, scientific exploration, literary insight into the human condition, economic and political systems, the experience of the poor and of the wealthy, the various cultures that shape human communities, and most importantly the religions of the world. This commitment to inter-human conversation, built on respect and willingness to learn, makes progressive Christians suspect to conservative Christians who are dedicated to building sharp boundaries around Christian truth.

Progressive Christians see themselves as living within a river of life that is never static. Older formulations and ways of living that no longer serve the cause of human flourishing need to be reshaped or radically altered. While progressive Christians respect the traditions they have inherited, they refuse to be enslaved by them. Where life-giving convictions are enshrined in these traditions, they frequently need to be recast in the language and thought forms and in response to the needs of contemporary living. So, for instance, many progressive Christians understand God as creative love present within all of life and luring humanity and creation towards its fulfilment, rather than as a distant ruler who controls creation from afar and who intervenes in miraculous and powerful ways.

Progressive Christians value the Christian Bible and respect the holy books and traditions of other faiths. We welcome scholarship that helps us understand, demystify and interpret these ancient words so that they may offer direction to those seeking to serve the purposes of God. They believe that all forms of fundamentalism—biblical, organisational or theological—are prisons that diminish human life and often serve to justify violent and anti-human behaviours. Progressive Christians are not imprisoned by what the Bible says. The biblically endorsed prejudice against homosexuality and the ambivalent attitude towards women, for example, are set aside as serious denials of the essential dignity of every person, who the same Christian Bible declares are made in the image of God. Where violence is sanctioned within the biblical story this is not regarded as providing religious sanction for contemporary imperialistic adventures by so-called Christian nations.

The heart of Christian living and conviction is found for progressive Christians in the way of life pioneered by Jesus, called the Christ. Progressive Christians seek to be shaped by the way of life taught and embodied by Jesus while also dwelling in conversation with the world in which they live. Both elements are important.

Progressive Christians value critical study of the gospels as part of their continuing search for the initial life-affirming impulse that brought Christianity into being and tended to be submerged by later heresy hunting, crusades and willing involvement in the imperial designs of successive empires. Jesus is understood to be an embodiment of the purposes of God but not necessarily the sole embodiment of those purposes. The world needs Jesus, but not as a creedal prison or an offer of salvation that, if not accepted, leads to death in this life and the next. The world will be a better place if together we can weave the hospitality, peacemaking energy, generosity and forgiveness apparent in the ministry of Jesus into every area of human living. Jesus, we suggest, represents an evolutionary possibility for the human family.

Progressive Christians believe humans are responsible for the sort of world we live in and tend to be critical of contemporary economic, social and political structures that serve the interests of wealthy nations and persons, lead to wars shaped by imperialist mentalities and the degradation of creation in the interests of wealth creation.

Progressive Christians are convinced that along with a sharper concern for issues of justice and peace and care for creation, we need also to be developing ways of living more deeply in the love of God. We talk a lot about spirituality. Some ancient pathways to God are being rediscovered and, most importantly, many people are learning to live within the larger pool of spiritual wisdom represented by the other religions.

It is important to recognize that progressive Christianity is part of the Christian Church and seeks the renewal of Christianity as a source of renewal within a tired and often violent world. Though often embarrassed by the actions and beliefs of other Christians, we cannot deny we belong to the same family. You will be aware there is a battle going on within Christianity between those who seek a more open and socially committed stance and those who seek the retention of older and often life-denying and divisive theologies and styles of living. Progressive Christians, while existing within current denominational expressions of Christianity, are often uncertain as to how much energy they can devote to changing the minds and hearts of co-religionists who march to a different tune. If the progressive components of the great religions of the world were to work together in the search for a more just, peaceful and creation-caring human community we might not only contribute to human well-being but also contribute to the renewal of our respective religious traditions.

Further Reading

L. C. Birch, *Science and Soul.*
M. J. Borg, *The God We Never Knew.*
J. B. Cobb, Jr., *Lay Theology.*
———, *Reclaiming the Church.*
C. H. Evans, *Liberalism without Illusions.*

Being a 'progressive' Community in the Bible Belt

John Shuck

The First Presbyterian Church of Elizabethton, Tennessee[1] is a progressive Christian community in the midst of the American Bible Belt. We are in the Tri-Cities metro area (Kingsport, Bristol, Johnson City) not far from the Appalachian Trail. It is beautiful country. Folks are friendly and well-mannered. You can't beat the weather, mild in both winter and summer with just the right amount of rainfall for a temperate rain forest.

Roan Mountain is less than thirty minutes from the church and is home to "one of the richest repositories of temperate zone biodiversity on earth".[2] If you take the trail to the Roan High Bluff, you will find a sign that talks about the bluff and the flora and fauna that live there. The sign was funded and placed there by my congregation. My church folks do love the mountains and trees and they fight to preserve them. Southern Appalachia is home to roots music, mountain culture, and Jesus.

Many people claim to live in the Bible Belt. I don't doubt that. I don't want to get into a spitting contest about it, but I think East Tennessee is the rhinestone on the buckle of the Bible Belt. You can't throw a rock without hitting a church. Everywhere you look you will find crosses and church signboards with aphorisms such as:

"Stop, drop and roll won't work in hell."
"Think it's hot now? Hell's hotter."
"Evolution is man-made. Creation is Bible."

I am not from here. This is the first time I have lived in the South. I am not really a Yankee, though. My home is Montana and I can appreciate a good mountain and the independent fighting spirit of those who are embraced by the mountains. My family and I have made a home here. My spouse, Beverly, teaches music at a local high school and directs our congregation's music program.

I left my last church willing to go anywhere in the country to serve a progressive community. I wanted to do ministry rather than fight about doing ministry and found a progressive community nestled in the hills of Appalachia. If you were to ask folks in my congregation what this church is about, you might hear answers along these lines:

"We're not fundamentalist."
"We are liberal . . . sort of."
"We accept gays."
"We question things."
"We don't take the Bible literally."
"We believe in social justice."
"We care about the environment."

My predecessors, Revd and Mrs John and Carolyn Martin, served here for thirty-three years. They introduced the congregation to depth psychology, process theology, and the historical-critical method for interpreting scripture. Among many accomplishments, the Martins reached out to the university community (East Tennessee State University) and encouraged the congregation to preserve the natural beauty of the area. Under their leadership the congregation became an oasis for people growing out of fundamentalism. The congregation has had a quiet presence in the community ("a well-kept secret").

I was called to poke the nest and get the word out about us. This I have done through the internet and the media, and through encouraging the congregation to embrace some important progressive causes. We are one of three "More Light"[3] congregations in Tennessee that fight for equality for LGBTQ people. We are also affiliated with The Center for Progressive Christianity[4] and Every Church a Peace Church.[5]

For folks at my congregation, Jesus is green. Our largest committee is the Peacemaking Committee. For twenty-five years it has encouraged the congregation to be active in environmental issues in addition to social justice and peace concerns. Recently we hosted a concert to raise funds and awareness to prevent mountain top removal strip mining from coming to Tennessee. We have supported efforts to introduce a 'bottle bill' in the Tennessee legislature to assist in recycling by requiring a refundable deposit to be charged for bottles and cans. We have written letters to support ending the death penalty. We have marched in Washington to end overseas wars and for marriage equality.

I have been blogging for about five years at *Shuck and Jive*.[6] The blog is intentionally provocative. I use it as a springboard for theological exploration and to share ideas on secular and church politics. It has turned out to be an effective outreach tool. Even as it frustrates the conservatives in my denomination, it resonates with others, like Bill:[7]

> I think your theological views are extremely refreshing and germane for the twenty-first century. Maybe we can finally get out of the Dark Ages we have been stuck in for centuries. . . . This stage of my life is the ONLY time I ever wanted to go to church and it is because I finally have validation for the religious perspective that I developed myself in a vacuum. I finally have a community!

Bill joined us after he saw an article in the paper about Evolution Sunday. The Sunday closest to Darwin's birthday has become one of our biggest days. Evolution Sunday (now Evolution Weekend) was started by Dr Michael Zimmerman[8] at Butler University for the purpose of showing that science (particularly evolutionary theory) and religion can coexist. Because of evolution's controversial nature in the Bible Belt, we tend to get good media attention. On Evolution Sunday we celebrate science in worship, tell our fourteen billion year cosmic story in poetic form, host lectures, visit the Gray Fossil Site and Museum,[9] and generally make a big deal of it.

In February 2011, Ken Ham of the infamous 'Creation Museum' in Kentucky came to Johnson City for an 'Origins Conference'. Mr Ham wrote a post critical of my congregation on his blog, "Does Elizabethton Presbyterian Church Teach Heresy?"[10] You can't ask for better publicity than that. Out of the blue, I received this email:

> Dear Reverend Shuck,
> We just made a donation to the FPC of E and thought you might enjoy knowing how/why it came to be.
> My husband is facebook friends with a (misguided, and I say that with love) fundamentalist cousin in California. She posted about the Origins Conference in Johnson City, where my sister lives. My husband saw a reference to your church and pursued it to learn more about your activities. He was so impressed with the openness represented, he sent me the link to your website. I was impressed too, and we decided to make a donation.
> We left Christianity for 'Paganism' some time ago because we couldn't find a church that gave our hearts enough room to be comfortable. (Paganism also allows us to acknowledge the feminine in the Divine, something that's especially important to me.) But based on what we read, and if we didn't live in NJ, we would probably attend services and participate in your congregation's many pursuits, because we do know Jesus is the man.

So those silly creationist folks led us to you and to donating, and we are the richer for it. Thanks for being who you are. Next time we get to Johnson City, we hope to see you on Sunday morning!

Those are the kinds of emails I receive on a fairly regular basis.

Because my congregation encourages me to be unabashedly out there in the media and on the blog about theological ideas, our congregation touches lives. It is rewarding to hear from those who understand what is at stake regarding being open about scholarship. This email from a woman who reads my blog regularly is a case in point:

> Seeing things from the inside (of church life) for so many years, I appreciate your candid nature and your willingness to share the theological knowledge and questions that usually only highly educated theologians are privy to. I truly hope that this is changing in all churches . . . that we 'common folk' can all be trusted to 'grow up' and participate as adults with access to full information in religious education and religious questions—not be treated as children who have to be bullied or frightened into certain beliefs because we are incapable of understanding anything more.

That is what we do in a nutshell.

There are many more things I could share about this amazing congregation. I don't have enough space to talk about our 'Jesus Seminars on the Road', full moon meditations, solstice and equinox celebrations, drumming, dancing, and what all. We are a little bit Pagan, a little bit Christian, and a little bit rock and roll.

Don't be fooled. This is serious work. We are in the Bible Belt. But the entire country is in the Bible Belt in a real sense. Spiritual bullying is a reality wherever you go. We are a church for those who have been burned by church, and we need more of these communities. With that I give the last word to this email, which sums up why we do what we do:

> Dear Mr Shuck,
> After reading your blogs, sermons and the shuck and jive that you post, I wanted to let you know how much I admire and appreciate the work that you do in 'my community'; the GLBT [gay, lesbian, bisexual, and transgender] community. My family was very involved in church—and still is. I remember growing up a young girl and knowing that I was 'different'. . . . Although I appreciate and have many fond memories of being in the church, I have always struggled with acceptance and finding my fit . . . especially in a church/religious atmosphere. Often I shy away from any event that has to do with religion—not because I dislike GOD or dislike church, but because of the 'non-acceptance of everyone'. . . especially the GLBT community. I have been told that GOD doesn't hear my prayers anyway. . . .

. . . Due to the ridicule and bigotry that I have experienced in the past (and present) with religious affiliations, I have not entered the doors of a church in over ten years. The few times I have been to a church during my adulthood was to 'dart' in and listen to the choir (I attended a few all-Black churches) and 'dart out' so no one would grab me and try to save me from what was written all over me—my lesbianism....

I spent my graduate studies doing research on GLBT youth and the statistics of GLBT suicide is astronomical. Oh how I wish there was a place where adolescents could have the support and acceptance that they crave. . . . My ultimate passion is to work predominately with GLBT youth—yet, being in the 'bible belt' where being different is an instant ticket straight to hell—our children will continue to feel less than, disowned, hated, ridiculed and even seen as not worthy. . . .

Mr Shuck, I guess what I am saying is . . . thank you. Thank you for giving me hope, thank you for supporting my community, thank you for accepting me and most importantly, thank you for letting me know that GOD does love me and that I am OK.

Being progressive in the Bible Belt is not really about theology, philosophy, or politics. It certainly isn't about being a religious brokerage house. It is about being human and being in community. We are all Earthlings finding our way. For Earth's sake, be kind.

Notes

1. www.fpcelizabethton.org
2. www.appalachian.org/protected/roanhighlands.html
3. www.mlp.org
4. www.tcpc.org
5. www.ecapc.org
6. www.shuckandjive.org
7. www.shuckandjive.org/2007/12/is-christmas-political.html
8. http://blue.butler.edu/-mzimmerm/
9. www.grayfossilmuseum.com
10. www.blogs.answersingenesis.org/blogs/ken-ham/2011/02/07/does-eliza-bethton-presbyterian-church-in-tennessee-teach-heresy

Further Reading

M. Fox, *Original Blessing*.
M. Gold, *Crisis*.
H. Taussig, *A New Spiritual Home*.

New Wine and New Wineskins: Shaping a 'progressive' Community

Ian Lawton

Jesus told a challenging parable about the danger of putting new wine into old wineskins. The analogy falls down if you reverse it, because old wine is well-placed in new wineskins. But when it comes to twenty-first century spirituality, C3Exchange is modelling new wine in new wineskins.

Some churches put old wine into new wineskins. Old theology, such as praying to a theistic God for divine intervention and looking to Jesus' death for eternal salvation in the hereafter, are placed in contemporary, often highly creative, form. People jump and dance to rock songs while evangelical lyrics about a pre-scientific worldview bounce along high-definition screens. Other churches put new wine into old wineskins. New theology focused around mystery, love and justice is placed in a traditional, often repetitive, form. This style is well summarized by the statement made to me in several liberal settings: "Say whatever you want but don't mess with the liturgy". This leads to an inevitable disconnect between the message and the medium.

C3Exchange (previously known as Christ Community Church) has evolved over the last eight years from a 2002 Shiraz in an antique bottle to a 2010 Merlot in a contemporary carafe, open and flowing. In 2003, the winegrowers in these parts invited me to take the community on the next leg of its evolving journey. It has mainly been a process of connecting the new theology with a form that was consistent and inspiring. In short it has been a process of living up to our mantra that we are an alternative to church as usual. What follows is some of what we have discovered to date.

Naturalism

In the most general sense, it has been a process of defining how a naturalistic community functions as opposed to a supernaturalistic community. We ask some searching questions.

What does prayer mean beyond asking an external God to alter the course of history and intervene in our lives in unexpected ways? What is worship beyond honouring a supernatural God and 'his' creation when an understanding of evolution requires no creator? What does it mean to gather in specially designated places and inviting God to enter the space when we believe that divine presence is always present, in all places? What is outreach when we feel no need to convert people to a particular form of Christianity? What is pastoral care beyond the 'cure of souls', when we no longer believe that the soul is an invisible part of people, distinct from mind and body, bound for another world? What is the role and value of the Bible when we are no longer held to a literal understanding of a divinely inspired text with timeless and unquestioned authority? What place do we give sacraments such as Eucharist and Baptism when we believe that all moments are sacred teachers?

Our Sunday gatherings are a time of inspiration and shared wisdom. We incorporate outstanding local musicians who sing songs that weave around a theme. We sing chants and group songs, and include readings and prayers that build the theme. We encourage each other to live fully in this life, and to take responsibility for the choices we make. We glean wisdom from all traditions, even though many of us are most familiar with the Judeo-Christian tradition. The Bible is one source of inspiration, although we urge each other to critique and reinterpret its words. Pastoral care is a matter of compassion and mutual empowerment. We strive to be whole people, healthy in body, mind and spirit. We celebrate babies as new members of the community, but not to achieve anything eternal or otherworldly for the child.

In our independent context we have no particular form or annual rhythm to follow. There is no central authority to which we are accountable, nor is there any single shared tradition. We are people of many faiths and no faith. We come with varying degrees of interest in the Christian story, and diverse expectations.

When we realized that our previous name and the large cross towering over the outside of the building were misrepresenting who we are, we began a community conversation. With very little internal drama, and a great deal of national interest, we changed the name to C3Exchange and removed the cross. C3Exchange reflects the exchange of ideas that takes place, as well as indicating our physical street address.

Core Values

We have created a community form and rhythm based on a series of core values we discerned. These values guide our Sunday morning experience as well as the many programs, children and youth curricula, community fairs and outreaches we host. This is how a typical year flows at C3Exchange.

In January we look at *universal values* through the eyes of different spiritual traditions. This is not interfaith dialogue in the sense of comparing and contrasting traditions. It is an attempt to live more peaceful lives and build a more peaceful world while looking to different traditions for inspiration. Some of these universal values include unity, compassion, action and balance.

February is our month of *inquiry*. We look at recent scientific advances to see how they inform our minds and guide our spiritual lives. This includes understanding the hemispheres of the brain, and how the brain feeds spirituality through meditation and consciousness.

In March we look at *gender* from the perspective of yin/yang complementarities. This includes the divine feminine, masculine spirituality, and active and receptive modes of living in tune with the universe.

April and May bring both *Easter* and *Earth* season together, which is a beautiful synergy. We emphasize the natural elements of the Easter story more than the supernatural miracles. We speak of resurrection all around us, and the need for humans to honour the patterns of death and rebirth in nature.

In June and July, we focus on issues of *personal development* and *intimate connections*. We look at issues such as trust and forgiveness, and study books such as *Blink* by Malcolm Gladwell, *Mindful Loving* by Henry Grayson and *A New Earth* by Eckhart Tolle.

August is our *wellness* month. We focus on nutrition, emotional health, yoga, relationships and spiritual practice such as prayer and meditation as being core components of health.

September is *Homecoming*, and *community* is our focus. We usually set the tone for the coming year by reminding each other of our core commitments as a community that is a subset of a global village.

October brings an emphasis on *sexuality*. We celebrate coming out day, and affirm sexuality as a good and beautiful part of our spiritual lives.

In November we focus on *activism*. We explore national and global issues in relation to our core commitment to be the change we wish to see in the world.

December is a time to reinterpret the *Christmas story* in a universal and naturalistic way. We spend some time deconstructing the story and much more time reinterpreting the story in a way that emphasizes the birth of hope in all of our lives.

Outreach

One of our mantras at C3 is "heads, hearts and hands". We seek cognitive resonance, intimate connections and effective action. You aren't expected to leave your brain at the door and doubt is encouraged as part of a healthy process of self-reflection (heads). C3Exchange is a community where you can ask questions in good company. We also seek to live lives of compassion where we support each other in the joys and sorrows of life (hearts). We also take personal responsibility for the world we leave for the next generations (hands).

We have no interest in converting anyone to any particular religious belief. Rather, we reach out to people where they are and encourage them to be more of who they are. We participate in a bimonthly program that houses homeless people. We are involved in local alternate energy think tanks. We support education programs in Nepal, and local education efforts in a neighbouring town.

Our community partnerships match our core values. We participate in local green initiatives and wellness networks. We collaborate with local Center for Inquiry (CFI) groups and participate in local interfaith events. These community initiatives come from the people of the community, and are led by community members.

Governance

Our organization's governance evolved from an eldership model to a board of trustees that is elected by members who gather at our annual meeting. We no longer feel the need to have elders who watch over the spiritual life of members. Now the board oversees a series of committees and task groups that facilitate the smooth running of the community. It is a movement from top-down to bottom-up governance. We encourage people to become members as a mark of commitment but we don't require any statement of faith as a criterion for membership.

Recently we initiated a redesign of our lobby area. The vision and manner of undertaking this project epitomizes the inclusive spirit of C3 Exchange. A small group of members met and shared the vision for an open space with architects, staff and city officials. Once the plans were approved, the work began and each Sunday more and more people enjoyed the evolving space. They adopted a mantra: "We are making a difference and we are having fun doing it."

This mantra captures the essence of C3Exchange. We are growing, making a difference "and we are having fun doing it". If the day ever arrives where this inclusive spiritual community stops making a difference in people's lives, or becomes a drudgery to maintain, this will be the day to put the cork back in the bottle. In the meantime, we are having too much fun to quit. After all, life is a cabernet and our job is to sing our unique song with spirit.

Further Reading

K. Armstrong, *A History of God.*
J. Campbell, *The Hero with a Thousand Faces.*
E. Fromm, *The Art of Loving.*
J. S. Spong, *Jesus for the Non-Religious.*
P. Tillich, *The Courage to Be.*
E. Tolle, *A New Earth.*

Pushing Boundaries: The Jesus Seminar and New Testament Scholarship

Gregory C. Jenks

The Jesus Seminar is a continuing academic project sponsored by the Westar Institute, and founded by Robert W. Funk. After a distinguished career in New Testament (NT) scholarship, Funk set up the Westar Institute as an independent religion think-tank to engage in research, and to act as an advocate for religious literacy. While only one of several seminar programs established by the institute, the Jesus Seminar proved to be the longest running and the most controversial.

During its first fifteen years (1985–2000), the Jesus Seminar identified and assessed all available traditions about Jesus from the first three hundred years of the Common Era. The material was not limited to the four canonical Gospels of the New Testament, but included all the relevant texts that have survived from antiquity. More than fifteen hundred sayings attributed to Jesus and 387 reports of events involving him were painstakingly examined. Since 2000, the focus has turned more towards exploring the implications of the earlier research for present and future expressions of Christianity, while continuing new research into Christian origins.

Despite claims to the contrary by its critics, there is no distinctive methodology applied by the Seminar in its assessment of the Jesus tradition. Each Fellow is required to have an advanced graduate degree in biblical studies or some other relevant discipline, including the capacity to work with the texts in at least one of the original languages. However, there is no attempt to select those scholars with particular approaches or theological preferences.

In a very real sense, the Fellows of the Jesus Seminar come from the mainstream of contemporary biblical studies. They belong within that 'broad church' of critical biblical scholarship found in mainstream seminaries, religious studies departments, and theological faculties all around the world—and share essentially the same set of assumptions.

This article will consider a selection of issues relating to the Jesus Seminar. These issues can be grouped into three categories: methodology, process, and outcomes.

Methodology

There are three issues that concern distinctive aspects of the Jesus Seminar's treatment of the historical Jesus question.

The Sayings Come First

Beginning with and focusing on the sayings attributed to Jesus, rather than the narratives about his actions, seems to be the most significant assumption of the Seminar. This is both a simple and a significant change of perspective. Events only happen once in time, and lend themselves to legendary embellishment. Historical judgments about them are more difficult. Sayings, by their nature, will have been delivered and remembered in a variety of contexts; perhaps even by Jesus himself. They are more suited to preservation within an oral culture. They retain a residual 'voiceprint' even when being performed by later speakers. The Seminar's focus on the sayings resulted partly from the prior involvement of several of the original Fellows with parables research in the 1970s. It may have been a happy accident.

Gospel of Thomas

Another distinctive element is the Seminar's acceptance of the Gospel of Thomas as a valuable source for historical Jesus studies. This is now much more common, but not so in the mid-1980s. Thomas is a collection of sayings attributed to Jesus, some quite similar to sayings in the canonical Gospels and some that appear to be gnostic texts. Thomas has proved to be important for several reasons. It is independent of the canonical Gospels. It seems to preserve older material pre-dating even Mark, and its form is evidence that sayings collections may have been the earliest form of the Jesus tradition.

Jesus and Apocalypticism

A third distinctive aspect is the Seminar's willingness to challenge the dominant assumption that the historical Jesus is best explained as an apocalyptic prophet. If there is one emphasis of the Seminar that appears to be unique within NT scholarship, it is perhaps the judgment that Jesus was not an apocalyptic firebrand, but more a teacher of sacred wisdom within the tradition of ancient Israel. This view arises not from a bias against apocalyptic, but from a close study of the parables that extended over many years in North America but was largely ignored elsewhere.

What the Jesus Seminar has proposed is that the voiceprint of Jesus that emerges from a study of the parables and other sayings is one that seems to be in tension with the traditional representation of Jesus as an apocalyptic teacher. That conclusion is not accepted widely—as yet. But it is not found only among the Fellows of the Jesus Seminar. It is a significant minority report. It presents a distinctive alternative, and has shaped recent debate in the field.

The Seminar Process

In terms of process, the following three items are important to note even if they do not have the same significance as the three issues already mentioned.

Collegiality

The collegial and collaborative character of the Seminar's work is very different from the traditional model of individual scholars working in solitude surrounded by their books. It has resulted in a new social reality that is highly valued by the Fellows who enjoy working together and value one another as colleagues, even when differing strongly over specific issues. The one hundred or so Fellows at any one time are a community of scribes gathered around the Jesus tradition.

Voting

Early in its history, the Seminar made a deliberate decision to vote on specific proposals at the end of each piece of work. Bringing each discussion to closure by framing specific propositions and voting on them focuses the attention of both the presenter and audience, and it allows the consensus within the group present for that session to be measured. It has meant that conclusions—however tentative and incomplete—are reached, rather than the question left open for ongoing discussion as usually happens in academic discourse. The four colours are derived from the traditional Red Letter Bibles, but allow two extra categories. In addition to "Jesus undoubtedly said this" (Red) and "Jesus did not say this; it comes from a later stage in the tradition" (Black), the Fellows allowed themselves two further categories: "Jesus probably said something like this" (Pink) and "Jesus did not say this, but the ideas contained here are close to his own" (Grey). While highly controversial, such voting is, in principle, no different from the voting that lies behind the decisions on which words to include in a critical edition of the Greek New Testament and which variants to relegate to the footnotes.

Talking Out of School

The Jesus Seminar is an activity of the Westar Institute and, as such, it is part of Westar's agenda as an advocate for religious literacy. The results of the Seminar's work have therefore always been reported to the wider public in non-technical terms, most famously in *The Five Gospels* with its four color-coded texts and its provocative inclusion of the *Gospel of Thomas*. In particular, the final weighted average generated by the voting process provides a helpful way for the Seminar to communicate its decisions to a wider constituency. The Seminar has 'talked out of school' and not kept its conversations within the privacy of the academic guild.

Outcomes from the Seminar

Finally, it is important to say something about the outcomes or results from the Jesus Seminar.

Scepticism

In some significant respects, the Jesus Seminar as a group is less radical than many individual NT scholars both within and outside the Seminar. The finding that only 18 percent of the sayings attributed to Jesus and 16 percent of the deeds are probably authentic has to be considered in context. The data is comprised of all the extant Jesus traditions from the first three hundred years, not just the canonical materials in the New Testament. If the focus is narrowed to include only the findings concerning the canonical Gospels, we find that John is mostly voted Black while the Synoptics have considerable percentages of Red and Pink. It has been estimated that the Seminar gave about 50 percent of the canonical materials a Red or Pink rating. This is more sceptical than conservative Evangelical scholars, but less sceptical than many mainstream NT scholars.

Profiles of Jesus

The profiles of Jesus that have been developed by different Fellows of the Seminar show considerable variety, along with some predictable common elements. Typically, they understand Jesus more within ancient Jewish wisdom traditions than within the apocalyptic traditions. In addition to the major studies by leading members of the Seminar, there is now a convenient collection of profiles prepared by different members of the Seminar.

Theological Implications

The theological and ecclesial implications of the Seminar's findings, like those of any scholarly process, require a process of reception. For some people they will be unacceptable, while others will experience them as liberating insights. In the longer term, the impact of the Jesus Seminar may be found more in its role as an expression of the contemporary unrest over traditional religious formulations than in any specific finding on the historicity of a particular saying or deed. The implications of the Seminar's work for the churches are increasingly being explored by specialist theologians. Both the methods and the findings of the Jesus Seminar tend to be highly valued by religious progressives, and the Seminar has evolved into a *de facto* think-tank for progressive Christians around the world. The Seminar's commitment to a public constituency may turn out to have been one of the most radical and most influential of its many decisions.

Further Reading

M. J. Borg, *Jesus*.
D. Boulton, *Who on Earth Was Jesus*.
J. D. Crossan, *God and Empire*.
R. W. Funk, *Honest to Jesus*.
R. W. Funk, R. W. Hoover, and the Jesus Seminar, *The Five Gospels*.
R. W. Funk and the Jesus Seminar, *The Acts of Jesus*.
_____, *The Once and Future Jesus*.
R. W. Hoover, *Profiles of Jesus*.
_____, *The Historical Jesus Goes to Church*.
R. J. Miller, *The Jesus Seminar and its Critics*.
_____, *The Future of the Christian Tradition*.

Biblical and Modern Worldviews of the History of the World and Human Life

Roy Hoover

The Biblical View	The Modern View
1. The origin of the universe God created the heavens and the earth and all of the forms of life in them in six days by commanding them into being (Genesis 1). God rested from his creating work on the seventh day, thus establishing it as a day of rest for as long as the world lasts.	**1. The origin of the universe.** The universe came into being fifteen billion years ago, or so, following a "big bang." Life on earth in its many forms has evolved and developed across hundreds of millions of years.
2. Space The earth occupies the center of the whole cosmos. The sun, moon, and stars circle around it.	**2. Space.** Space is many light years in extent and seems to be still expanding. The earth is one of several planets orbiting the sun in a solar system that is part of the milky way galaxy.
3. Human origins God created human beings in his image, made them male and female, commanded them to propagate and fill the earth, and delegated to them authority over and responsibility for the care of the plants and animals God had created (Genesis 1:26-31; 2:15).	**3. Human origins.** Human beings emerged comparatively late in the history of the earth from earlier forms of life and continue to be sustained by the whole ecosystem of the planet.
4. God God is the world's lord and king; he rules over it from his throne high in the heavens.	**4. God.** God is the symbolic term we use to refer to the ultimate reality and mystery with which we have to do. Theology is and always has been the constructive work of human beings and is useful only

insofar as it succeeds in depicting the way things really are and in pointing out how we may live humanely amid the realities of the world.

5. History

God is directing the course of history to its final consummation which he determined for it from the beginning.

5. History

Human beings are characterized by self-conscious, self-transcending intelligence and imagination. This capacity gives us the ability to create culture and to shape history. It also give us the inclination and ability to search for and recognize the meaning of our experience in the world, which we often express in the form of a religion.

6. Bible

God revealed, through Moses, the basic law by which human life is to be ordered, and sent prophets, apostles and other messengers to communicate his will to humankind. These revealed truths, recorded in scripture, make the Bible the Word of God.

6. Bible

God [esp. the rule of God] is the principal subject of the Bible, not its author. The writings-- of priests, prophets, wisdom teachers, psalmists, anonymous gospel narrators, and apostles-- that have been collected to form the Christian Bible are an irreplaceable source of information about the origins of the characteristically Jewish and Christian ways of viewing the human condition and a primary resource for theological reflection and public worship.

7. Jesus

God sent his only son, Jesus Christ, to preach the gospel and to die on the cross to save us from our sins. God raised Jesus from the dead and will likewise raise all who believe in him. This incarnation of the eternal son of God

7. Jesus

Jesus of Nazareth was the pioneer and exemplar of a new form of ancient Israel's faith that emphasized its universal rather than its ethnic meaning. The message Jesus preached was about "the Kingdom of God," a vision of marks the beginning of the consummation of all things, which is even now playing out under God's providential direction.

life ruled by the union of power and goodness. The political and religious establishments of that time regarded the threat to their legitimacy posed by this vision sufficient reason to execute him.

8. The future

The resurrected Jesus will return on the clouds of heaven at the end of history when God will defeat the powers of sin and death and bring into being his kingdom which will have no end.

8. The future

The literal statements about the resurrection lost their literal meaning when the modern view of the world displaced the ancient. The real core of ancient resurrection faith is the recognition that justice and moral virtue are indispensable for a truly human life, and that human life can be transformed in the direction of greater fulfillment.

The 'Second Coming' of Christ Will Only Happen When . . .

John Dominic Crossan

Although the challenge of Jesus emphasized the *present* reality of the Kingdom of God on earth, the necessary participation of his companions in its arrival, and their collaboration with God in its establishment, early Christians still wanted to know about the *future*—possibly as a flight from the message of their *present* responsibility. But, be that as it may, two very different models, two major mega-metaphors, were used in the New Testament to imagine that future consummation. One comes from Paul of Tarsus in the 50s, the other from John of Patmos in the 90s. Note, in what follows, that expressions like 'second coming' or 'return' of Christ never appear in the New Testament itself.

The models used by both Paul and John of Patmos agreed that the climactic end of what Jesus had inaugurated would happen *soon*, in the very near and not in the far distant future. *Soon* meant, in effect, within the author's own lifetime. On that point, both authors were flatly wrong, off by two thousand years—and still counting.

When he wrote to the Thessalonians, Paul expected the coming of the Lord within his own lifetime. He said that "we who are alive . . . will be caught up in the clouds . . . to meet the Lord in the air" (4:17). Later, after and probably because of his near-execution at Ephesus, he could write to the Philippians that "my desire is to depart and be with Christ" (1:23). By then he could imagine dying before the return of Christ but he still presumed that it would occur within his own generation's lifetime or at least very, very soon. Even after that remark to the Philippians, he could write in 1 Corinthians about "the impending crisis" since "the appointed time has grown short" with "the present form of this world . . . passing away" (7:26–31). And still, as late as his letter to the Romans he could write that, "salvation is nearer to us now than when we became believers; the night is far gone, the day is near" (13:11–12).

The message of 'soon' is reiterated like a mantra across the entire book of Revelation. It is announced at the very start: "The revelation of Jesus Christ, which God gave him to show his servants what must *soon* take place; he made it known by sending his angel to his servant John" (1:1). It is still proclaimed in the very end: "The one who testifies to these things says, 'Surely I am coming soon.' Amen. Come, Lord Jesus!" (22:20). In between, Christ repeats, "I will come to you soon" (1:16) and—three times—"I am coming soon" (3:11; 22:7, 12). In other words, John agrees with Paul—as indeed with Mark (9:1) and Matthew (10:23)—that Christ would return to earth soon—and, as I said, all of them were equally wrong on that expectation.

But my present concern is not with Paul and John on the *time* of Christ's return but with their divergent visions of its purpose and method. For Paul, the (second) coming of Christ would be a *non-violent* celebration of our collaborative success. For John, the (second) coming of Christ would be a *violent* repudiation of our collaborative failure.

Paul's metaphor-model for the coming of Christ is the joyful visitation of the emperor or an imperial legate to a peaceful city during the *Pax Romana*. This is evident from the twin technical terms he uses in 1 Thessalonians—*parousia* for the visitor's advent and *apantēsis* for the visitor's reception:

> For this we declare to you by the word of the Lord, that we who are alive, who are left until the coming the Lord (*eis tēn parousian tou kuriou*), will by no means precede those who have died. For . . . the dead in Christ will rise first. Then we who are alive, who are left, will be caught up in the clouds together with them to meet the Lord (*eis apantēsin tou kuriou*) in the air; and so we will be with the Lord forever. (4:15–17; see also 2:19 and 5:23)

As the imperial visitor approaches the city, the first to greet him will be—as it were—the honoured dead whose stately tombs lined the edges of the main road outside the gates (think, for example, of the north road into Phrygian Hierapolis). And, of course, after both dead and living aristocrats had greeted the visitor, he accompanied them into their city for feasting and celebration—he did not turn around and go straight home.

That metaphorical vision of the Kingdom's consummation is summarized even more succinctly in 1 Corinthians. It is called, once again, the 'coming' (*parousia*) of Christ (15:23) and described like this:

> Then comes the end, when he hands over the kingdom to God the Father, after he has destroyed every ruler and every authority and power. For he must reign until he has put all his enemies under his feet. (15:24–25)

The 'coming' (*parousia*) of Christ is to consummate and celebrate the Kingdom of God established on a transfigured earth and therefore ready to be handed over "to God the Father . . . so that God may be all in all" (15:24, 28). That language from imperial visitation during the common urban experience of the *Pax Romana* never appears in John's Revelation. He uses the ordinary Greek verb 'to come' (*erchomai*) and that leaves his vision open to a violent rather than a non-violent consummation.

Where does John get such a metaphor-model of violent imperial arrival, and how would it be persuasive after more than a hundred years of the *Pax Romana*—especially for those seven rich cities of Asia Minor, the richest province of Rome's empire? What is John's model for Christ's (second) coming?

The clue is all the emphasis on the Emperor Nero, who was already dead for thirty years when Revelation was written in the 90s under Domitian. Recall, for example, the warning that "this calls for wisdom: let anyone with understanding calculate the number of the beast, for it is the number of a person. Its number is six hundred sixty-six" (13:18). The standard scholarly wisdom is that 666 designates Nero because in Aramaic—with letters also serving as numerals—the seven letters of NRWN QSR (Nero Caesar) indicate the numbers 50 + 200 + 6 + 50 + 100 + 60 + 200 = 666.

On June 9, 68 CE, Nero committed suicide to escape assassination. He left behind a reputation for crimes so monstrous that the senatorial and aristocratic classes of Rome had clearly rejected even his memory. But he also left behind a very different reputation among the lower classes of Rome and even among upper classes in the east. A Roman emperor who competed with others by performing on his lyre and racing in his chariot was popular precisely among those groups. And it was there that the legend of Nero *redivivus* was born and survived— even to the time of Saint Augustine over three hundred years later.

That legend—as attested by both Roman and Jewish sources— claimed that Nero had not died but had fled eastward beyond the Euphrates. From there he would soon return at the head of Parthian imperial armies to destroy the Roman Empire. Sources not only mention that belief, they also cite pretenders who claimed to be Nero *redivivus*. The coming of Nero *redivivus* will be far from the nonviolent imperial visitation of the Roman peace. It will be the violent imperial visitation of the Parthian revenge.

Rome will be destroyed *soon*, announces John, not by Nero *redivivus* but by Christ *redivivus*. Not Nero backed by the Parthians but Christ backed by the angels will come—and come soon—to destroy Rome. In that transfer from Nero to Christ, the eschatological consummation retains all the violent imagery of imperial warfare. It is the counter-violence of Christ-as-Nero whose Coming will destroy the violence of the Roman Empire. That is the model and metaphor that controls the Revelation from Patmos.

Eschatological consummation will indeed be a Great Final Feast for the entire world—as promised by Isa 25:6. But, says John of Patmos, it will be a feast for carrion crows and vultures: "Come, gather for the great supper of God, to eat the flesh of kings, the flesh of captains, the flesh of the mighty, the flesh of horses and their riders—flesh of all, both free and slave, both small and great . . . and all the birds were gorged with their flesh" (Rev 19:17, 18, 21).

The Second Coming of Christ is not an event that we should expect to happen *soon*. The Second Coming of Christ is not an event that we should expect to happen *violently*. The Second Coming of Christ is what will happen when we Christians finally accept that the First Coming was the Only Coming and start to cooperate with its divine presence.

Further Reading

J. D. Crossan, *God and Empire.*

Why I Can No Longer Say 'The Nicene Creed' . . .

Noel Preston

I am more interested in understanding faith as a way of seeing and trusting reality . . . which, in turn, supports a way of living with integrity and authenticity. In my own case I recognise that I cannot dispense with 'beliefs' altogether, even if their 'truth' is metaphorically rather than literally true.

As a traveller in the new millennium, my faith must be credible, intellectually sustainable and coherent with contemporary cosmological understanding[1].

In my experience, religious groups and their leaders have been inclined to be too wordy. We have tended to major on statements, confessions, doctrines, encyclicals, and explanations that are often a substitute for action. This verbosity too often impedes the human journey toward practical wisdom grounded in 'a spirituality' which is life giving. It creates a lopsided faith—faith that constrains experience of the eternal mystery by downgrading the mystical, while overemphasising beliefs at the expense of the way we live (i.e., expressing faith through our ethical and communal life). So the dictates of orthodoxy stifle the possibility of orthopraxis.

I have a particular difficulty with creeds. Historically (though there have been exceptions as with Quakers and Anabaptists), the classical creeds of Christendom have been used to sort out the 'theologically correct sheep from the incorrect goats', and thereby, to buttress audacious claims about authority and truth through decrees which broker communion with the divine. I call this 'creedalism'. Creedalism feeds off the powerful need we humans have for certainty and control in the face of uncertainty and vulnerability. In its hierarchical institutional forms, Christianity—whether Catholic, Protestant or Orthodox—has, at least since the Constantinian compromise of the fourth century, been prone to this tendency. This tendency has even infected such a contemporary, and partly liberal and democratic, form of church as the Uniting Church in Australia. In that denomination some have invested its *Basis of Union* document with scriptural authority and creedal status.

I am firmly resolved I can never say or assent to the traditional creedal forms of Christianity known as the *Apostles' Creed* or the *Nicene Creed*. That said, in public worship I am prepared to compromise with

words, images and phrases that may be in use by others whose integrity as worshippers and disciples I am not inclined to question. For
example, in conducting the baptisms of my grand-children recently
I have been happy to include the 'Statement of Faith' written for the
United Church of Canada which is included in a list of resources for
worship by the Uniting Church in Australia Liturgical Commission.

My disenchantment with the Nicene and Apostles' Creed is longstanding and parallels my journey to a non-theistic understanding of
Christianity. On this journey I have become increasingly sensitive to
the words we use in liturgy, including the words of hymns couched in
imagery of a pre-twentieth-century worldview. But creeds are a particular case. They say, presumably, what we *actually* believe. They require
a more uncompromising, literal commitment. In my youth we extended the creedal exercise to catechism questions and answers, which
unmistakably defined what we believe, and bound co-religionists together. For understandable reasons (not just reasons of relevance), the
catechism and its definitive attempts to describe the indescribable have
disappeared in most denominations. It is time for changing the creeds
if we are to have them at all.

The Nicene Creed as a Case in Point

From the point of view of the prevailing bishops aligned with Rome
and Constantinople, the Nicene Creed (originally adopted 325 CE,
amended 381 CE) was about stamping out heresy and creating an 'orthodoxy' which suited the religion they had constructed. The Nicene
Creed was adopted in the face of the Arian controversy. Arius, a Libyan
presbyter, had declared that although Jesus Christ was divine, God
actually created him, and "there was a time when he was not". This
made Jesus less than God, the Father, and contradicted the doctrine of
the Trinity and so provoked a serious controversy. But Arius' view only
reflects the diversity of teaching and beliefs about Jesus that characterised Christianity in its early centuries, stemming from the first century
CE when there was division between the Jewish faction, which did not
attribute divinity to the rabbi from Nazareth, and the Pauline faction,
which developed an elevated notion of the Christ as divine. Modern
biblical scholarship has revived knowledge of this debate. Indeed,
many scholars maintain the Nicene Creed confirmed the admission of
Hellenistic philosophy to Christianity, a process that was necessary to
break Christianity's ties with Judaism, as Adolf von Harnack argued.

By the fourth century the time was ripe for a political settlement
with the Roman Empire. The bishops who prevailed at Nicaea were

happy to be in league with Roman Imperialism, a far cry from the first-century church. The 'heresy' they sought to eradicate can therefore be seen in another light—Rome's ecclesiastical and military need to stamp out elements which refused to submit to the Roman line. The Nicene Council, from this viewpoint (and it is generally so regarded by church historians), resulted in the imposition of universal (Catholic) dogma by an imperial ruler and politician rather than by consensus coming from within the body of the Church itself. Its theological legitimacy is questionable from the beginning.

The political and social history of the Nicene Creed discredits these words for many of us. They were given birth in the context of the Constantinian compromise, which ushered in the era of Christendom. Though now arguably redundant, that pact with the Roman Emperor led to a religion sometimes corrupt and an institution which served the objectives of imperialism and often became preoccupied with its own maintenance rather than its mission, unrecognisable as an instrument of the Jesus story.

Furthermore, these early creeds were designed within a cosmological framework that is no longer accepted—the three-tiered universe of a pre-evolution creation myth. The language of the creed with its allusions to 'the resurrection of the dead' and Christ's 'ascension', 'seated at the right hand of God' come from a worldview that predates contemporary science. Moreover, it reflects a theistic view of 'God' rejected by many current theologians.

The most disquieting feature of both the Nicene Creed and the Apostles' Creed, is what they omit. They say nothing about the central teaching of Jesus in Matthew, Mark and Luke: the Reign of God and its ethic of compassion and social justice—key themes of the biblical prophetic tradition. Rather than affirm 'the Jesus way', the bishops' council of Nicaea produced a document of esoteric doctrine and a formula of salvation that became an instrument of church control. Adherence to the Trinitarian faith that is summarised in this creed remains the test of who is in communion with Rome and/or the World Council of Churches.

Because of their longstanding acceptance in Christendom and the fact it is generally acknowledged by the major Christian denominations, there is presently reluctance by church councils, synods and ecumenical gatherings to question the ancient creedal formulations. Some might even opine, "Regardless of its words, the Nicene Creed represents what we Christians have in common." Others would be shocked to think that the theological essence of what Nicaea was about—Trinitarian Doctrine that contains an elevated view of the divinity of Jesus the Christ—is being questioned.

Frankly, Nicaea doesn't speak for countless, thinking progressive Christians. It dangerously distorts the Jesus of the gospels and sounds like gobble-de-gook in a twenty-first-century service of worship.

Literally understood, the Nicene Creed enshrines very questionable theology that, I hazard to suggest, is not really believed by a majority in the pews of mainline denominations. As instances, I cite the Virgin Birth, Substitutionary Atonement, the Second Coming and even, perhaps, a literal Bodily Resurrection. Some of my theologically trained friends would counter: "I get by with these expressions by demythologising them without literally believing them." I find that approach dishonest and an unnecessary stumbling block to a credible, contemporary representation of the gospels, to say nothing of the confusion it may set up for less theologically trained pew sitters.

And So . . .

A fair analysis concludes that 'creeds' have often been instruments of control, inquisition and domination, to sort out the sheep and the goats. Granted, in local church communities, this may not seem to be the case in our day. But it still begs the question: what credible purpose do such creeds serve? Whatever the answer, they seem to send a subtle message about 'faith': it is more important what we believe than what we do. That, of course, is an unbiblical position that calls to mind the reported (and paraphrased) admonition of Jesus: "Why do you call me Lord, Lord, but do not act on the things I say?"

In what is often now called the 'emerging church', the emphasis is on 'how we live rather than what we believe'[2]. Of course we continue to have beliefs and, collectively or individually, progressives may need to articulate contemporary creeds, but they are likely to be simpler, briefer and reflect a credible worldview while emphasising the values of the 'Jesus way'. Rather than insisting on orthodox answers about matters of belief, living the questions (orthopraxis) would seem to represent a more authentic spirituality for our times.

> And the point is to live everything,
> live the questions now.
> Perhaps you will gradually,
> Without noticing it,
> live along some distant day,
> into the answer.
> —Ranier Maria Rilke

Notes

1. N. Preston, *Beyond the Boundary*, 291.
2. T. Harpur in M. Schwartzentruber, *The Emerging Christian Way*.

Additional Notes

- The origin of the Apostles' Creeds seems obscure. Catholic tradition has at times attributed this statement to the original Twelve. Today scholars are more inclined to the view that this creed emerged centuries later to summarise Catholic doctrine and as a baptismal confession in the churches of Rome. Other critiques may be made of many creeds and statements of faith that come from the era of Christendom, including the Reformation Westminster Confession of Faith.
- For a fuller discussion of the Arian controversy and its significance in evaluating questions of the "divinity of Jesus the Christ", see J. A. T. Robinson, *The Human Face of God*, 109ff.
- For a lucid account of the context for the Nicene Creed, including a revealing quote from Bishop Eusebius, see R. Holloway, *Doubts and Loves*, 172.
- For an informative analysis of the role of creeds and a discussion of attempts by the United Church of Canada to update creeds, see G. Vosper, *With or Without God*, 91–102. Also, "On Saying the Christian Creeds with Honesty" is the title of chap. 1 of Bishop Spong's *Why Christianity Must Change or Die*, 18–19.

Further Reading

C. H. Hedrick, *When Faith Meets Reason*.
N. Preston, *Beyond the Boundary*.
M. Schwartzentruber, *The Emerging Christian Way*.
J. S. Spong, *A New Christianity for a New World*.

This We Can Say
A 'progressive' Affirmation
Rex A. E. Hunt

Critics are quick to point out that progressive Christians seem to know what they *don't* believe. But do they know what they *do* believe?

I, and many others who call ourselves 'progressive Christian', have heard this charge several times. Well . . . a group of folk in my last parish, inspired by Gretta Vosper's congregation in Canada and their Affirmation, embarked on such a journey—of shaping an Affirmation which expresses the characteristics of a progressive Christianity. It was an attempt to move beyond saying what we don't believe, to affirming what we do. Reconstruction rather than just deconstruction.

After a couple of months listening and reflecting and writing, the *Canberra Affirmation* resulted as one among three attempts. Is it a final,

definitive statement? No. Life continues to evolve and so do our experiences of life and the sacred. Change is! But some of us have parked
here for the moment.

The *Canberra Affirmation* is as follows:

As progressive Christians in the twenty-first century, we are uncomfortable with rigid statements of belief, as we recognize our
understandings are shaped by life experiences within cultural and
environmental contexts. Yet, there are some common understandings which continue to shape our lives, both individually and in
community with others. These we seek to affirm and celebrate:

- We celebrate that our lives are continually evolving in a web
  of relationships: continuous with historical humans and their
  societies; with other forms of life; and with the 'creativity' present at the origins of the universe. Over billions of years this
  'creativity'—the coming into being of the new and the novel—
  has undergone countless transformations, and we and all other
  life forms are its emerging products. Thus we are called to live
  in community, respecting all human beings, all life forms, our
  planet and universe.
- We affirm there is a presentness in the midst of our lives, sensed
  as both within and beyond ourselves, which can transform our
  experiences of this earth and each other. Various imaginative
  ideas have been used to describe this presentness: 'God', 'sacred', 'love', 'Spirit of Life'. We recognize all attempts at understanding and attributing meaning are shaped by prevailing
  thoughts and culture. Ultimately our response can only be as
  awe-inspiring mystery beyond the limits of our ability to understand our world and ourselves.
- We honour the one called Jesus, a first-century Galilean Jewish
  sage, nurtured by his religious tradition. A visionary and wisdom teacher, he invited others through distinctive oral sayings
  and parables about integrity, justice, and inclusiveness, and an
  open table fellowship, to adopt and trust a re-imagined vision
  of the 'sacred', of one's neighbour, of life. As we, too, share in
  this vision, we affirm the significance of his life and teachings,
  while claiming to be 'followers of Jesus'.
- We receive the Hebrew and Christian scriptures known as the
  Bible, as a collection of human documents rich in historical
  memory and religious interpretation, which describe attempts
  to address and respond to the 'sacred'. It forms an indispensable part of our tradition and personal journeys. We claim the
  right and responsibility to question and interpret its texts, empowered by critical biblical scholarship as well as from our own
  life experiences. We accept that other sources—stories, poems
  and songs—imaginative pictures of human life both modern

and ancient, can nurture us and others, in a celebration of the 'sacred' in life.

- We recognize there are many paths to the 'sacred'. We respect the diversity and pluralism of truth-claims, often in the midst of serious disagreement. In and with this diversity we honour the integrity and meaning of each religious tradition and the people who practice them. We reject all attempts to convert others to any fixed body of belief which they would not come to through their own open, free and considered explorations.
- We acknowledge that a transformative path of inclusion and integrity involves living responsible and compassionate lives in community with others. Such a path asks us to adopt values supporting social equality and connectedness. It entails non-violent peacemaking and considered forgiveness. It invites passion and action for social justice, and stewardship of the earth and all its life forms. It encourages humour, challenge, and acts of generosity. At its centre is an awareness of oneness: one with the 'sacred', with ourselves, with others, with the universe.

Since sharing this Affirmation with others, it has been supported and adopted by several, criticized by others, used in study groups in Australia, New Zealand and the USA, and commented on in sermons, lectures and liturgies. It has also inspired Australian hymn writer George Stuart to write six original hymns—each hymn addresses one of the Affirmation clauses.

Those hymns follow:

(i)   Creativity – The Canberra Affirmation 1
Tune: 'Austria', 87 87D

When beliefs and rigid doctrines,
Like stone statues cold as death,
Discipline us into silence,
Rob us of life-giving breath;
We can voice our great discomfort
As we recognize the truth
That our life and all our living
Give us insight from our youth.

We would celebrate evolving;
In the webs of life we bond
To the cosmos and our family,
Humans here and those beyond;
Thus we're called to live together
With respect for all that is,
For the cosmos and our planet
With respect for all that lives.

'Creativity' is present
Ever since before the start;
Brings to birth such great abundance;
Gives birth to a loving heart.
With this birthing of the novel
'Creativity' transforms;
Energy and life emerges;
Beauty seen in all its forms.

So we celebrate the myst'ry;
Stand in silence; look with awe;
Countless years in billions ended
Since the opening of the store
Of variety and brilliance,
Of the life-force and of grace;
It's amazing and so wondrous
We can claim to have a place.

(ii) Presentness – The Canberra Affirmation 2
Tune: 'Ascalon', 668D

There is a 'presentness'
In our midst that we confess;
Sensed both within and beyond us all;
This 'presentness' can be
Transforming constantly
In each event and overall.

We give this 'presentness'
Many names which do express
The faith of those with religious creed;
'God', 'Sacred' and 'Divine'
'Love' and 'The one true vine'
Can prompt the caring act and deed.

We recognize these names
Are but only passing frames
For all the pictures we have been taught;
Each image we attempt
Can never be exempt
From all prevailing views and thought.

To this grand mystery,
Our response can only be
Far and beyond what we understand;
For our ability
To search infinity
Can never match such high demand.

(iii) Jesus – The Canberra Affirmation 3
Tune: 'Triumph', 87 87 87

We would honour one called Jesus—
Wisdom teacher, Jewish sage;
Nurtured by his own tradition
And religion of his age;
Long ago he took his journey; setting forth from Galilee.

Through distinctive oral sayings,
By the parables he told
Of inclusiveness and justice,
Of integrity so bold
He invited others trust in his great vision for his day.

Life, one's neighbour and the 'sacred'
Re-imagined when he taught;
Table fellowship was open—
Symbol of his warm support;
As we too share in his vision, we affirm and follow him.

(iv) The Bible – The Canberra Affirmation 4
Tune: 'Regent Square', 87 87 47 extend

We receive the Hebrew Scriptures
And the Christian Scriptures, too,
As collections, human writings
Rich in mem'ry and review;
These describe attempts, responding
To the 'sacred', sensed as true.

Indispensable, this Bible
Is part of our heritage,
In tradition, pers'nal journeys
It finds us at every stage;
Reading, list'ning and debating,
Finding wisdom for each age.

Yet we claim the right to question;
Take responsibility
To interpret texts and stories,
Searching each quite critically;
Then empowered with life's schooling
Wrest its wisdom honestly.

We accept that other sources—
Stories, poems, many a song,
And imagination pictures

Of our life, both weak and strong,
Join the process of our searching
For the 'sacred'; all belong.

(v) Paths to the sacred – The Canberra Affirmation 5
Tune: 'Ewing', 76 76D

We recognize the 'sacred' is sought in many ways,
With diff'rent paths to travel, with diff'rent passageways;
Midst serious disagreement we still respect, with grace,
Diversity of truth-claims; for each can have its place.

We honour diff'rent meanings and much integrity
Surrounding each tradition in this diversity;
We also honour people with righteous piety
Who practise their faith-teachings with poise and dignity.

Attempts to convert others to sets of fixed belief
Is not part of our program, sustained or even brief;
For we reject the process if it is not their choice
In open explorations through which they have their voice.

(vi) Values – The Canberra Affirmation 6
Tune: 'Tallis Canon', 88 88

Transforming is the path we take
With others, to community;
This path involves compassion bold,
Inclusion and integrity.

The values this path asks of us
Is to adopt, uphold, support
Equality, connectedness
In social action, noble thought.

This path entails a peaceful stance;
It seeks non-violence in its heart;
And with forgiveness at its core
Has harmony its counterpart.

This path invites a passion strong
In stewardship of all the earth,
For all life forms and nature's charm,
For us to recognize its worth.

This path encourages and prompts
Good humour, challenge, deeds of grace;
With acts of generosity
To bring a smile to every face.

The centre of this path we find
A oneness, we can all rehearse,
With self, the 'sacred', others too;
A oneness with the universe.

Further Reading

R. W. Funk, *A Credible Jesus.*
G. Stuart, *Singing a New Song 2.*
G. Vosper, *With or Without God.*

Stepping Out with the Sacred
'progressives' Engaging the Divine

Val Webb

It is no wonder that the contemporary progressive movement has emerged under a postmodern umbrella where truth is no longer seen as absolute, the authority of knowledge and office is no longer sacrosanct and personal experience has claimed its rightful place as a test for authenticity. No longer is access to theology locked within the halls of the ordained or chosen. Many serious theological books share space in public bookshops, and the new atheists are promoting a user-friendly atheism that raises timely questions for religion. Rather than something abstract and elitist, theology is always the attempt by humans to talk and think about God from their own experience and within their own context. We are each therefore responsible, albeit with guidance from others, to create something functional, not obtuse, that actually works in our lives.

Many scholars today have abandoned the old man God in the skies judging who's 'naughty and nice' and breaking natural laws to reward some and not others (I use G-O-D as a three letter symbol without specific gender or theological baggage). Instead, they describe the Sacred *within* the universe, whether called Energy, Presence, Love, Spirit, Ground of Being or Life. Such imagery allows us to talk within our contemporary scientific world about the wondrous universe we share and the mystery we *all* seek to unravel, whether described in religious, natural or scientific terms. This does not reject all biblical imagery—there are many places where biblical writers imagined the Sacred thus, for example, the beautiful metaphors of Psalm 139 in response to the question "Where can I go from your Spirit? Or where can I flee from your presence?" (v. 7). John's Gospel speaks of "know[ing] the Spirit of truth because that spirit abides with you and will be in you" (14:17) and Paul describes the Divine to the Athenian philosophers as that in which "we live and move and have our being", as their Greek poets also said (Acts 17:28). With this language, we reclaim the transcendent All-pervasiveness, where transcendence means unlimited and unbound rather than elsewhere; and Immanence (the Sacred with/ in us) is possible *because* of this transcendent limitlessness.

Re-imagining the Sacred is not about taking some nips and tucks in an old idea. It is a total paradigm change with endless repercussions for established doctrines. These doctrines were not spelled out in the Bible but, rather, are theological systems shaped around ancient philosophical arguments by stringing together disparate Bible verses (and leaving awkward ones out) in order to formulate a seamless explanation of Divine thought and activity. The creation story, Adam and Eve's disobedience, original sin, atonement theories and the Trinity metaphor all became beads on this string. Cut the string at any point and the whole thing falls apart. Over the centuries, cuts *have* been made, but those in power busily knotted the string together again. That day has passed and, not only do we have a handful of loose beads and a piece of tattered string, we have also discovered a host of forgotten beads under the couch or behind the fireplace, waiting to add their story to the mix, including women, gays, the earth and other religions. Progressives are restringing the beads on a new piece of thread, giving weight to previously neglected beads and removing or reinterpreting some of the old ones.

If we speak of the Sacred in everything and everyone, or the Sacred in which we live and move, this includes *everyone*, Hindu, Christian, atheist and Sikh, which brings us to a whole new imaginative place. We can no longer seek and explain the Sacred from our cultural and religious imagination only. If the Sacred infuses everything, can we talk about Jesus as the only or most authentic incarnation, especially if we have never investigated incarnation stories in other religious traditions? Can we claim God is present only for those who pray the right words? Can we talk about spiritual and secular as different compartments of experience? Such a change *necessitates* engaging with other religious traditions to see how *our* Divine appears in those different venues. A theologian once said that to know one religion is to know none, which, when we think about it, is true, although most of us have acted within only one religion all our lives.

While interfaith dialogue is very important, this is a plea beyond dialogue—that progressives seek to reconstruct their images of the Sacred beyond just Christian perspectives and language, a journey that will enrich our lives and open doors to a smorgasbord of wisdom. If we are not interested in how other religions experience the Divine we seek, we perpetuate our exclusivity and restrict our possibilities for transformation. Progressives often seem more willing to integrate their contemporary God-images with physics, cosmology, ecology and biology than with people on the same spiritual search—exclusivity dies hard. This does not mean we all come to the same conclusions since the point of the progressive movement is to be part of the cosmic dance, not locked in new boxes of other peoples' conclusions with a new set of 'must-hold' beliefs.

We will discover that, in describing God as Energy and Creativity infilling the universe, we are newcomers on the block. From the Sioux tradition, Black Elk said "For the Great Spirit is everywhere; he hears whatever is in our minds and hearts, and it is not necessary to speak to him in a loud voice." Indigenous Australians see the land as full of knowledge, story, energy and power. The Indian greeting *namaste*, with hands together and a bow, means "the Divine in me greets the Divine in you". Shinto teaches there is not a single place in all the corners of the world where God is absent, and the Qur'an says, "To Allah belong the east and the west: wherever you turn, there is the presence of Allah, for Allah is all-pervading, all-knowing" (2:115). To these, we can add the words ascribed to the apostle Peter, "Truly I perceive that God shows no partiality, but in every nation anyone who fears [God] and does what is right is acceptable to [God]" (Acts 10:34-5). Given all this, progressives may have more in common with other religious traditions than with traditional Christian God-images.

When Christian claims of uniqueness and superiority (and the theology that supported them) dissolve, we find ourselves reconnecting and mending barriers. In our rediscovery of the earth as sacred and our responsibility for its care rather than exploitation, we are borrowing language, concepts and rituals from indigenous traditions we once tried to destroy, and finding ourselves more in line with the celebration of nature than with many church worship liturgies. As for ethics, we discover that our assumption that the Golden Rule is of Christian origin simply shows our isolation and ignorance—it existed in many religions long before Jesus. Ancient Sumatran wisdom says, "Let all your undertakings be pleasing to you, as well as others. If that is not possible, at least do not harm anyone." Zoroastrianism praises the person that "refrains from doing unto another whatsoever is not good for itself". From the Hindu Vedic writings, "Do nothing unto others which would cause you pain if done to you." Confucius said, "What one does not wish for oneself, one ought not to do to anyone else," and

Plato reiterated, "May I do to others as I would that they should do to me." From the Jewish Talmud, "What is hateful to you, do not to your fellow human being: this is the whole Torah: while the rest is the commentary thereof," and from Buddhism, "Hurt not others in ways that you yourself would find hurtful."[1] The words ascribed to Jesus, "So in everything, do to others what you would have them do to you" (Matt 7:12) seem strangely less unique, and Matthew's Jesus acknowledged this, adding "for this sums up all the Law and the Prophets".

At the Parliament of the World's Religions in Australia in 2009, some seven thousand people from across religions listened to how others engaged the Sacred and how this shaped the way they lived. During the opening plenary, Zoroastrian, Hindu, Jain, Buddhist, Sikh, Jewish, Christian, Muslim, Baha'i, Aboriginal and Shinto blessings were offered, representing a plethora of wisdom and human transformation stretching back through time. In seven days of meetings, I heard no one making superior or exclusive claims for their beliefs, except the Christian lobby outside with a sign proclaiming Jesus as the only way, truth and life and the atheists beside them offering ten thousand dollars to anyone who could prove there is a God.

Progressives are busily reinventing themselves in response to failures within our Christian tradition, yet we are surrounded by people from other religious traditions, who have long worked at engaging the Divine and who will share their discoveries if we read their sacred writings and listen to their wisdom. We share human desires and a planet in turmoil. Should we not also share our hopes and solutions, not in order to convert each other but to live and work together? Religion scholar Ursula King says we need more 'world believers' who, like world citizens living in more than one country yet retaining a sense of 'home', have deep roots in one faith but relate to, and learn from, faiths *other* than their own—spiritually multi-lingual and multi-focused people. This, I believe, is the progressive challenge.

Notes
1. A. Krishna, *One Earth One Sky One Humankind.*

Further Reading
U. King, *The Search for Spirituality.*
V. Webb, *Like Catching Water in a Net.*
_____, *Stepping Out With the Sacred.*

Not Forgetting the Children!
A 'progressive' Christian Spiritual Curriculum

Deshna Ubeda

Let me tell you a story.

A Spanish missionary was visiting an island when he came across three Aztec Priests.

"How do you pray?" the missionary asked.

"We only have one prayer," answered one of the Aztecs. "We say, God, you are three, we are three. Have pity on us."

"A beautiful prayer," said the missionary. "But it is not exactly the one that God heeds. I'm going to teach you one that's much better."

The padre taught them a Catholic prayer and then continued on his path of evangelism. Years later, when he was returning to Spain, his ship stopped again at the island. From the deck, the missionary saw the three priests on the shore and waved to them.

Just then, the three men began to walk across the water toward him.

"Padre! Padre!" one of them called, approaching the ship. "Teach us again that prayer that God heeds. We've forgotten how it goes."

"It doesn't matter," responded the missionary, witnessing the miracle.

And he promptly asked God's forgiveness for failing to recognise that God speaks all languages, in all ways, to all people.[1]

Too many progressive Christians today are afraid of new language, new metaphors and new stories. Too many times I have visited so-called progressive Christian churches and for the life of me I can't figure out why they call themselves progressive. The question that always comes up in those moments is: What are the children hearing? How are they making sense of this direct dichotomy?

It is time to shift. It is time to evolve. We cannot speak to our children in a language that is no longer relevant. We cannot expect them to relate to a culture and period of history they don't belong to. This is our challenge. This is what we are being called to do, today. Change or die. Progressive Christianity must rise to this challenge or we will be leaving our children with no foundation on which to build their beliefs.

Children today hear a mythical story of a man, a hero born to save them, and half the world says it is the truth and the other half is so confused, disparate and quiet that it really has nothing to say. Should they reject this belief altogether then? Should they chalk it up to the craziness of the older generations? What happens when their friends begin telling them they will go to Hell (and burn for all eternity) if they don't believe in its truth? What happens when, with access to all of the world's information, they begin to question the myth? When they begin to learn about the mysteries of the universe, the unknowns, the billions of people with different beliefs? What happens when they learn that these beliefs cause the majority of the wars fought? What happens when they turn to their community and look there for answers and their pastor stands up each Sunday and reads from the Bible—but is afraid to say what she or he really believes? What happens, is they are left with nothing but a blank confusion or, worse, a deeply seeded fear.

A number of years ago, we at *ProgressiveChristianity.org* began pondering what we were called to do within the progressive Christian realm. We interviewed thousands of people, churches and major leaders in the progressive Christian field and came to the conclusion that one of the main things missing was a progressive Christian curriculum for our children. We were forgetting the children!

Children's curriculum hasn't kept up with the evolving path of today's progressive Christianity. We are long past the debate of whether god is a he or a she. People in today's field are talking about the vastness of this universe and the miracle of how humans evolved. We are talking about string theory, multiple dimensions, and how interconnected all beings are. The majority of children's curriculum in faith communities today is still totally Bible centred, using little to no other myths, stories, or wisdom traditions. Most of them treat the Bible as history and talk about God as a powerful deity that has human qualities, using such words as: wants, hears, listens, needs, gives, receives, asks, does.

I understand why this is. It is easy to intellectualize progressive Christianity, but talking about it with our children is another story altogether. For how do you explain that which is unknown? The dilemma many face is trying to combat these other belief systems that claim to know the answers. When your belief system is open to the unknown, what answers do you have for your children? So, in fear of saying "I don't know," do we ignore the questions?

We must remember that Jesus did not give his followers the answers to the day; he gave them a way of being. He offered an experience of life, a door to the kingdom of God. He wasn't talking about

Heaven or Hell; he was talking about the day to day life. Love your neighbours! Love your enemies! God is within!

Therefore, in order to teach our children about the path of Jesus, from a progressive Christian point of view, we need to create curriculum that is focused on a way of being, a curriculum that is relevant and intelligent—one that doesn't contradict the scientific knowledge of our time. A curriculum for today's world needs to be radical—just as the teachings of Jesus were radical for his time.

When we set out to begin writing a children's curriculum that would be utterly unique and pertinent, we faced many challenges. For one, how do you define what progressive Christianity is when half the people in the field don't exactly agree on it! How do you talk about who or what God is when no one could ever give anyone an answer to that question? How do you push the edges of people's awareness without leaving behind those who are not ready to be pushed? How do you create a curriculum for multiple denominations, levels of inclusion, varying stages of progressiveness, and a huge variety of small groups and individuals all over the world?

Well, we started with finding great writers and an incredible artist. Our team has inspired us in their innovation, their wisdom, and their ability to take complex ideas and present them in such a way that is appealing to children as well as the teachers.

We also began the hard work of coming to some agreement on the tenets of progressive Christianity and what our mission for this curriculum would be. We got our Board members together and invited a handful of progressive scholars and thinkers to join us in the discussion. We interviewed leaders in the field. We asked the hard, gritty, sometimes embarrassing, personal questions one needs to ask themselves when they are affirming what their beliefs are, and we talked openly, without judgment, as best we could. We asked each other: What is God to you? Do you believe Jesus was real or a myth? Why do you follow the path of Jesus? What is so special about it to you? What can we let go of? What can we create? We talked about diversity, forgiveness and our experiences as children. We argued and laughed and cried and sang.

Then we put the questions out to our affiliates, our readers, and the amazing writers to see what people really were currently thinking within progressive Christianity.

There began to form a picture in our minds of the kind of curriculum we wanted to create. We wanted to teach our children to listen and respect all people, to think of the world as family, to celebrate and care for the earth, to see God within each other, to be able to concentrate and control their energy. We wanted to offer them a way of life that centred on the teachings of Jesus but also valued the teachings of other wisdom paths. We wanted a curriculum that doesn't force our beliefs on these young minds and hearts, but allows them space and supplies them with encouragement to ask questions and find within themselves the answers. We wanted to be able to give them a new language so they could feel comfortable discussing their beliefs with others.

Little by little the curriculum came together and transformed into an exquisite taste of this path we hope to inform our children about. It is a path of compassion, of wisdom and non-judgment, of prayer and stillness, gratitude and inclusion. Now we have seen the curriculum completed, we can without doubt, proudly present it to the world as the most important thing *ProgressiveChristianity.org* has ever done. We offer it as an example of how we *can* make change in our world.

It is my belief that forgetting the children, or not putting in the work to offer them something valuable, would be the biggest mistake we could make as thinking and compassionate human beings. It is crucial that we guide them into this world and, as they forge their own beliefs and ideas, support them in that exploration. It is also my belief teaching our children to think for themselves and follow a path of compassion is by far the most important responsibility we have as human beings.

Notes

1. From Leo Tolstoy's short story "The Three Hermits" (*Tri Startsy*)

Further Reading

J. Burklo, *Birdlike and Barnless.*

S. Dermond, *Calm and Compassionate Children.*

S. Dermond, et al., *A Joyful Path: Spiritual Curriculum for Young Hearts and Minds.*

M. Dowd, *Thank God for Evolution.*

L. Geering, *Coming Back to Earth.*

M. Morwood, *Children Praying a New Story.*

B. Sanguin, *Darwin, Divinity, and the Dance of the Cosmos.*

———, *The Emerging Church.*

Singing the Theology that Can Shape 'progressive' Christianity

Andrew Pratt

A Place for Hymns?

Hymns were first defined as 'praise of God sung'. If this is all they are in the twenty-first century, their relevance must be questioned. But they have become much more. The medium has evolved.

The starting point for a study of Christian hymns is set amid the Psalms and other Hebrew Bible Poetry, Prophecy and Wisdom writing. In these genres we find not just praise of God, but questioning, exploration and the signs of a dynamic, evolving faith; its expression and development. This faith is, in words used in a different context by Sydney Carter, 'nothing fixed or final'. It is more exploration and discovery than belief and dogma.

It is clear that the writers of the Hebrew Bible were feeling their way. The images of God that they use are sometimes contradictory. Their understanding of the Divine is a work in progress. Yet we declaim and so often judge, we codify and the spirit of God is diminished and emasculated. Somehow the church needs to reclaim the prophetic spirit that permeated the Hebrew Bible, to enable new adventures of faith, new discoveries of the unfathomable grace and freedom of God. In this process the whole concept of 'God' must be open to question. This is notwithstanding the fact that within the Hebrew Bible the process of codifying was already taking place as laws were formulated and ideas concretized.

What is critical to our understanding is that within the Hebrew Bible, where we discern movements of faith and the formulation of ideas about God, we also find poetry and arguably music, and this is not limited solely to the Psalms. Scholarship suggests the whole of the Hebrew Bible was marked for cantillation[1] enabling it to be sung[2].

Put this alongside the scholarship of Walter Brueggemann and an interesting hypothesis begins to develop. Brueggemann wrote of 'prophetic imagination'. It's a useful term. What he pointed to was the capacity of the prophets and the psalmists to push back the boundaries of expectation, even to the point of changing firmly held theological opinion by the use of imagination set free through the medium of poetry. Ezekiel, in writings so brimming over with metaphor and symbolism that they have inspired umpteen books on the subject of extra-terrestrial intelligence, not to mention innumerable biblical commentaries, enabled the people of Israel to move beyond the idea of a God contained and constrained by the Jerusalem temple to an image of a God who was with them in exile and who could breathe life into the dry bones of a spiritually dead society. Beyond that is a vision of resurrection to new circumstance out of an inconceivably tragic situation. What carried this prophecy beyond being simply cold words on a scroll was the fact that the prophecy was, in all probability, pointed, involved cantillation[2]. Hebrew Bible texts were predicated on the principle of them being sung. Put this alongside the concept of prophetic imagination and we are presented with a medium that was potentially, intrinsically dynamic. Indeed, Bruggemann points out that the task of the poet is pastoral and because of this s/he

> wants his community to think afresh, decide afresh, and act freely. He knows that this is a terrifying possibility. We are frightened nearly to death, to run any risks, to stand out in the crowd, to go against conventional opinion.[3]

Past Practice

Historically hymn writers have paraphrased scripture or framed creedal statements in poetry[4]. Some writers have moved from this to interpretation offering a polemic to opposing opinions[5]. What is interesting here is that the way in which the polemic is framed has come about as the writer has tried to make sense of doctrine. It can be a small step from here to developing novel insights that may extend the scope of doctrine or move it in entirely new directions. When this happens, the charge of heresy or at least lack of orthodoxy raises its head.

"Gather Us In, Thou Love That Fillest All", by George Matheson is a case in point. The hymn was regarded by twentieth-century liberals as far-sighted, offering an inclusive, multi-faith view of religion. Christopher Idle, however, makes this comment about it:

> Evangelical books avoid such universalism. Are latter-day liberals reading more into it than Matheson meant? The author consistently defined his doctrinal position as 'broad', distinct from the evangelicalism which nurtured him. [...] Nor would it be top favourite in the nearby mosque or temple.
>
> > 'Gather our rival faiths within thy fold.
> > Rend each man's temple veil . . .
> > In many ships we seek one spirit-land'?
>
> 'O no we don't!' cry the deeply offended Muslim and his Indian or Burmese neighbours. Matheson certainly sees the lordship and love of Christ as the supreme unifying force; but he flies far beyond Ephesians 1:10, the text given as his starting-point.[6]

For the progressive Christian this altogether misses the point. Starting with the text, Matheson has done one of two things, or perhaps a combination of them:

1. He has interpreted the text in the context of universalism.
2. He has tried to gain a greater understanding of the text for himself and in doing so has pushed the bounds of orthodoxy.

It is uncharitable to assume that he simply 'rode light' to the meaning of the passage.

As we have seen, the danger of his approach is that of heresy. But heresies sometimes help us frame what we really believe. Most of the historic creeds have come into being as defence against distortions of truth. But as someone once said, "What is truth?" The moment we think we possess it we are, perhaps, captives of our own arrogance. Creeds can have a positive purpose, but equally they can be a straitjacket. And so as we write and sing we strain that jacket at the seams and sometimes, hopefully, burst out of it completely.

Historically that challenge, that exploration, has so often been found in the words of poets, especially those who have allied their writing to music. It is no accident that in the Hebrew Bible the challenge to ingrained views came from the poets while those of a less creative, perhaps more authoritarian nature, defined laws that would constrain and repress people and limit their understanding of God's grace, let alone God.

In the New Testament we hear of worship in hymns, psalms and spiritual songs, yet the role of the poet at this time was taken over, perhaps, by those who related pragmatic practice to experience and made theology 'on the hoof'. While Paul would reflect to provide an empirical belief structure for the emerging Jewish sect, Peter met people, sought to embody something of the spirit of Jesus and, in consequence, challenged developing beliefs and rigid expectations. Rules were broken, new norms established. The negative side to this was the subsequent codification of these norms rather than the recognition that they, in themselves, were provisional. The canonization of thoughts, poured out in letters in a response to crises, stifled much of the dynamic that had broken free of law. It is ironic that the spirit of one growing out of Israel, literally one who strives with God, whom Cupitt describes as, "the blasphemer, heretic and could be destroyer of the Law, Jesus",[7] should be quenched.

What is interesting is the spirit never entirely evaporated. From time to time through history it has re-emerged and at times has been carried on imaginatively by hymn poets.

Progressive Practice

In the twenty-first century Don Saliers has said of hymnody, that it asks us "to say some things that we don't truly think we believe until we sing them"[8], enabling us to sing with our lips those things which we still have difficulty grasping with our intellect. As we sing we are challenged, convinced, changed as questions are asked and hymn poets open us to new possibilities. To what extent is there evidence of this sort of progressive exploration in the words of twenty-first century hymn poets?

Let me give a few examples of the directions that are being taken. Brian Wren's well known though little used hymn, "Bring Many Names" (1986) challenged gender stereotypes and anthropomorphic language relating to God by reversing the stereotypes, opening people as they sang to a broader possibility in the description of God while still retaining essentially orthodox categories. Graham Adams, a less well known but nevertheless competent author,[9] has often re-written older texts to explore better what they express in a contemporary context, so "O Little Town of Bethlehem" becomes, "O Troubled Town of Bethlehem". Fred Kaan's last collection of hymns was entitled, *The Only Earth We Know* and was moving towards consonance with Don Cupitt's expression of a grounded, 'solar' Christianity which has no need of anything beyond the possibility of corporate human experience.

Antipodean hymnody has provided challenging and thought-provoking texts from Shirley Erena Murray, Bill Wallace and Colin Gibson, while Mary Louise Bringle, writing in the USA, intentionally addresses with great competence areas and issues on the edge of Christian orthodoxy.

Perhaps the greatest stimulus to progressive hymn writing has come with the attempt of those who have sought to answer theological questions posed by twenty-first-century experience. How do we respond to a tsunami? What is the essence of truth when scientific 'truths' are shown to be provisional? How can faith be re-expressed in a postmodern context in which hierarchy ceases to be acknowledged while images of God are predicated on metaphors of rule, kingdom and authority? And what of faith itself when metaphysical notions of 'god' no longer hold sway, while people continue to thirst for things spiritual?

The Way Ahead . . .

It is my contention that what is now needed is a re-discovery of prophetic imagination among hymn poets to explore and push the boundaries of doctrine in order that the needs of people can be met. At best hymn poets will be pushing at the boundaries and often destroying them, testing the limits of our faith. Writers will be challenging norms and opening up new possibilities. Yet the nature of the way in which hymns work makes this challenge all the more threatening to those who would exercise power, for this tool is potentially subversive and transformative. Think of a football crowd singing their team's anthem. Think of the power, struggle, violence, that can take place on and off the pitch. Think of those taken into slavery in the Americas who found themselves bound together by experience, and sometimes by shackles, singing their spirituals, literally singing for their lives. If others really grasped the power of singing, they might be worried, very worried.

Notes

1. For an introduction to cantillation see "Hebrew Cantillation Marks and Their Encoding": http://www.lrz.de/~hr/teamim/intro.html#synt viewed 9/12/2010.
2. S. Haïk-Vantoura, *The Music of the Bible Revealed.*
3. W. Brueggemann, *Hopeful Imagination*, 103.
4. J. H. Newman. See "Firmly I believe, and truly" as a classic in this genre.
5. C. Wesley. See "What shall I do my God to love, /my loving God to praise", which makes an Arminian statement over against Calvinist double-predestinarianism.
6. C. Idle, *Grace Magazine*: "That in the dispensation of the fulness of times he might gather together in one all things in Christ, both which are in heaven, and which are on earth; [even] in him" (Authorised Version).
7. D. Cupitt, *Theology's Strange Return.*
8. D. Saliers, *Music and Theology.*
9. See G. Adams, *Christ and the Other*, for an introduction to his theology.

Further Reading

S. E. Murray, *Touch the Earth Lightly.*
J. Nelson-Pallmeyer and B. Hesla, *Worship in the Spirit of Jesus.*
A. Pratt, *Reclaiming Praise.*
————, *Whatever Name or Creed.*
W. L. Wallace, *The Mystery Telling.*

Hearing the Voices
How 'progressive' Christian Thought Enhances Interfaith Relations

Lorraine Parkinson

Traditional Christian theology is greatly challenged by its encounter with other faiths. I will spell out implications of Christian beliefs which can place roadblocks in the way of productive and positive relations with other faiths, in particular with Judaism and Islam. I will also propose that the theological emphases of progressive Christian thought offer a way to harmonious interfaith relationships.

Christian-Jewish Relations

In the first two centuries CE, Christian anti-Semitism encouraged hatred of Jews and Judaism. St Gregory of Nyssa called the Jews "slayers of the Lord, murderers of the prophets, adversaries of God, advocates of the devil, brood of vipers, assembly of demons, wicked men, haters of righteousness". St John Chrysostom said he was concerned about Christians celebrating Jewish festivals. His 'concern' is best described as hatred of the Jews: "It is unfit for Christians to associate with a people who have fallen into a condition lower than the vilest animals." In the sixteenth century Martin Luther said of the Jews of Germany: "What shall we do with this rejected, condemned Jewish people? We cannot quench the fire of God's wrath, nor convert them. With prayer and in the fear of God we must exercise a sharp compassion in the hope of saving a few of them. I shall give you my sincere advice." He then listed seven measures against the Jews, including burning their homes, synagogues and sacred books, and forbidding the teaching of Judaism to their children. Tragically, Luther's instructions were revived by the Nazis as justification for their systematic murder of the Jews.

For twenty years after World War II, Christian theologians were too stunned by the Holocaust to say anything substantial about it. When the first official Christian-Jewish dialogues took place in the 1960s, there looked to be insurmountable obstacles to it because of Christian doctrine and ways it had been implemented. A monumental task of theological rethinking, healing and reconciliation was needed.

Christian-Muslim Relations

Historical Christian attitudes to Islam also include the demonization of Muslims. Crusaders called Muslims 'pagans', meaning 'godless', and Christian scholars added to their virulent anti-Semitism an equally virulent Islamophobia. But Karen Armstrong (*Dawn*, June 2002) reminds us that the Qur'an does not rule out the revelations of Judaism or of Christianity. The cause of most difficulty in Christian-Muslim relations is the Muslim doctrine of monotheism, alongside Islamic understandings of the Doctrine of the Trinity. The twentieth-century Christian theologian Karl Rahner argued that Judaism, Christianity and Islam all professed monotheism, but Judaism and Islam had "failed to achieve (that monotheism) which finds expression precisely in the doctrine of the Trinity". For Rahner the crucial difficulty was Christian understanding of the concept 'person'. He dismissed completely the idea of God communicating through human agency. "The mediation itself must be God," he said, "and cannot amount to a creaturely mediation." This cannot be reconciled with Muslim belief in Mohammed as the human mediator of the word of God (or Allah).

Real progress in relations between Christianity and Islam was made by the Christian theologian Hans Küng. Küng's assessment of Mohammed likens him to the prophets of Israel; a visionary, who had a personal relationship with God, but who insisted upon unconditional obedience, devotion and submission to this one God. One problematic area between Muslims and progressive Christians is the progressive view of scripture as a 'human product' (to quote Marcus Borg). Muslim scholars argue that this implies human authorship of the Qur'an, which they emphatically deny.

The Doctrine of Original Sin

Although not official doctrine, the Doctrine of Original Sin continues to be taught in the Roman Catholic catechism. It is denied by the Eastern Orthodox Churches and is not official doctrine, for instance, of the Uniting Church in Australia. Yet it remains the foundation stone for the whole edifice of Christian doctrine. It refers to the biblical story where Adam and Eve succumbed to the serpent's temptation and 'fell' into sin. Progressive Jews see no source of human sin other than the evil actions of individual human beings. For them Eve disobeyed God's order, but Adam did nothing to stop her, nor did he refuse to follow her lead. Adam and Eve had to learn by their mistakes to become responsible human beings. Progressive Christian thought echoes this view that the fruit is symbolic, representing the development of humans as moral agents. For traditional Christians the doctrine of original sin underlines their conviction that people of other faiths must be converted to escape God's condemnation.

Islam teaches that all humans are innocent at birth and become sinful only when they consciously commit a sin. It regards atonement theories of the Cross as the invention of those who declared themselves Christians. Islam believes that one person's sin cannot be transferred to another; nor can a person's reward be transferred to someone else. The Qur'an, in Surah 17, verse 25, says: "Who receiveth guidance, receiveth it for his own benefit: who goeth astray doth so to his own loss. No bearer of burdens can bear the burden of another: nor would We punish until We had sent a message [to give warning]." The Qur'an has Adam and Eve repenting and turning to God for forgiveness: "Then Adam received some words from his Lord, so He turned to him mercifully; surely He is Oft-returning (to mercy), the Merciful" (2:37). Muslims also refute the idea that sin is passed on to the sinner's offspring. This is in accord with progressive Christian thought.

The Doctrine of Atonement

Of five classical theories of atonement, the 'satisfaction' and 'substitutionary' ideas are most popular with traditional Christians. It is hardly surprising that a 'moral' theory of atonement, where Jesus risks his life to show human beings how to become 'fully human', is most helpful for progressive theologians. The topic of salvation was not discussed by the World Council of Churches during the first decades of Christian-Jewish dialogue. This was due to traditional Christian belief in the central role of Christ in atonement, and also meant avoidance of the subject of Christian evangelism. In the first WCC symposium on salvation (1986), Rabbi David Rosen saw personal salvation as being "allocated a portion in the world to come" through repentance and reconciliation with God. He said divine attributes of God such as mercy and compassion make it possible for 'at-one-ment' with God to be effected through sincere contrition.

The traditional Catholic position is: "No salvation outside the church." Yet alongside their own faith commitment, liberal Catholic scholars embraced the Jewish concept of salvation set out by Rabbi Rosen. This pluralistic stance is also the progressive Christian approach, which opens doors to positive and hopeful dialogue. Vatican II also refers to salvation for Muslims:

The plan of salvation also includes those who acknowledge the Creator, in the first place among whom are the Muslims: they profess to hold the faith of Abraham, and together with us they adore the one, merciful God, the judge of humanity on the last day.

Muslims believe that salvation comes in the afterlife from God's recognition and acceptance of individuals, dependent on their virtue, obedience and/or good deeds.

Progressive Christians see the cross as the cause of Jesus' death, not as the entire purpose of his life. They explain the cross as Jesus' willingness to risk his life for the sake of his fellow human beings. This was not to save them from their sin, but to remain true to the way of life he bequeathed them through his teachings. Jesus knew that reconciliation with God comes not through the blood sacrifice of a human being, but through individual repentance and forgiveness. The progressive Christian conviction that salvation does not rely on belief that 'Jesus died for my sins' has a profoundly positive effect on interfaith relations.

The Doctrine of the Incarnation

In the early Christian era it was decided that Christ was both truly God and truly human. Because he was now recognised as God incarnate, the church began to worship him. Prayer was directed to Jesus and forgiveness of sins was believed to be effectual only through his name. Belief in the divinity of Christ can be a huge stumbling block in interfaith relations. For Judaism and Islam this belief is not only triumphalist but a contradiction of Christianity's claim to be a monotheistic faith.

The Doctrine of the Trinity

Recognition of the Doctrine of the Trinity as man-made tradition releases Christian dialogue partners from triumphalism. Progressive Christians do not believe in a Triune God revealed through the Holy Spirit as Father, Son, and Holy Spirit; through the Son as Father, Son and Holy Spirit, and through the Father as Father, Son and Holy Spirit—a circular argument if ever there was one! Yet historically, that piece of theological-speak has undergirded Christian persecution of other faiths. The idea of God as 'three persons' prompts Jewish and Muslim charges that Christianity is not a monotheistic faith.

The 'Second Coming' of Christ

Progressive biblical criticism recognises the 'second coming' as contextual belief. The American Jewish organization 'Jews for Judaism' says:

Time makes the Christian doctrine of the 'second coming of Christ' lose all credibility. If Jesus promised to come back shortly and the disciples expected so strongly to see Jesus return and establish the kingdom of God and neither event occurred, for what can the church still hope? In essence, Christian theological speculations on the 'second coming of Christ' represent nothing more than the systematization of a mistake.

Progressive Christians have no problem with that, although most Muslims believe Jesus will return to earth before the Day of Judgment to defeat the *Dajjal* (Antichrist). The hadith, a record of the sayings and deeds of the Prophet Mohammed, says: "The Hour will not be established until the son of Mary descends amongst you as a just ruler."

The Future of
Interfaith Relations

Progressive Christians rely on humility in interfaith relations. They understand that no faith is the single source of knowledge of God and of ultimate human values. Each faith has its own knowledge of compassion, justice, freedom and peace. On that shared ethical foundation different faiths can meet positively and productively, with respect and cooperation. It is no coincidence that progressive Christian thought has emerged at a time when Christians are able to hear and learn about other faiths.

Further Reading

K. Armstrong, *The Battle for God.*
J. Chittister, et al., *The Tent of Abraham.*

What They Told Us in Seminary
but We Never Got to Preach About!

Nigel Leaves

I have to admit that the two years I spent at seminary (1984–86) preparing for ordination into the Anglican (Episcopalian) Church, were among the best of my life.

Not only was the seminary located in one of the prettiest cities in England, but also it offered a theologically liberal teaching staff that presented with total honesty the latest trends and fashions in biblical, feminist, liberation, and pastoral theology. We were, to use a modern idiom, 'at the cutting-edge', primed to drag the Church kicking and screaming into the latter part of the twentieth century. With a sprinkling of full-time female students, we were one of the first 'mixed-gender' seminary classes. We accepted their God-given right to be ordained priests and even bishops almost fifteen years before most of the Church decided to grant them full clerical status. We were equally proud to number among our ranks openly gay ordinands (no hiding in the closet here!), and we were armed with cogent theological, biblical and ecclesiastical arguments that together with their 'life partners' they were to be welcomed as future priests of the church. Furthermore, we were encouraged each week to create imaginative liturgies that would broaden the scope of a church based on the prayer-book. Our finest achievement was a 'Computer Eucharist' that anticipated what in today's internet age would be categorized as: 'virtual church'. It was heady stuff; and I loved it!

The Church we both envisioned and were encouraged to embrace was 'open, inclusive and life giving'. Indeed, our motto might have been the words attributed to Jesus in the Fourth Gospel: "I have come that you might have life and have it abundantly" (John 10:10). It was a bold, radical, transformative vision that would be echoed a few years later by John Shelby Spong in his mantra: "Live fully, love wastefully, be all that you can be; and dedicate yourself to building a world in which everyone has an opportunity to do the same."[1] This, we agreed, is what it meant to believe in God, to be a disciple of Jesus; and what the Church of the future was called to be. This is what we were taught in seminary. The future looked bright!

How wrong we were, how disappointed we were to become, and how unprepared we were for the day-to-day reality of the ordained priesthood!

The Church proved to be light-years away from the giddy heights of the seminary experience. Enthused with the hope of being able to change and transform humanity, I soon learnt I had to struggle within and against an ecclesiastical culture that was determined to preserve the *status quo*.

"Keep your nose clean; don't rock the boat for the next three years, learn from the way *I* do things" was the admonition of my 'training Rector' ('training' understood as discouraging independent thought). It was like being sent back to kindergarten to be the 'obedient child', following dutifully in the steps of 'the master' and listening respectfully to the wisdom of 'one schooled in priestly ways'. One was to learn the prescribed set of 'manual acts' for the Eucharist, the appropriate clerical/liturgical attire, and a long list of regulations governing one's

conduct in parochial affairs—even on one's 'day off'. In this last particular my Rector was eccentric to the point of wackiness. The young
lady I was dating at the time (also an Anglican minister) lived a couple
of hours drive away, and my Rector was scandalized that I should presume to meet her except in the social context defined by himself and
the congregation. Despite his best efforts to derail the relationship, it
survived and that lady and I have been happily married for more years
than we care to remember.

The idiosyncrasies and churchly conservatism of this worthy mentor were unfortunately reflected in a considerable portion of the congregation. It was difficult enough to persuade some of them to drop
the seventeenth-century language of the 1662 *Book of Common Prayer*
for a modernized version, let alone consider elements of the theological radicalism I had been imbued with at seminary. How could one
even begin to discuss such ideas as inclusive language, sexual identity,
liberation from unjust structures or patriarchy, and realm of God values when people stoutly refused to address God as 'You' instead of
'Thou'? We were singing from different hymnals, and as a mere curate
I was supposed to acquiesce to their wishes.

To be sure, a few forward-looking parishioners were ready
to embrace new ideas, but they were in the minority and the cards
were stacked against them. I had some wonderful private conversations with people who dared, as the prophet Joel puts it, "to dream
dreams"—and who wanted the church to become the open, inclusive
community that Jesus preached. But once they learned about my radical ideas, they expected me to preach what I believed, and were often
disappointed by the Sunday morning sermon. I was torn between ap-
peasing my Rector (and thus keeping my job) and justifying their view
of me as a champion of the new Christianity. I did succeed to some
extent, for I was able to get a well-to-do congregation to experience life
in a lower socio-economic parish as part of a social justice project, and
I managed to pass on some new theological insights in various parish
education programs[2]. But for the most part I was trained to celebrate
the Eucharist and officiate at the Church's rites of passage—baptisms,
marriages, and funerals. The existing church would continue *semper
eadem*, in the same way forever. What was needed was *faithful* (even if
not particularly competent), *obedient* (certainly not questioning), *exem-
plary* (not necessarily life-affirming) priests who would hand on to suc-
ceeding generations 'the faith as it had been revealed to the apostles'.

The obvious disconnect between the vision of the seminary and
the reality of life in the parish caused many of my fellow seminarians
to leave the ministry. A former Anglican priest offers this attestation to
the high dropout rate of clergy:

When I left after thirteen years, I was behind the game. Only a quarter of my college leavers' year completed those thirteen years in parish ministry. Another quarter left and then went back, with varying degrees of reluctance and varying plans for the future. The rest have left with no intention of going back.[3]

It is both a sad commentary and a sharp indictment that so many potentially visionary leaders of the church were in effect driven away by an organization that refused to embrace anything new and innovative—especially after investing so much in their theological education. Worse than a waste, it is a tragedy.

The tragic irony is that the seminary I trained at was so far ahead of the church I was being prepared for. And in many ways that same situation remains today. The theology taught to the next generation of priests and deacons is serviced through secular universities whose programs embrace the latest biblical, hermeneutical and methodological approaches. Ideas about 'God', 'Jesus', 'the Church', etc., are not necessarily filtered through a denominational lens, but are presented in a sweeping overview of what has been written in the past and what is being written and spoken today. Seminarians rub shoulders with secular humanists as they both seek to discover 'the historical Jesus'. As one who now sits on the other side of the lectern, I often discover that the seminarian is far more theologically and ecclesiastically radical than the 'seeker after Truth' sitting next to her. And yet, the Church they are being sent to is not necessarily prepared to receive their theology. It daily proves to be an intellectually stimulating process.

In short, some of the disconnect I experienced as a young curate all those years ago still remains. How does the Church envision its own programs of theological education? Does it really want its future ministers to embrace the habits of critical thinking inculcated in its educational modules? Consider, for example, the feminist criticism that arose some three decades ago—the complaint that 'the church is irredeemably patriarchal'. To what degree has the Church been responsive to that challenge? Why has it done so little to revise its sexist liturgical language? Could it not have more forcefully addressed the systemic issues of status, class, race, sexuality and gender that many find at best anachronistic and at worst offensive? In short, is the Church serious about *thealogy*[4]? And if not, then why does it let its seminarians be exposed to such ideas? Does it expect them to obediently forget what they learned at seminary and enter into the glories of ministry with a pre-school theology that will not offend the faithful in the pews?

Concerning the clergy it is often said that to learn when they attended seminary, one need only examine their bookshelves and see when most of their theological books were written, for they don't tend

to buy new ones when they get into a parish. Likewise, many newly ordained ministers sell back to the seminary the recommended theological books, because they sense that they won't need them again. More
often than not they restock their shelves with conservative texts that
will be acceptable to parish nominators (search committees) who just
might happen to glance in at their study. In short, how practical, how
relevant, is the current process of theological education?

It is my contention that what is *taught* in the seminary should be
applied in the Church. If the seminary experience is to prove useful,
it cannot be simply a training regimen to be endured or a warm-up
round with little relation to the main event. Rather, it is a vital resource
for enabling the Church to become theologically liberated and renewed. The seminary and the Church need to become partners in the
revitalisation of an institution in decline. Parishioners should not look
forward to moulding the new curate in their own image, but to being
challenged and invigorated by a visionary proclamation of good news
that transforms their situation and the world at large.

I have argued elsewhere that only 'good theology' will save religion[5]. That same 'good theology' might go some way toward saving
the Church. Indeed, the fundamental role of seminaries is to produce
and pass on 'good theology'. To neglect that vital function is to settle
for rearranging the deck chairs on a doomed steamship, to accept becoming increasingly irrelevant in a world that finds us both archaic
and, worse yet, 'dishonest'.

Notes

1. J. S. Spong, *Eternal Life*, 212.
2. N. Leaves, "A Journey in Life", 25–40.
3. M. Hampson, *Last Rites*, 13.
4. Some feminist theologians prefer *thealogy* to *theology*, thus incorporating the feminine into the divine.
5. N. Leaves, *Religion Under Attack*.

Additional Notes

- I thank the Revd Harvey Ray from the USA for the insight into what happens in many Episcopalian seminaries where the 'seminary theology' is to
be 'got through' and not acted upon because the local church isn't ready
for such ideas.
- For an excellent analysis of the way the church has been afraid to disseminate new understandings of God, Jesus, etc., see J. Good, *The Dishonest
Church*. I thank Robert Semes for alerting me to this vital book.

Further Reading

N. Leaves, *The God Problem*.
———, *Religion Under Attack*.

Florence Nightingale
'progressive' Theologian

Val Webb

At the age of seventy, Florence Nightingale wrote, "When many years ago, I planned a future, my one idea was not organizing a hospital but organizing a religion." While Florence came down in history as the 'Lady with the Lamp', the heroine of the Crimean War (1854–6), this designation disguises the woman who, on her return, began half a century of poor reform, including writing a new religion for the poor. We need to take the lamp from her hand and properly illuminate this brilliant woman who changed Victorian England.

Florence was born in 1820 into an upper class Unitarian family but raised Church of England. Her Cambridge-educated father taught her 'like a son'—five languages, history, science and philosophy. As a child, Florence was religiously absorbed and unhappy with her rich, idle life compared with the poor villagers on her family's estates. She was frustrated by the band-aid help of soup and advice given by the upper class without any systemic reform, supported by Church of England theology that claimed God ordained people rich or poor, thus the class system was not open to change.

At seventeen, Florence received her first call from God to serve the poor, but her family thwarted her repeated attempts to respond. At thirty, Florence went with friends to Egypt and, unbeknown to family, visited a German Protestant Deaconess training centre. Here she discovered a religious order without vows where women could train to serve the poor. When she wanted to volunteer in a hospital on her return, the family again sabotaged her plans, and Florence wrote an autobiographical fiction about a woman who welcomes death rather than her fate in the family. At thirty-three, Florence finally extracted herself to become the volunteer administrator of a home for destitute governesses, attracting the attention of Secretary at War Lord Sidney Herbert, who sent her to the Crimea. Her experiences there among poor soldiers who fought and died for a ruling class that oppressed them made her even more determined about her vocation.

After returning from the Crimea, Florence retired into monastic seclusion and invalidism, yet her productivity was not diminished. She analysed her extensive Crimean notes on diseases and deaths, designed the first hospital record forms and persuaded Queen Victoria and key parliamentarians to initiate a Royal Commission into Army

Health, whose working party met in Florence's home. This led to a Royal Commission into Army Health in India and recommendations from Florence for health and welfare reform in Indian villages. Her reputation spread. As well as poor reform at home, she was consulted on care of the wounded in America's Civil War and by *both* sides in the Franco-Prussian War. She drafted the British delegation's proposal to the Geneva Convention and made recommendations about colonial indigenous health.

The Nightingale School of Nursing opened at St Thomas' Hospital in 1860 from funds raised in Florence's honour. The Fund directors had pestered Florence, while still in the Crimea, to start this nursing school on her return, but her now-clear call was to reform the Army's medical services. Florence submitted designs for the nursing school but was not involved until over a decade later and then from a distance. Her *Notes on Nursing* (1858) was written not for hospital nurses but for women caring for sick family at home. The image of Florence the nurse is based on twenty months in the Crimea and a nursing school in which she did not work. Since Florence was rarely seen in public, this image persisted rather than a woman determined to change the world.

Why did Florence become an invalid recluse? Some argue chronic Crimean fever, others psychological reasons and others an escape from family. I argue it was in line with her religious call. Before going to Egypt, she spent time in a Paris convent learning the spiritual disciplines she followed all her life. She contemplated joining a religious order, or forming her own, but instead formed an order of one—herself. Her seclusion, reform work and disciplined life where people, including family, visited by appointment, was a monastic life. When she celebrated her jubilee, Florence dated her fifty years from her first call.

Florence was a prodigious writer. Her letters and manuscripts in the British Library comprise one of their largest collections, and sixteen volumes of her works are being published. Florence translated the medieval mystics in preparation for a book and edited the final translations of Plato from Greek to English by Benjamin Jowett, Master of Oxford's Balliol College. In 1860, she completed an eight-hundred-page manuscript offering a new religion for the poor, including a fifty-page rage on how Victorian families 'murder' their daughters. Florence knew that challenging the class system required challenging the theology that God *ordained* people rich or poor. She wrote her 'new religion' amidst other theological challenges—biblical criticism, the Oxford Movement, Darwin (*The Origin of Species* had just been published)—all demanding new explanations. Some of the working class had become agnostic, but Florence wanted a religion that gave them *hope* without throwing God out altogether. Florence's topics included the concept of God, universal law, Divine will, sin and evil and family life and her conclusions paralleled the Anglican Broad Church publication *Essays and Reviews* (1860) which led to its authors' heresy trials. Florence sent her draft to six prominent thinkers, including John Stuart Mill, who urged publication and quoted her in a ground-breaking parliamentary speech on women's rights. Benjamin Jowett called it "the imprint of a new mind". It was not published, however, because it needed editing and Florence was overextended with reform work.

Florence's new religion reflected much of today's progressive thought. Calling herself a mystic, she believed everyone could experience the Divine within themselves without need for clergy, religious rites or institutions. She identified with the mystical language of abiding in God and God in us in John's Gospel and understood Jesus as sharing God's *task*, "to do the will of him that sent me and to finish his work" (John 4:34), rather than Jesus *as* God. She disagreed with mystics who withdrew from or renounced the world—"There will be no heaven unless we make it"—and was wary of ecstatic states and self-contempt that focused on self, not others.

Rather than accept a bundle of infallible doctrines formulated from ancient texts, Florence stood with the poor and asked the contextual question, "What is good news in this situation?" From there, she went to scripture to find answers. There are a few biblical passages about poverty stemming from laziness or ineptitude, but most name poverty as the product of social inequities and injustice for a class held in poverty by oppressors, against which Hebrew prophets railed (Isa 3:13–15). Florence found the plight of the poor *central* to the biblical message and God demanding their empowerment. Challenging prevailing theology, Florence taught that the Spirit was in everyone, rich and poor, and everyone is called to discover God's universal laws and work towards improving society—bringing in God's reign.

How can we know God's laws (thoughts), and who is God anyway? All we can say, Florence said, is that we recognize a power superior to our own, exercised by a wise and good will that organizes the universe through scientific laws discoverable through statistical study. Florence called statistics a 'sacred science' because statistical analysis transcended narrow individual experience to reveal God's thoughts (laws). Florence rejected a God who intervened in human affairs at will with supernatural acts, seeing natural laws as more reliable than revelations delivered through culturally bound language and people. For Florence, God-images evolved. Early humans sought a powerful God to protect them, offering sacrifices, worship and prayers. An arbitrary and powerful God needing appeasement was no longer necessary and some virtues attributed to an all-powerful God, like defeating one's enemies and miraculous feats of deliverance, were no longer seen as virtuous. When King William IV declared cholera a judgment on a sinful nation and asked for prayers, Florence said, "It is a religious act to clean out a gutter and to prevent cholera; . . . it is not a religious act to pray (in the sense of simply asking to take cholera away)."

For Florence, Goodness was an appropriate God-image and she advocated a moratorium on God language in order to reshape divine metaphors. She saw God embodied (incarnated) *as* the universe; thus, humans share this divinity. Our life purpose is to organize the world so *everyone* can be open to this divine indwelling. If God's spirit is incarnate in everyone however, incarnational, Trinitarian and atonement theologies must be rethought because they localize Divine activity to *one* incarnation and a single day's suffering, ignoring God's suffering, work and passion across eternity. She proposed a 'Trinity' of God as universal thought, purpose and will; the Son as *all* humanity indwelt by God, with Jesus the most perfect model, and the Holy Spirit the divine in us communicating God's will. As for Anselm's atonement theory of God requiring a sacrifice to appease Divine offence over human sin, Florence called it barbaric, originating in an era that demanded punishment for wrong-doing rather than reform. Dismissing original sin, Florence saw no evidence humans were created righteous or unrighteous, but born with a divine nature, albeit immature, to evolve to perfection through learning God's laws. Mistakes are made out of ignorance, and evil and suffering happen but, by discovering God's laws, we move from ignorance to perfection with the help of the Spirit—and also human 'saviours' sent, like her, to help in difficult times. Her new religion, therefore, encouraged the poor to change their situation rather than accept the status quo.

Florence was a pioneer feminist theologian. In Victorian times, women were valued only as wives and mothers. Single women cared for sick relatives and children at home, worked as governesses for the rich, or worked in factories or prostitution, depending on their means. Florence decried women's lack of identity, waste of talents and mind, and their trivial, boring lives, longing for a female saviour to bring in much needed reforms. Since women were financially dependent on father or husband, she advocated paid work for women of all classes. In her day, a husband, even if separated, could claim his wife's inheritance; married women could not own property, make a will or bring a lawsuit; a man could divorce his spouse for adultery but not a woman and, if a wife left a drunken, abusive husband, she could not take her children. Women's education was also thought a waste, except for 'accomplishments' for marriage, so Florence initiated ways to empower women by training orphan girls for work in Poor Houses, health missioners to educate cottage women and education and reform for prostitutes. She was not actively involved in the woman's vote because she thought these few votes for upper-class women would take parliamentary time away from these more pressing needs. When bachelor academic Benjamin Jowett first read Florence's writing about women, he assumed her experience unique and thought her 'tirades' weakened her other arguments. He did not recognize the ground-breaking moves she was making, first to validate women's experience and then to challenge religious rules based on cultural assumptions held in place with selected Bible verses.

Further Reading
B. M. Dossey, *Florence Nightingale.*
V. Webb, *Florence Nightingale.*

The Art of Public Theology
A Case Study
Clay Nelson

Christmas 2009 a billboard put up in front of the church brought St Matthew-in-the-City in Auckland, New Zealand to the world's attention. In a matter of hours it had over seventy thousand hits on Google. Within days it was printed in every major daily newspaper in the world and many small local dailies as well. A museum in Switzerland asked to include it in its collection of contemporary art. It was debated in blogs, on talk radio around the world and even on the BBC. It was protested, praised, and painted over, and eventually stolen twice. Over a year later it lives on. Its image is found all over the Web. Local and international media to this day wonder what newsworthy billboard will follow it.

What was the cause of such a ruckus? It tastefully portrayed a man and woman lying in bed awake. The man looked dejected. The woman looked wistfully heavenward. The caption read, "Poor Joseph. God is a hard act to follow."

Its impact in both the religious and secular worlds was impossible to predict. But in the aftermath, there has been considerable reflection on why it happened and can it, as a graphic example of doing successful public theology, be replicated?

My conclusion is there was a certain amount of luck involved, not unlike hitting the Lotto, but it wasn't a random lighting strike; the congregation had put up a lightning rod. Even with the lottery one has to buy a ticket.

Before exploring ways to put up a lightning rod, it would be helpful to work with a common understanding of what 'public theology' is in the progressive context.

It was not a common term thirty years ago during my own theological training. Church historian Martin E. Marty is credited with coining the term in 1981, but just because it took that long to name it isn't to say it didn't exist. Public theology is the product of a burgeoning and increasingly diverse secular society usurping the authority of the church in western culture. Without the immergence of public theology, Christian perspectives could have been shut out entirely of the raucous marketplace of ideas that influences our post-modern society. In that marketplace the church is just one of a multitude of often conflicting voices. In the midst of the cacophony, it is hard enough to be heard never mind being taken seriously.

For the sake of this conversation, I would define public theology as engagement with the culture with the expressed hope of facilitating transformation. My definition has one particular limitation. It leaves open the question of what kind of transformation is being sought. The answer depends on the Christian being asked.

Evangelicals are committed to recreating Christendom as measured by biblical scripture as they or tradition interprets it. Their primary concern is convincing the public sphere to hold 'right beliefs'. Their worldview is individualistic and focused on personal responsibility. They seek power to impose it.

Progressives prefer a society where church and state are separate, but are committed to making the ethical teachings of Jesus of Nazareth, as they interpret them, universal in both. Their concern is moving the public sphere to 'right action'. Their worldview is communitarian and focused on social responsibility. They seek to convince the collective whole to embrace it and live it out.

Efforts at public theology by these two groups have been quite different and frankly the evangelical branch of Christianity has been more successful to the detriment of progressives. In this reality the first thing progressives must do in order to engage society is to differentiate themselves from evangelical and, yes, orthodox Christianity.

It may seem counter-intuitive, but in order to have a credible voice with those outside the faith we must be willing to challenge traditional understandings of faith. The progressive challenge is to put forward a vision of Christianity that makes sense to those outside of the faith. On one level that should be easy. A progressive view of Christianity does not require magical thinking or blind adherence to dogma and doctrine or a rejection of science. Problematically, progressives are usually enfolded within a conservative institution. Holding an opposing view to the traditional one is neither comfortable nor easy and, for the clergy, can be hazardous to one's career.

What follows is a case study of how one parish has stepped up onto the soapbox. While the historical accidents that enable this congregation to do progressive public theology may be unique, the hope is it will inspire other acts of progressive public theology in the wider church. The only caveat is: it is an art, not a science.

A Public Theology Case Study

St Matthew-in-the-City was one of the earliest churches formed in Auckland, but as luck would have it, it was formed on 'the wrong side of the tracks'. Most, but not all of the sources of local power were situated on the other side of town. By 1930 all were. From its inception it was a place that served, out of necessity, the powerless. Its location shaped its mission.

What wasn't luck is that for fifty years its middle and lower class members raised money to build a stone church. When finished it became the envy of both sides of the tracks. Its neo-Gothic architecture became a prominent landmark in the city centre and still is.

What was luck was the development around the church that followed. It included major tourist attractions, financial institutions and all the major New Zealand media outlets. The street the church sits on became the busiest surface street in the country. Perhaps most importantly, our nearest neighbour is the Auckland City Mission, one of the largest and most prominent social service agencies in the city reminding us daily of our mission to the disenfranchised.

What wasn't luck was St Matthew's commitment to social justice. It began as a school to educate the children of the neighbourhood, walked for Maori land rights, helped organise New Zealand resistance to apartheid, actively participated in efforts to make New Zealand a nuclear-free zone, helped found the first GLBTQ congregation in New Zealand when homosexuality was still illegal, fought for the ordination of women and is still working for the ordination of gay and lesbian candidates, conducts civil unions for gay and lesbian couples, has promoted anti-smacking laws and is in partnership with the City Mission to build a state-of-the-art social services centre on their land and ours.

Such a history should have made it easy to do progressive public theology, but that was not the case. The downside of being fiercely inclusive is holding diverse elements within the congregation's embrace. Building community out of such a theological, liturgical, and socioeconomic mix was made all the more difficult by the fact most of the congregation did not live within the parish boundaries, but came from a wide geographical area.

It was into this parish mix Glynn Cardy was called as Vicar in 2004. As he began to build his team, I was immigrating to New Zealand. My first Sunday in New Zealand I attended St Matthew's because of an act of public theology. A large banner that flew from the bell tower drew me in: "Make Poverty History".

In the pew sheet was a notice that they were looking for someone who had communication and marketing skills, as well as proficiency in website development. Having acquired qualifications in web development, I applied. At the interview I shared my vision of creating a virtual progressive church online. Two weeks later I was employed to start building it. A month later Glynn broached the subject of my also serving as a priest in the parish.

Glynn and I are in many ways quite different from each other, but, as luck would have it, we discovered we have the kind of rare synergy forged in close friendship, common purpose and a willingness to break the rules. Through our writing and preaching we began climbing further and further out on our progressive theological limb. Putting it on the web for all to read committed us further to continuing our progressive journey. Eventually the congregation began to notice that what we were preaching was often being refuted by language in our Prayer Book and the hymns. But putting aside the Prayer Book in the Anglican tradition is not something done lightly.

The opportunity to begin making the liturgy congruent with our theology came in 2006 in planning a U2charist—a Eucharist using U2 music instead of hymns to support the UN Millennium Goals. At the time U2charists were sweeping across the US, but they were just putting Bono's music into traditional liturgies. I asked Glynn, the poet on the team, to write a liturgy that reflected progressive theology for our U2charist. That was the beginning of our liturgical renewal. We now have several liturgies we use during different seasons of the church year.

In retrospect, how we approached liturgical renewal and the content of the liturgies themselves accomplished what none of Glynn's predecessors had been able to achieve—they formed St Matthew's into a more theologically cogent community. A few, of course, are not happy about not using the Prayer Book, but to their credit they accept that the new liturgies represent the community. A few have left, but many more have come. In the last four years worship numbers have grown by a third. Even better, the congregation is considerably younger and more diverse than before. They are proud to be part of a church on the edge. This was never more evident than when the furore hit over the billboard. A few were uncomfortable with it, but only one member of the congregation left because of it. The vast majority was totally supportive and happy to defend St Matthew's billboard to their families, friends, co-workers and neighbours.

Liturgical renewal not only helped us to form a community, its theology also under-girded the development of the Christmas billboard and the decision to go forward with it. In other words, doing progressive public theology requires a progressive community.

What Other Lessons Have We Drawn from This Experience?

There are five. The most important lesson is the realization that being an inclusive church has its limits. Yes, all are welcome, baptized or not, Christian or not, to receive communion. But we should not be concerned if some choose not to be included. Progressive Christianity should not be concerned that some are offended by our message. Our view is that Jesus wasn't.

The second lesson is related—unity is highly over-rated. Many of our colleagues in the diocese were not pleased with us because they believe the church should speak with one voice. This idea is laughable. The church has never spoken with one voice. The challenge is educating the rest of society to that fact.

The third lesson is that in a secular society that rarely looks at the church, one cannot be too bold in doing public theology. We make headlines sometimes by making fun of ourselves or challenging sacred cows, standing up for the GLBTQ community or working for peace.

We also make headlines by sending out media releases on topical issues. We send letters and opinion pieces considered controversial for publication in the *NZ Herald*. As the media feeds on controversy, they are published more often than not.

The fourth lesson concerns issues around freedom of speech. Our experience is the biggest threat to our freedom of speech is our selves. Self-censure is a much bigger threat to getting our message out than anything our detractors or the institution can do to silence us. Fear is at the heart of silence or failure to act.

The fifth lesson learned is that in today's information age, the best place to engage society is online. We now work to direct controversy created by billboards and articles to our website or Facebook page. We send press releases out to pertinent websites and blogs as well as the mainstream media.

Conclusion

Whether or not St Matthew's will have another billboard that is as successful is open to question, but the necessary groundwork has been laid. In the meantime, there is no question we have succeeded in differentiating St Matthew's from other churches. As a result more people outside of the church are interested in what we might have to say. We may still only have a soapbox to stand on, but we now have a bigger megaphone for doing progressive public theology.

Further Reading

M. Benedikt, *God is the Good We Do.*
H. Cox, *When Jesus Came to Harvard.*
L. Geering, *Such is Life!*
The Jesus Seminar, *The Future of the Christian Tradition.*

The Healing Narratives
The Importance of a 'progressive'
Theological Approach
John W. H. Smith

Our interpretation of the healing narratives as recorded in the gospels has had a profound, and in many cases, negative impact on the way the church has responded to people with illness and disability. In the last two decades there have been two important influences in reshaping our understanding of the healing narratives. The first has been the influence of people, either with disabilities or those associated with them. The second has come from a scholarly focus on the New Testament by scholars from the 'historical Jesus' school and, in particular, from the Jesus Seminar and Westar Institute.

The healing narratives are an important part of the 'ministry' of the historical Jesus of Nazareth, and they form a significant collection within the canonical gospels. There are twenty recorded healing narratives, twenty-three if you include the three stories of the 'raising of the dead'. Ten of these twenty-three stories are told three times, four are repeated twice and nine are told once. They cover a wide range of illness and disability and can be classified into physical disabilities, sensory disabilities, chronic illness, mental illness and fever. It is important to recognize these stories are but a small sample of the rich healing ministry of Jesus. For as we read in Mark 1:32–33, "That evening at sunset, they brought to him all who were sick or possessed with demons. And the whole city was gathered at the door." It is interesting to note also there has been little scholarship and research around this particular area considering the significance of the size of this activity.

The traditional interpretation of the healing narratives has been to emphasize the importance of the divinity of Jesus. Many of these narratives have been interpreted as miraculous healings. This is seen more to be the case if we include the three instances of the 'raising of people from the dead', as examples of Jesus healing ministry. The conclusion is that Jesus is seen to be more than human. A second traditional interpretation is 'healing' is dependent on one's faith, or in the case of the man with paralysis the faith of friends, in the healing power of Jesus. The logical consequence of such an approach is that if a person is not healed or cured — and there is a difference, discussed below — then somehow it is the person's faith, or lack of it, that is the reason. Either that or God is using this person as an example, or is punishing this person because of some perceived sin. Many people with disabilities or illness have felt alienated from the church because of these traditional interpretations.

In the last two decades such interpretations have been brought into question by some important and potent forces. The first is the movement towards a more 'inclusive spirituality'. This movement has originated out of a concern for the lack of social justice for people with chronic illness or disability regarding acceptance and access to mainstream religious communities. This movement has concentrated its efforts in raising to consciousness the importance of the spiritual dimension of people's lives regardless of illness or disability. Further, participants in this movement have seen their role as advocating on behalf of people who are seeking to be recognized as people with spiritual needs regardless of their special concerns. A person with cerebral palsy, sensory disability, down syndrome or bi-polar is still a person with a spiritual dimension to their being and should not be made to feel personally responsible for their condition. Nor should they accept that some vengeful interventionist God, simply to prove a point, is responsible for their condition.

We are grateful to the many pioneers in this movement such as Kathy Black, David Pailin and Nancy Eiesland, who have challenged theological interpretation and religious practice by advocating for the rights of people disadvantaged by illness and disability. They have alerted us to the logical excluding consequence of inappropriate theological formulations and exclusive liturgies.

Coupled with this movement has been the significant rise of New Testament scholarship surrounding the importance of the 'historical Jesus' and the resultant theological understanding that flowed from such scholarship. The work of John Dominic Crossan in his book *The Birth of Christianity*, which includes a chapter devoted to "The Meaning of Healing", helps raise the important distinction between healing and curing.[1] Crossan does what he does better than almost anyone else; he places the issue of illness and healing not only within a historical context but also within a cultural and political one. More than this, we need to recognize the importance of how our theological interpretations are fashioned and coloured by our historical, social, and cultural contexts and what impact these have on the practice of our faith. Often healing requires acceptance by the community, of the person who is ill or disabled, as we witness in the story in Mark 5:24b–34 of the woman with a persistent vaginal haemorrhage. In this story we recognize that the social isolation which the condition creates is due to an unrealistic interpretation of the 'purity laws'. Acceptance into the community is part and parcel of the healing process. Not only is this woman suffering the debilitating effects of her illness, she is also suffering from the psychological effects of the social rejection, because the purity laws forbid her to enter into normal intimate social activity. Jesus' actions in calling her 'daughter', a term of endearment, bring her back into community by removing her social isolation. Clearly, to remove the stigma attached to a disability requires more than a rethinking of our theology; it requires a social revolution.

Stephen Finlan in his book *Problems with Atonement* has also raised a valid theological perspective based on a 'historical Jesus' interpretation of the healing narratives. Finlan emphasizes the point that healing occurs before the death of Jesus, hence healing is not dependent on a theology of the atonement. It is important to understand that when Jesus announces "your faith has made you whole", which he does six times in the healing narratives, this phrase is in the past tense. Jesus therefore does not see salvation or healing being dependent on his sacrificial death. People who related to Jesus and were the recipients of his declarations knew that God's saving or liberating power was already available to them, and was not dependent on his soon-to-occur execution.

Jesus continually points to the 'God activity' in these circumstances and makes no request of those receiving his healing power to believe in him as the 'Saviour' of the world. Healing is not dependent on such a belief. Therefore one must question the concept of a supernatural God whose divine intervention is made possible by the sacrifice of Jesus. Finlan stresses that "salvation and wholeness are freely available without any mediating transaction and faith means trusting in God's straightforward generosity".[2]

Unfortunately the church continues to perform activities and holds to theological assumptions and liturgies that support an orthodox and out-dated understanding of the healing narratives, the consequence of which isolates, and in some situations, demonizes people with illness and disabilities. As Crossan explains, when illness strikes, the appropriate response by family, friends, the health system and support groups such as a community of faith, will vastly affect how the illness develops and more importantly, how healing can take place.

One of the many questions raised by an examination of the healing narratives is whether Jesus is curing a disease by an intervention in the physical world, or healing the illness through an intervention in the social world. I do not believe the human Jesus could cure the disease of leprosy, but he did heal the man's illness by refusing to accept the disease's ritual uncleanliness and social isolation. In so doing Jesus forces others to either reject him from their community or accept the leper within it as well. It is the human Jesus who reaches out to touch the man with leprosy and in so doing makes himself ritually unclean. He responds to this man not because he is a divine being, but out of compassion for the man's condition. This very act challenges the rights of society's boundary-keepers and shifts the balance of power. Such an interpretation may destroy the 'miracle', but miracles are not necessarily changes in the physical world so much as changes in the social world, and it is society that dictates how we see, use and explain the physical world.

There is much work still to be done in highlighting New Testament scholarship on the reinterpretation of the healing narratives. It is by concentrating on the importance of the humanity of the 'historical Jesus' that will give structure and credence to the movement towards the practice of 'inclusive spirituality'. These two movements are intricately entwined because one is the logical extension of the other. Together they become a powerful transforming force for our communities of faith.

The implications of a progressive theological reinterpretation of the healing narratives will have a profound and positive impact on people who feel alienated and marginalized by mainstream Christianity through illness or disability. However, the most important aspect of bringing progressive Christianity together with the movement for inclusive spirituality is, it will give our understanding of the healing narratives an intellectual integrity.

Notes

1. J. D. Crossan, *The Birth of Christianity*, 291ff.
2. S. Finlan, *Problems with Atonement*, 114.

Further Reading

K. Black, *A Healing Homiletic.*
J. D. Crossan, *The Birth of Christianity.*
N. L. Eisland, *The Disabled God.*
S. Finlan, *Problems with Atonement.*
D. A. Pailin, *A Gentle Touch.*

God or Mammon?
Toward a More Humane, Just and Environmentally Sensitive Economic System
Keith Rowe

Among the streams that flow into contemporary progressive Christianity is what is loosely called the 'Social Gospel', a movement often identified with the work of Walter Rauschenbusch (1861–1918), an American Baptist, pastor to the poor, theologian and critic of social and economic structures, along with attitudes and theologies that create and/or perpetuate injustice. He recalled the church to the prophetic search for a just society.

Among present-day progressive Christians, the work of *Progressive Christians Uniting* and in particular of John B. Cobb Jr. provides intellectual leadership in articulating a critique of contemporary society and the social norms and systems by which it is shaped. While their work touches on issues of race, gender equality, interfaith understanding, care for the environment and peacemaking, the focus and integrating centre of their work is a theological critique of Free Market Economics (FMC), the taken for granted global economic system within which most people live, prosper or suffer.

The economic system within which we live is a taken-for-granted way of ordering our life together. The word 'economics' comes from the Greek words *oikos* (household) and *nomos* (law or management) and refers to the management of the human household. God is portrayed in scripture as like a household manager wanting to ensure no one is deprived of what they need and greed is curbed by care for neighbours. Serious and critical discussion of economics tends to be discouraged in many Christian churches lest it prove to be divisive, yet it is an all-pervasive influence on all our lives.

Harvey Cox[1] has described how, when in the 1990s he began to study the finance and business pages of the newspaper, he found himself entering into an alternative religion complete with systems of salvation, arguments about free will and predestination, temples for worship, a priesthood and even an eschatology or predictions about the end of the world. The free market functions as an omniscient God, and heretical departures from orthodoxy, particularly by nation-states, can be punished. Even the most holy of objects are transfigured into commodities re-valued according to the whims of the market. Sticker prices function like the sign of a cross on a child's forehead. Everyone and everything has a market value. Cox concludes: "Of all the religions of the world the religion of the market has become the most formidable rival (to the traditional religions) because it is rarely recognised as a religion." According to its logic there is no other name in heaven or earth by which we can be saved. John Cobb describes this all-pervasive religion, this thoroughly imminent and involved god, as 'economism', a view that the economy is the most important part of society and that other dimensions such as politics and education (and even religion?) should serve it.

While masquerading as a value-free science, economism is built on dangerous values and attitudes easily identified by those shaped by the way of Jesus.

1. FMC is built on the fundamental assumption that growth in monetary value is a primary goal in the well-adjusted life and is an inevitable producer of national and individual happiness. Personal worth is measured by wealth, and national health is measured by the rise or fall of the Gross Domestic Product (GDP) a measurement based on the value of all financial transactions and making no distinction between transactions that promote human wellbeing and those that damage the community. Some economists, progressive Christians among them, are developing alternatives to GDP as a measurement of communal wealth that, like the Genuine Progress Indicator (GPI), distinguish between welfare enhancing and communally destructive activities, identify environmentally sustainable from environmentally destructive forms of consumption and recognise the social capital represented by volunteer work and other undervalued contributions to communal well-being.

2. The engine of growth in FMC is human greed encouraged by aggressive and frequently misleading advertising. The impression is created that we all need more of everything and that retail shopping is the pathway to salvation. Personal and national debt is encouraged so that consumption may grow. Oliver James has coined the term 'affluenza' to describe the personal and collective passion to possess. Inherited religious wisdom that greed/desire is an attitude that damages life is ignored or derided.

3. In regarding the individual as the primary unit in life, FMC departs radically from the Christian view that human individuality finds its fulfilment in community. A test of any economic theory or practice is whether it builds good human community and enables people of varying social circumstances to live together in collaborative rather than competitive ways. Too often natural communities are destroyed by the demands of the market for cheap labour. John Cobb claims "since community has no value in economic thinking, it is not surprising that traditional communities everywhere have been undercut and that the life of new communities is fragile and temporary".[2]

4. Unrestrained economic growth fuelled by the growth needs of the 'developed' world is leading to environmental destruction on an unprecedented scale. The environment simply cannot sustain the desire of those in control to ensure continuing economic growth as currently defined. It is claimed that for all the earth's people to enjoy a Western middle class life style, four more planets the size of the earth would be needed as a resource base. This contrasts dramatically with the biblical understanding of humanity as stewards of the good creation, a commonplace understanding among indigenous religions.

5. The near unanimous conclusion of progressive theologians is that our current economic system has brought us into a serious crisis in all areas of life and has so modified our understanding of human possibility and the conditions that promote happiness, that it must either collapse or be radically modified. John Gray, former advisor to Margaret Thatcher, claims the present system cannot be fixed and that we are at "the fag end" of a particular kind of capitalism, debt-based finance capitalism, and we will need to live with uncertainty for a period till a new economic paradigm emerges[3]. In the meantime, he suggests, banks should be returned to their role as service agencies and "cease to be gambling joints", and the welfare state be strengthened so there may be security for the vulnerable during this period.

Progressive Christians have valuable insights to offer as they, along with others of good will, seek ways toward a more humane, just and environmentally sensitive economic system. Economic policies and their impact on the human family especially the most vulnerable need to be widely discussed among progressive Christians and involvement in public and political debate on economic matters become a natural outcome of congregational life. Members of progressive congregations can provide mutual support in resisting economically and legally encouraged 'addiction to affluence'. A rediscovery of the prophetic vision for communal living along with empathetic knowledge of how the economy impacts the neediest are starting points for the discovery of a contemporary progressive expression of the social gospel.

Notes

1. H. Cox, "Living in the New Dispensation".
2. J. B. Cobb, Jr., *Postmodernism and Public Policy,* 166.
3. J. Gray, *False Dawn.*

Further Reading

"Covenanting for Justice in the Economy and the Earth: The Accra Declaration of the World Alliance of reformed Churches", 2004: www.ch/documents/ACCRA-pamphlet.pdf.

J. B. Cobb, Jr., *Resistance.*

H. H. Daly and J. B Cobb, Jr., *For the Common Good.*

C. Hamilton, *Growth Fetish.*

P. F. Knitter and C. Muzaffar, *Subverting Greed.*

P. Rauschenbusch, *Walter Rauschenbusch, Christianity and the Social Crisis in the 21st Century.*

Exploring Eco-Theology

Noel Preston

The Christianity of my boyhood didn't have much to say about the natural environment. In fact, my early Methodist formation was not only human centred but rarely discouraged our misuse of natural resources or questioned what we called progress. Indeed it was something of a heresy to imagine you were nearer to god in nature than you were in church on a Sunday, while many of my fellow believers regarded the biblical account of creation as literal fact. Things have changed. Pope John Paul II called for "an ecological conversion" and even certain American evangelical Christians have become ecological converts. Initiatives described as 'eco-ministry' abound. Theologically, liturgically and practically, in the new millennium religion is greener.

The question is: how much new wine can these old wineskins hold? My assumption is that, by and large, even the greener churches have not substantially embraced the new paradigm required of an eco-theology.

Meanwhile, the Genesis mandate that we, *homo sapiens*, are to have dominion over the Earth haunts us in the guise of global warming, the threat to eco-systems and loss of biodiversity, depleting energy sources, a deepening water crisis, international security flashpoints, crimes against humanity, gross inequalities between and within nations, and absolute poverty and destitution facing 1.2 billion of a human population rushing toward nine billion. The situation is unsustainable. Collectively our global consumption of resources is 1.23 times that of our ecological footprint. That is, we humans are already using one and a quarter planet Earths. At the same time, the affluent 20 percent of the world's population controls and uses approximately 80 percent of the Earth's resources.

So we have this double-edged urgent challenge: to achieve environmental sustainability on the one hand and a fairer and more equitable distribution of resources and life opportunities in the human community, on the other. This double-edged challenge is what is now termed *eco-justice*.

Moreover, any theology or spirituality which is not eco-centric (i.e. centred on the Earth and its life forms) is grossly inadequate because it fails to take seriously the reality of life it rests on a faulty narrative if you like—and, furthermore, it does not provide humanity with the motivation and nurturance to make the journey into the future which will sustain the community of life. At its core, progressive theology or religion must be eco-centric. Eco-theology is not an 'add on' to mainstream theology or religious practice, a mere development of the unchanging, dogmatic centre. This is not a flavour-of-the-month theology or sub-set of systematic theology like some regarded 'political theology' or 'feminist theology' or 'pastoral theology'. This is the main game.

A Brief History of Eco-Theology

What we call 'process theology' is the major foundation for (neo-Christian) eco-theology. As the term 'process' implies, this is theology that takes seriously the processes of life, a more organic view than one that is propositional, evolving largely out of a platonic worldview. Rejecting so called dualistic ways of understanding the world, a process view of God emerged, articulated by Paul Tillich as 'the ground of our being', opening the way for a departure from traditional theism to what may be termed pan-en-theism, defined more precisely and discussed further below. In Australia this has been best interpreted by the lay theologian, Charles Birch, whose primary field was biology. Meanwhile Catholic theology, which had richer sources to draw on than the Reformation fathers, was influenced by the work of a palaeontologist who was also a Jesuit priest, Pierre Teilhard de Chardin, whose writings harmonise with process theology and its holistic approach. Teilhard de Chardin moved the essential theological focus from redemption to creation. His worldview radically situated the human story in the context of 'the Universe story'.

In the past thirty years or so the voices in this conversation have multiplied. Within non-Catholic academia, Sallie McFague and Jurgen Moltmann are significant contributors. Key Catholic thinkers who are reframing their tradition include Thomas Berry, an American Passionist priest, Matthew Fox, the trailblazer for what he called 'creation spirituality', and feminist scholars such as Rosemary Radford Reuther. An Australian Catholic whose work has attempted to stay faithfully within his Catholic tradition is Denis Edwards. So, for example, Edwards is concerned to give a Trinitarian account and a theology of the Eucharist rich in ecological themes.

What Eco-Theology is About: An Overview

This growing conversation suggests to progressives that an ecological reformation of Christianity is

1. *Inclusive not exclusive,* not just in the sense of gender, race or species but also in rejecting a fundamentalist mindset. It recognises that the 'truth to live by' may be revealed in varying and multiple ways.

2. *Mystical rather than literalist;* that is, it centres on an experience of transcendence which is connected to life's mysteries and uncertainties while it is triggered more by connectedness with the cosmic community of life than it is by codified religious forms.

3. *Eco-centric and not anthropocentric;* that is, it rejects human-centred theology which subtly endorses our species' destructive dominance of nature through human technology, in favour of a view which takes seriously the intrinsic value of all life.

4. Shaped by an over-riding sense of the *goodness of life rather than its undeniable tragedy,* which suggests that life's purpose is more about celebrating original goodness rather than seeking salvation from original sin.

Points 3 and 4 particularly represent a departure from what has been a dominating and dualistic understanding of human nature in Christianity, separating 'man and nature', 'spirit and flesh' and so on. (To those who know some church history, these points reflect the theological battle between ancient church teachers, Augustine and Pelagius.) The triumph of Augustinianism contributed to a theology that places the human over nature.

Freed from the need to dominate (a consequence of anthropocentrism) and empowered by a different, holistic and eco-centric way that trusts the processes of life, a focus on *right relating in the community of life* emerges to underpin an ethic and spirituality compatible with eco-theology. Therefore any credible creed will affirm that life is much bigger than our individual human failures and successes and that our nobility as a species is contingent on relating rightly to all life forms from a position of responsible dependence within the biosphere. It follows that loving our neighbour includes loving nature.

From this style and standpoint eco-theology rewrites or discards traditional doctrines. It is beyond the scope of this short essay to itemise these changes except for the following notes on key planks of traditional Christianity.

Three Crucial Questions

What about the Bible?

Christianity is a religion grounded in biblical revelation. But, biblical revelation must be continually tested against revelation of nature itself. Despite a strand in the biblical witness which hints at the immanence of Yahweh in creation, and while there is clear teaching about the requirement for humans to be good stewards of nature's resources, the Bible's patriarchal and anthropocentric orientation dominates. Eco-centric themes are not very visible, even though scholars (such as Norm Habel) have valiantly and helpfully advocated re-reading the Bible 'from the perspective of the Earth'.

What about God?

The Universe story of life's evolution indicates that there is no place for a being who is unchangeable and in absolute control in such a dynamic and continuously creative process. That process is both purposeful and chancy. At the same time we can say that this process is imbued with an awesome and mysterious force of being and becoming which transcends any particular being. An understanding of God that takes seriously this view is termed 'pan-en-theism'—as distinct from 'pantheism', which simply says 'everything is God', or 'theism', which objectifies god as a being separate from the cosmos. A pan-en-theistic theology allows us to take eco-centrism seriously while preserving the idea of transcendence. In this worldview there is no 'elsewhere God', 'a god-out-there', but rather 'an everywhere God', 'the ground of our being'.

The New Testament core statement that 'God is Love' fits with pan-en-theism. Love is that energy, that quality in the process which shapes life's relationships rightly, in ways that are more harmonious, empowering, joyous and just, reflecting, if you like 'the Divine'. The everywhere God is an embodied god, the god within all bodies 'in whom we live and move and have our being', in much the same way as the mystics often speak of their experience of God. From an eco-centric understanding, God transforms our relationship to nature because the earth itself, Gaia, is 'the body of God'.

I draw the crucial conclusion for so called 'progressives', that the main dividing line across the communities of spirituality and religions is that between theism and pan-en-theism—this is a particular challenge within the Abrahamic faiths.

What about Jesus Christ?

The stories which explain ourselves to ourselves matter. In the twenty-first century such stories must be set within the over-arching story, the Universe story of life. So, what place does the Jesus story have in eco-theology? How will a neo-Christian eco-theology speak of Jesus the Christ? The answer to these questions acknowledges that the Jesus story is no more than a significant account within the story of human evolution set as it is within the Universe story of life.

I do not pretend to be a gospel scholar trying to uncover the original Jesus. Obviously we must disown those versions of that story which lead to 'Jesusolatry', and which surely cause Jesus himself to turn in his grave. Central to those distortions are theories of atonement that reduce the Jesus story to make him a Saviour who is sacrificed to win a theistic God's agreement to forgive sins. The story of this prophetic, healing and mystical teacher who brought hope to his Galilean contemporaries has much to contribute twenty centuries on, because it challenges the oppression of the vulnerable and marginalised.

More than the Jesus of history, the Christ of faith, is the pre-occupation of most of those who explore eco-theology from a Christian background. Matthew Fox's *Coming of the Cosmic Christ* is one significant formulation of this re-mythologising. In brief, Fox's thesis is that the historical Jesus introduces us to a Christ who is the underlying reality giving an inherent sacredness to the Cosmos. Fox cites authorities from St Paul to the medieval mystics who talk this way: "in him were created all things in heaven and on earth: everything visible and invisible" (Col 1:16). An ecologically (and mystically) informed approach to what is traditionally called 'the incarnation' has been put this way by Niels Gregersen:

> Understood this way, the death of Christ becomes an icon of God's redemptive co-suffering with all sentient life as well as with the victims of social competition. God bears the cost of evolution, the price involved in the hardship of natural selection.[1]

Another line of inquiry about the place of the Jesus story in eco-theology would be: what is it that nurtured Jesus' spirit, which sustained and motivated him? It is a question that provides clues for an eco-spirituality. Jesus had a strong sense of an 'everywhere-here-and-now' God whose kin-dom is within us. As a mystical prophet, Jesus operated out of a strong sense of unity or 'oneness' with his God giving him a deep awareness of oneness with all, with himself, with other human beings, with all other beings and, I suspect, as he spent nights in prayer on the hillsides of Galilee, oneness with the starry heavens and the cosmos.

How Then Are We To Live?

Religious progressives have frequently touted what is more than a half-truth: that it is more important how we live than what we believe. So, briefly, what are the practical consequences of eco-theology, the lifestyle and political commitments which should be its outcomes? Eco-theology certainly raises radical questions about what prayer or worship means, but more than that, it calls for clear action to care for the resources of the Earth. On the one hand, eco-theology's profound sense of the interconnectedness of all bespeaks a spirituality which nurtures our awareness that 'one is all and all is one', while on the other hand, it issues in compassion for all, which takes form in programs of eco-justice.

Notes

1. Quoted in D. Edwards, *Ecology at the Heart of Faith*, 59.

Further Reading

B. McKidden, *Eaarth.*
S. Ogden, *Love Upside Down.*
N. Preston, *Beyond the Boundary.*

When Christ Is Cosmic

Bruce Sanguin

Jesus continues to be the central character of the Christian faith, and will remain so for as long as there are people for whom a Christian identity still matters. Therefore, how we imagine what was going on with him and through him matters a great deal.

For example, if we imagine Jesus to be an emergent form of Earth—an occasion of miraculous cosmic and planetary creativity—we ground the Jesus story within the universe as we know it to be. Salt waters coursed through his blood, ancient bacteria were alive in his gut, and the neurons that fired in his grey matter were gifts of an ancient exploding supernova. He was, in short, a child of Earth and Cosmos. Before the various and necessary doctrines and dogmas developed to address the mystery of Jesus, he represented, inside and out, soul and body, an occasion of cosmic coalescence and creativity. The evolutionary pressure coursing through the whole universe also gave birth to Jesus. In short, I believe that it's important to present him as a child of Earth and Cosmos and not only a child of Heaven.

Highly educated Christians still speak of Jesus being 'sent' to Earth by God. This *Star Trek* version of Jesus' arrival on the scene ("Beam me down, Scotty") is reinforced when we read the story of Jesus birth without interpretation. Clergypersons may appreciate that the myth of the virgin birth was the early church's way of saying this peasant Jew (and not the guy wearing the laurel wreath and the toga) is God's only son. But without an explicit interpretive framework, the layperson is left thinking Jesus arrived on the scene having circumvented all the evolutionary, deep-time history that actually constitutes our humanity. Let's realize that Jesus is kin with star fields, our solar system, the Earth's bio-systems and all creatures—and see how that impacts our mission to repair Earth. By grounding Jesus' humanity in the evolutionary narrative of the universe, the ancient doctrine that affirms Jesus' full humanity takes on a more precise and empirically accurate meaning. His humanity is an expression of an evolving cosmos. It took 13.7 billion years to produce Jesus. Once this terrestrial identity is established, we can employ what Michael Dowd calls "night language" to the Jesus event. For example, we can enjoy the biblical language of the Holy Spirit 'overshadowing' Mary to describe the Mystery of Jesus' conception.

I recently participated in a Eucharistic service at which the body of Christ was offered as a tasteless, sterile wafer. Nothing could proclaim with more power Jesus Christ's essential disconnection from Earth—Christ as cardboard. Don't get me wrong. There was much about the ancient liturgy I appreciated. But the symbol of the body of Christ should taste like it came from Earth: yeasty, whole grain, locally ground, and baked in a wood-fired oven. The aroma should trigger salivation. Salivation as salvation! Our instinctual desire for food is a sacramental expression of our spiritual yearning to become one with the divine.

Walking along the shores of the Atlantic Ocean in Narragansett Rhode Island, almost twenty years ago, I received a sacrament of another sort. The whole cosmos was fed to me as the living body of the Christ. I awoke to an identity that included, yet transcended, my psychological self. I received my cosmic identity. I knew myself to be the presence of the universe coalesced after 13.7 billion years in this transient presence with the name of 'Bruce'. But I also knew that the warm rocks under my feet were the presence of the cosmos, and the screeching gull drifting by sounded like the call of the Divine insisting that I step through forever into this moment. Evolution itself had arrived, as the presence of love, wanting to express itself through me, in me, and as me. I knew more deeply than I knew anything that I was one with the universe and one with Spirit—expressing Itself in all this diversity.

I want Christians to know that our Common Creation Story, given to us by science, is a sacred narrative. It is another scripture declaring God's handiwork. When this story of sacred emergence is presented as the sacred context of the Judeo-Christian text and tradition, and that Jesus showed up as a sacred manifestation of this process, the reality of what we call 'God' comes alive.

Much theology assumes that to be human is to be a separate and fallen creature. My Barthian seminary professor taught me that creation, too, was fallen. But God 'sent' Jesus into the world to redeem me, if I believed the right things, as eventually 'He' would redeem all of creation. It is our *belief* in separateness that constitutes our fall and our failing, but there is not actually any separation, anywhere. This insight is the gift of the 'new' cosmology.

We need to allow our theology to be updated by scientific evidence, and wherever our theology and actual facts clash, science wins every time. For example, empirical, evolutionary evidence doesn't support the metaphysical assumption that we have fallen from some primordial perfection, and that this fall renders us 'sinners'. We now know we have three brains (some say four) stacked on top of each other: a brain stem; the reptilian and mammalian, predisposing us to indulge instincts that evolved under different evolutionary conditions; and our prefrontal lobes. As well, our brains have two distinct hemispheres associated with different functions and states of consciousness. It could be said we have four or five natures, not one, which are in daily 'conversation' with one another. That conversation is more often than not heated. The science of brain chemistry was unknown to Paul when he wrote that he was a man undone—doing the very things he didn't want to do and refraining from those things he did want to do. He chalked up this instinctual war between his 'members' to sin. Today scientists speak of 'mismatched instincts'—one part of our brain will forever try to convince us that we can never get enough sugar, salt, and fat from a time in our evolutionary history when the threat of starvation was real. The diet industry has capitalized on the messages from this part of our brain. When confessions of sin are not grounded in this scientific understanding of what makes us tick, these rituals perpetuate a kind of chronic helplessness requiring repeated divine rescue missions. Instead, we could teach that the very act of becoming conscious and making choices *is* the presence of Spirit in our lives.

American philosopher, Ken Wilber, reminds us that, scientifically, we are moving "up from Eden". We are evolving in a biased direction of increased complexity, unity, consciousness, and compassion. The modern worldview and associated theological models are dismissive of any notion of progress. They point out the many, undeniable atrocities of the twentieth century to support their case. Yet, taking the long view of Big History it seems undeniable that the cosmos is moving toward what A. N. Whitehead calls an increase in value.

Is there evidence of this? While not denying our continuing propensity for violence, the last fifty years has seen an unprecedented social evolution apparent in the rights assumed in Western democracies by women, blacks, handicapped, and even other-than-human species—such as legislation passed in Ecuador conferring rights to the animals and ecosystems. There are many progressive Christians who lament that what was started in the 1960s civil rights movement in the U.S. fizzled out. They see only regression. Yet as I write this, the people of Egypt, Libya, Saudi Arabia, and Mauritius are expressing an impulse for freedom and democracy that has already seen one dictator fall. To give one more example, the congregation I serve is privileged to practice an international ministry of marrying gay and lesbian couples. We could hardly imagine this would have been possible in society—let alone in a church—even twenty years ago! To repeat, we have not fallen from some perfect paradise. We are evolving. It is not therefore, religion's primary role to help us recover some lost state of wholeness through various rituals. It is the role of religious institutions to create habitats of creative emergence to support and foster a sacred evolutionary impulse to realize greater freedom and fullness of life on

Earth. The Cosmic Christ, emerged, not to save us from original sin, but to reconcile us with a profound unity that extends to whatever we mean by 'God'.

I want Christians to know that 'Christ' is not Jesus' last name. It's a title the early church gave to Jesus. It's the Greek word for 'Messiah' in Hebrew. There is a complicated history to the word. By the time the writer of John's gospel comes to give his account of Jesus as the Christ, he employs the Greek idea of the Logos, or the Word of God. Whereas for Jews, the Messiah is a very human figure who would come as priest and king to save Israel, the Word of God or Logos represented a kind of Platonic ideal—the Heart and Mind of God in which everything that was created came into being and was given life (John 1). Many scholars are convinced, as I am, that the Word of God was the Greek version of the Jewish tradition of Lady Wisdom—a feminine creative and creating principle. What matters is the early church believed the Christ/Logos/Wisdom/Divine Creativity took up residence in Jesus of Nazareth—the Word made flesh.

These days, my shorthand for all of this is simply 'Heart and Mind'. Jesus was transparent to, and enacted, Heart and Mind. His transparency, surrender and enactment issued in what he called the Kingdom of God, or the divine realm. This realm manifested in the interior life of individuals, in our relationships and our culture, in nature, and in our social and political systems. This realm is ever-present and ever-evolving in these four domains. To 'enter' this realm one must shed the self-sense of being a separate and disconnected individual. This sense of self must undergo a metaphorical crucifixion. As we die to our small self, we are raised to a self of both cosmic and transcendent dimensions. To follow Christ, then, is to submit oneself to the Heart and Mind that manifest in Jesus of Nazareth.

Jesus didn't want to be worshipped. I don't even think he wanted to be followed—if by 'follow' we mean creating a whole new religion around him. We're stuck with it now, and I make my living trying to keep it alive. But I'm pretty sure Jesus himself would direct us back to the original experience of actually entering and enacting the realm of God. Jesus did want people to know that what lit him up was also available to them—if they were ready, willing, and able to surrender their small selves and be transformed by Heart and Mind.

We live within a miraculous, evolutionary unfolding that is the allurement of Heart and Mind towards increased complexity, unification, beauty, love, and freedom. The whole universe, from electrons and protons to galaxies, and from single-cell bacteria to the intelligence of Gaia and the human mind is shot through with, and responsive to, the presence of non-coercive Heart and Mind.

The same Heart and Mind that was present in Jesus is also present in us. This means that as Christians what we are called to make of our lives is distinct from, yet connected to, the heart and mind of the first-century Jew, Jesus of Nazareth. This is because the divine Heart and Mind that is forever and always creating and loving, will inevitably be interpreted anew in the evolving consciousness of the human species. We are in the process of being divinized. To be in Christ is to consciously cooperate with a sacred evolutionary impulse to assume responsibility for realizing the Kin(g)dom of God on earth. The church will be renewed as we help people awaken to the desire of God to manifest in, through, and as us.

Further Reading

M. Dowd, *Thank God for Evolution.*
B. Sanguin, *Darwin, Divinity, and the Dance of the Cosmos.*
———, *If Darwin Prayed.*
K. Wilber, *A Sociable God.*

Songs of the Spirit for a Twenty-first Century Faith Journey
New Zealand Hymn Writers Respond

John Thornley

In what strange land will I sing your song,
   O God, my God?
To what new code must my heart belong,
   O God, my God?
The boundaries shift as the lines delete,
and the way back home is a tired beat:
there are new directions to take my feet
to follow you.
   —Shirley E. Murray

I did think of opening in the prosaic mode, but a song seemed a good place to start—and also, to end. I call them 'songs' not 'hymns'. It's part of the shift from a church-centred to a world-centred paradigm.

Shirley Erena Murray is New Zealand's best known hymn writer, sharing popular currency in church hymnody with Colin Gibson, who wrote the music for 'In what strange land'. The song is included in *Hope is our Song*, published by New Zealand Hymn Book Trust (NZH-BT) in 2009, and launched at a national hymn conference.

Founded in 1978 by several denominations, the NZHBT has now published four books, six CDs and one set of sheet music (an SATB setting of 'Hymn for Anzac Day').

Historical Roots

A brief history of the New Zealand HymnBook Trust is in order. The energising force for three decades was the Very Reverend John Murray, a former Moderator of the Presbyterian Church of New Zealand. His initial approach to the churches, in the late 1970s, inviting them to engage ecumenically in publishing NZ material, was not received warmly. In a short article published in *Music in the Air*, Summer 1999, John recounts that meeting, with acerbic brevity:

> I then put the proposal (for a new hymnbook) to the Joint Commission on Church Union for their backing. Surely they would see this idea as a God-given way of promoting ecumenical worship, and so the goal of church union itself? They were very friendly, listened to me, as some sort of diversion, it seemed to me, from the real work of creeds and statements of faith. They thanked me, wished me well, and moved on to the next item of business.

However, a door did open, with the proposal for a New Zealand Supplement to a new Australian-initiated book, *With One Voice*, and out of this came the setting up of the NZHBT by five churches in 1978. It launched its first all-NZ collection, *Alleluia Aotearoa*, in 1993. While governance remains with the churches, the effective work is done by the management team, supported by an editorial group.

The Trust's independent status is important; the exercise of greater control by church institutions would be gently, but firmly, resisted. A huge input of energy from volunteers at the local church base goes into active production and promotion of the Trust resources, including writing texts, composing tunes, teaching new songs to choirs and congregations, and celebrating, with intentional use of our own songs, Christmas, Easter and other high points of the church year.

The Trust's policy is to publish songs with new words and new tunes, that are ecumenical, contemporary and of Aotearoa NZ origin primarily but, with the Tasman ditch increasingly not an impassable barrier, finding a place within the Australian church and cultural setting.

A total of over 450 songs appear in the four published titles, and currently in preparation is a *Companion*, with Colin Gibson as author. Nearly one hundred names of creative wordsmiths/poets and composers/musicians appear in the books and CDs. Some writers of texts are also published internationally.

Because of their greater exposure, 'at home' and on the world stage, the second half of this article will focus on some words of Shirley Murray relating to theology, followed by some comments from Colin Gibson, relating to music settings.

Shirley Murray on Theology

In the Winter 2004 issue of *Music in the Air*, following interviews with Shirley, I published some of her thoughts under a subtitle 'Notes for an Incarnational Theology', when she was questioned on her use of imagery of the world as the Body of God and the church as the Body of Christ. She replied:

> My meaning was certainly to the World as 'the body of God', and the call to the Church to be the resurrected 'body of Christ'. Since you have picked up on this, I'll try to explain what it means in terms of my hymn-writing. For a start, it has to be with the parameters of reality being defined by the World, not the Church, in the broadest sense.
>
> I suppose I grew up believing that 'the Church tells you what the World is' (good/evil, heaven/hell) and the World should be brought into the Church in order to 'save' it. Now, I live in a World where all the parameters are being pushed out and we recognise few barriers between people and faiths. Hopefully, we learned a great deal about this in mission fields and aid programmes, and recognise that the Body of God is the World, not the Church.
>
> As to hymns, my immediate instinct was to avoid any language that sounded 'religious' in that it used, or over-used, pious expressions that are 'in-house'. This includes the whole concept of God/Jesus as King, references to the blood of the Lamb, eternal bliss and the like, along with an indulgence in sentimentality (for example, "Our blest Redeemer, ere he breathed his tender last farewell")....
>
> The whole thrust of 'Star-Child' (Shirley's carol, found in *Carol our Christmas*) is for the entire world to experience Christmas, from street kids to the forgotten elderly, and this has to be expressed in language we now relate to. Hence, in other places, such words as 'laser', 'website of love', 'stock markets', 'God's holy Internet', represent an attempt to make our imaginations work in the present world rather than the unreal past....
>
> Maybe our re-awareness of the full humanity of Jesus, rather than his divinity, is the point which allows us to move from Church language to 'secular' language, with a different style for the next context. . . . ' Telling the story' is a 'secular' thing, while preaching the doctrine the Church thing.

Here is Shirley Murray's complete hymn from my opening statement:

In what strange land will I sing your song,
  O God, my God?
To what new code must my heart belong,
  O God, my God?
The boundaries shift as the lines delete,
and the way back home is a tired beat:
there are new directions to take my feet
  to follow you.

With what new eyes will I see your hand,
  O God, my God?
By what new chart will I understand,
  O God, my God?
The old worlds wither away and die;
your new creation is like the sky,
with new-found galaxies spinning by,
  which dazzle me.

You test my faith in a different sphere,
  O God, my God.
You guide the cursor that brings me here,
  O God, my God.
For childhood things keep me in the past,
remembered hymns that still hold me fast,
familiar words that were meant to last,
  and sing along.

You put a new song into my mouth,
  O God, my God.
You lift my spirit to touch your truth,
  O God, my God;
you give me bread when I fear a stone,
you do not leave me to walk alone,
my heart will trust in your heart's unknown,
  O God, my God.[1]

Colin Gibson on Music

Shirley Murray has, on several occasions, commented on the importance of songwriters. "Without lively tunes and rhythms which are easy to sing, the writers of texts will find few singers." The revolution must not only be with new words, but also new music. As composer of new tunes, Colin Gibson was asked to reply to the question, "How does your own hymn-writing go beyond the traditional four-square choral-based hymn form?", and his reply appeared in an article in the NZ music journal, *Sound Ideas*:

Traditional hymns generally keep up a regular and even metrical stress pattern, providing sequences of crotchets or crotchet-and-minim combinations, for instance, with little use of dotted rhythms or quaver interruptions to their stately progress. I like to introduce, where possible and appropriate, more irregular rhythms adapted from contemporary folk, musical and pop idioms (such as, tango rhythms, syncopation, an unusual degree of rhythmic change) and variety within a melodic line and so on.

To put it briefly, I allow instinct to dictate the displacement of order when setting words. I have become aware that congregations used to the staid rhythmic patterns of older hymns find it very liberating to sing to the freer, 'jazzier' rhythms and stronger beat of contemporary secular music. The difficulty is finding an intermediate position between archaic regularity and anarchic freedom, both of which completely control and suppress spontaneity and independence.

Prophetic Word from Karl Barth

An on-going concern, shared among the enthusiasts, has been the slowness with which theological colleges/seminaries have taken on board hymnody (songs) as a critical component in ministry training. Courses offering knowledge and critiques of the variety of theologies and music styles for songs used in worship are conspicuous by their absence in most institutions of ministry training. Church leadership seems deaf to the prophetic words on singing by Karl Barth:

> The Christian community sings. It is not a choral society. Its singing is not a concert. But from inner, material necessity it sings. Singing is the highest form of human expression. . . . What we can and must say quite confidently is that the community that does not sing is not a community. And where it does not sing but sighs and mumbles spasmodically, shamefacedly, and with ill grace, it can be at best a troubled community which is not quite sure of its cause and of whose witness and ministry there can be no great expectation.[2]

A Closing Song

Let me close this short introduction to *Songs of the Spirit*, New Zealand style, with Bill Bennett's song for a southern hemisphere Good Friday:

> On a cool and autumn dawn,
>> as the sun awoke the eastern sky,
>> we decided you were such a risk

we abandoned you to die—
on a cool and autumn dawn.

On a cool and autumn morn,
    as the sun began to climb above,
    we nailed you to a kauri beam
as your wounded eyes spoke love—
on a cool and autumn morn.

On a cool and autumn noon,
    as the sun lit every watching face,
    you forgave our cries of heartless hate
with compassion and with grace—
on a cool and autumn noon.

On a cool and autumn day,
    as the sun began its western slide,
    'It is finished!' came your cry of hope,
confident of Eastertide—
on a cool and autumn day.

On a cool and autumn eve,
    in the fading light when hope seemed lost,
    in the tomb we laid your mortal bones,
waiting for God's Pentecost—
on a cool and autumn eve.[3]

Notes

1. "In What Strange Land"—Words: Shirley Erena Murray; Music: Colin Gibson. Words and Music © Hope Publishing Company. Book and CD. *Hope Is Our Song*, NZ Hymnbook Trust, 2009/11.
2. *Church Dogmatics* IV, xvii, 72.4.
3. "On a Cool and Autumn Dawn," © Bill Bennett, in book and CD, *Hope Is Our Song*, NZ Hymnbook Trust 2009/11.

Additional Notes

- Full details of the Trust's publications and how to order, within NZ, are on its website: www.hymns.org.nz. For Australians, a list of in-country retailers can be supplied on enquiry to the NZHBT office, email: info@hymns.org.nz.
- *Music in the Air* is a biannual journal published/edited by J. Thornley, exploring the creative arts and spirituality. Launched in 1996, it is planned to 'self-destruct' in 2016, with Issue 40. NZ hymn-writing and popular music have been two foci of the journal, reflecting the editor's interests.
- *Sound Ideas*, first launched as a print journal but now an e-journal, is published by the Music Department of the University of Canterbury,

Christchurch. The article cited: "The Catching of Values", by J. Thornley, vol. 4, no. 2, Jan. 2001 (www.nzsme.org.nz).

Further Reading

New Zealand Hymn Book Trust: *Alleluia Aotearoa* (1993); *Faith Forever Singing* (2000), *Carol Our Christmas* (1996), *Hope Is Our Song* (2009).

S. E. Murray, *Touch the Earth Lightly.*

W. L. Wallace, *The Mystery Telling.*

Living the 'progressive' Dream . . .

Stories from congregations self-styled as 'progressive'

Progressive Christianity

A 'Grassroots' Response

John Smith

Introduction

As information regarding New Testament scholarship surrounding the 'historical Jesus' has become public, it has generated a wealth of interest in the life of this peasant from Nazareth. Further it has provided an impetus for those who are challenging orthodox Christianity. The Jesus Seminar has been instrumental in igniting this interest, through its examination of the words and actions of the 'historical Jesus'.

It appears that for some considerable time in Australia and New Zealand there has been an enormous energy force hiding just below the surface of devout participation in the orthodox Christian Church, and we are now witnessing its emergence. Many people feel that for many years they have been living a form of schizophrenic existence when participating in orthodox Christian worship, while privately disagreeing with the language of the creeds, hymns, prayers and time-locked doctrines.

So how have individuals responded to what some have declared as the liberating experience of in Marcus Borg's words, "meeting Jesus again for the first time"? Taussig has given us a window into the North American response to this experience in his essay "The Search for Community and the Historical Jesus". This is recorded in the Jesus Seminar publication, *The Historical Jesus Goes to Church* and a more thorough analysis found in his book, *A New Spiritual Home*. As a result of Taussig's work, I determined to follow his lead and ask people who initiated progressive groups/communities of faith in the antipodes how they had responded to their experience in light of the recent historical Jesus scholarship. These groups had established alternative ways of seeking a relationship with the sacred armed with questions, doubts and courage to risk the way. The following chapter is the result of this search from a representative sample of these groups.

This research conducted in Australia and New Zealand is but a small journey into this phenomenon, and it suggests more work needs to be done. However a number of salient points can be gleaned from this exercise and I will refer to these after placing before the reader the stories of these groups and their personal journeys in faith.

◆ ◆ ◆

Something for the Spirit

"Something for the Spirit" began in 2005 among members of Ewing Memorial Uniting Church, as a regular monthly meeting to explore matters of faith and meaning, and to find a faith relevant to life in the twenty-first century. The name is deliberately non-churchy, allowing for maximum freedom of exploration and content.

The group began with the encouragement and support of the then minister, but leadership remains in the hands of lay people. A larger group of 16–20 meets once a month on a Sunday evening in a private home, a casual gathering around food and drink (wine and nibbles) and open to anyone interested. A second smaller group also meets monthly, midweek, with a similar format. To ensure this casual, 'meeting of friends' atmosphere, it is important not to meet at the church. (An exception is the occasion of a significant visiting speaker, when a larger venue is required.)

Many members are Ewing people, but several belong to other churches or to no church at all. The current minister of Ewing is a member but not the leader.

The activities have followed a pattern of discussion around an article, a talk, a DVD, or a book. We have been following fairly closely the thinking of the challengers to the traditional forms of Christianity: John Shelby Spong and Michael Morwood in the early days, then Marcus Borg, John Dominic Crossan, Lloyd Geering, Greta Vosper, Karen Armstrong, Matthew Fox and others. We've looked at gospels outside the canon, Christian mysticism, other major world religions, interfaith ministry, and atheism. It is emphasized that all ideas expressed are welcomed and there are no 'right' answers for the group, only for individuals. We are not seeking consensus.

The Seekers, St Leonard's Uniting Church

The name 'The Seekers' was chosen about ten years ago because our numbers were growing and it was felt we needed a name for clear identification. It was also recognized that our major activity was seeking where we were going on our religious journey.

The group was originally established about sixteen years ago as a classical Bible Study group that met once a month after church in a private home. But a couple of years later several members decided to broaden the group's life. With the change we started studying and discussing works by C. S. Lewis and Francis Macnab and gradually the group morphed towards a more progressive Christian outlook. Typically, each meeting was planned, and information and discussion questions circulated, one week before the meeting by email. The information could be progressive chapters of a book by a leading modern author, a newspaper article, a CD, articles, or comments off the Internet, and each meeting was loosely led by one of several leaders. We have tried many things—writing our own modern creed, packing Christmas shoeboxes for overseas orphanages, interviewing a Muslim woman about her faith, interrogating a succession of three ministers over the period on progressive subjects. Some members of our group helped to start another group in a church several suburbs away. One of our ministers presented and ran the program *Living the Questions* (attended by thirty-five parishioners) for twenty weeks, and this was most helpful to group members.

Our numbers have now grown too large for a single discussion group, so we intend to split into two voluntary groups for discussion only and share the rest of the time of the meeting together.

PAX: Progressive Acting Christians

PAX (Progressive Acting Christians) Centenary Suburbs is a small group of sixteen or so Christians seeking some answers on their journey in the Way of Jesus. Established in 2010, our name PAX is an acronym of the word "peace" in Latin, taken from *pax et bonum*. We initially looked at Progressive Anglican Christians (Toowong Pax group; see below) but as we had a number of Uniting Church members, we chose the word 'acting' to allow an ecumenical feel to the group. Our gatherings are weekly, in the evening. We have now completed the first DVD of *Living the Questions* (LtQ) as well as Dr Steven Ogden's *I Met God in Bermuda*.

Our group consists of a range of theologically minded people at different stages on their journey. LtQ helped to amalgamate our ideas and thoughts. Our ages range from forty-five through to seventy, which is good for healthy discussion, but no exuberance of youth from the younger set.

Our discussions are very healthy. Everyone is encouraged to input their 'bit', and even the quieter members have come out with their own philosophies on a subject. We predominantly examine the 'historical Jesus' research of Borg, Crossan, and Spong, but have also dabbled in modern theologians such as Tillich and Rayner. There is also a fair amount of book swapping to cross-fertilize ideas and philosophies, using such writers as McLaren, Vosper, and Webb.

There is a democratic air to our leadership with the majority making decisions or choices on content, evenings, dates, etc. We have also touched bases with the Toowong Anglican parish, which also conducts a PAX group and plan further joint meetings.

PAX is an enlightening aspect of our faith because it allows the asking of the difficult questions we have harboured down the years. It is amazing how people can be seen to be unburdening a load from their lives in the discussions of some of our evenings. Also, some members have revitalized their church attendance and participation because of a freeing up or understanding of the dogma and ritual in our worship.

The Rockhampton Explorers

About ten years ago, a couple perceived a need in the Central Queensland city of Rockhampton for a forum where people of any faith tradition could explore tenets of their respective faiths in the light of modern scholarship. As a result, they invited interested people to join a group that came to be known as 'The Rockhampton Explorers'. Since then, the group has met fairly consistently twice a month except in December and January.

The name reflects the group's thought that matters of faith (doctrines, liturgies, spiritual observances, religious teachings) should allow for new insights to be incorporated into how that faith is expressed, instead of being tied to beliefs about which contemporary scholars of religion and science have cast doubts.

Over the years, the group has been made up mainly of Anglicans and Roman Catholics with a few from other traditions. There are ten regular members in the group. Some have taken a 'sabbatical' from religious observance; some attend religious services occasionally; some attend church services weekly.

Apart from two retired Anglican priests and one retired Uniting Church minister, there appears to be no interest among clerical or leading lay members of any denomination within this city.

There has never been a set program, and the content has depended on who in the group is willing to prepare material. A Eucharistic-type liturgy has been written and experienced by the group and we are now in the process of preparing the outline for a funeral liturgy together with a number of choices for each part within the liturgy. Various books have been studied and discussed, such as *On Forgiveness* by Richard Holloway, *Who on Earth was Jesus?* by David Boulton, and *Meeting Jesus Again for the First Time* by Marcus Borg. The group also spent one year working through the material of *Living the Questions.* Members have also written their personal creed.

At the time of publication, the group is considering the field of ethics. When we decide to study and discuss a book or article, someone accepts responsibility to prepare notes and questions relevant to the material.

Chapel by the Sea, Uniting Church Bondi Beach

'The Chapel by the Sea' Uniting Church has been at work in the Sydney suburb of Bondi Beach since it was purpose-built some forty years ago in the heart of the Bondi Beach CBD.

The Chapel community meets each Sunday for worship in diverse styles at 9.00 a.m., 11.00 a.m. (contemporary, informal), 3.00 p.m. (a time of healing and wholeness with many on the edge of our community) and 7.00 p.m. Cafe Church. Cafe Church alternates among speakers, films and meditation using the resources of the Taize Community. We have enjoyed speakers of the caliber of Hugh Mackay, Greg Jenks, filmmaker Hayden Keenan, Bruce Petty, Keith Suter and Graham Long.

As well as worship we have a study discussion group (fortnightly) called 'Meeting Point' which, as the name implies, is a meeting of ideas. Our format is to view an audio-visual resource such as *Living the Questions* before discussion. Annually the Chapel hosts a weekend 'Future Dimensions Conference'. These conferences have the aim of relating faith to the questions raised by our modern context.

The Arts (music, song, dance and drama) and culture represent a large part of the Chapel's life. Regular art exhibitions are part of our life, while the Chapel has become a place where many from the community come to initiate ideas, such as the Waratah Community Land Trust, an alternative affordable method of housing, and Worldly Soles, an agency involved in sending shoes to the Third World needy.

The Chapel has a charitable arm primarily through its work with the homeless and marginalized at Norman Andrews House. There, food, shower and laundry facilities are provided along with counseling and legal and tenancy advocacy.

Interfaith work also lies close to the heart of the Chapel. Many of those involved at the Chapel come from different faith traditions: Jewish, Muslim, Buddhist and Hindu. Despite their different faith backgrounds they have found a home here. A recent initiative has been 'Sacred Fest' a series of cultural celebrations of different faiths. While it is not difficult to study different faiths, the aim of this is to allow people to experience those faiths.

Faith Explorers Group, Heathmont Uniting Church

Heathmont Uniting Church 'Faith Explorers Group', formerly the Thursday Faith Sharing Group, was formed in July 2001, with the encouraging support of the then minister, following a visit to Australia by American Episcopalian Bishop, John Shelby Spong. The name was chosen by a popular vote of members in 2006. The Group is affiliated with the Progressive Christian Network of Victoria.

Meetings are held every second Thursday of each month (except January) for a couple of hours, during which there is a discussion of selected material chaired by two study leaders. Such material has always comprised books, sermons, and writings by a number of progressive Christian clergy and scholars from a range of denominations, both overseas and within Australia. These include Karen Armstrong, David Boulton, Jim Burklo, Wendy Chew, Joan Chittister, Don Cupitt, Richard Holloway, Catherine Keller, Ian Lawton, Michael Morwood, Ched Myers, Diane Teichert, Alfred North Whitehead, Henry Nelson Wieman and Miriam Therese Winter—to name but a few.

Membership and average monthly attendance have grown steadily to a current membership and monthly attendance of thirty-seven and twenty-two people, respectively. This number includes members of the Heathmont congregation (15) and members of other churches and non-church-going people (14).

The group satisfies the pressing need of a growing number of people who no longer feel comfortable in attending regular worship or who have felt unwelcome by the institutional Church as they seek fellowship, the freedom of an open mind, and the sharing of experiences on questions of faith and practice, without restriction.

Faith Group, Toronto Uniting Church

For many years there has been a number of people associated with the Toronto Uniting Church who have been questioning the traditional emphasis of their Christian upbringing. As a result, particularly in the last fifteen years, these people have developed a variety of alternative methods to explore their faith questions. Further, they have aroused interest in alternative views of the Christian faith that emphasise the value of diversity. These alternatives have met, in most instances, with opposition from members of the faith community and the clergy.

In spite of these responses, the desire to pursue a faith journey that questioned Christian orthodoxy and, in particular, the liturgy, creeds and doctrines, continued to manifest itself. Groups were formed informally to allow members to study the thoughts of such writers as Crossan, Borg, Webb, Mackay and Spong.

In total there are about forty people who attend and enjoy the opportunity to express their doubts and concerns in an open and supportive environment. However, there is some resistance to entertaining alternative approaches within public worship.

St Matthew-in-the-City, Aukland NZ

St Matthew-in-the-City, Auckland, New Zealand, has been on a 'progressive' journey since its founding in 1843. However, our goal to be a beacon on a hill for progressive theology began during the tenure of the previous vicar, Ian Lawton.

An import from Australia in 2001, Ian began using a fledgling Internet to begin articulating a progressive theological view beyond the walls of the parish and applying it to secular culture. Within the parish he preached a progressive understanding of the Gospel, began opening up the building for secular use by the community that was often considered non-traditional use of a church, invited the likes of Jack Spong to speak, and began discarding the prayer book to develop a more progressive worship life.

The next and current vicar, Glynn Cardy, is also committed to building an inclusive congregation where everyone is welcome. He has used his gifts as a writer to publish his progressive views in secular and religious media. A year after his arrival he called Clay Nelson, an American priest with web development qualifications, to promote the church's brand on the Internet and in more traditional media. Clay's vision was to create a virtual progressive church online that would give support to progressives in locations where there were no progressive churches.

To strengthen the commitment of the parish to such endeavors opportunities to learn more about progressive theology beyond what was said in the pulpit were offered. Both *Living the Questions 2.0* and *Saving Jesus* were used as resources. Progressive conferences are held with keynoters that have included John Shelby Spong, Paul Oestreicher, Cynthia Bourgeault, and Joan Chittister. Controversial use of our billboard increased our visibility and built a sense of pride in the congregation about being risk takers. Lastly, several new liturgies were developed in consultation with the congregation.

The impact on the congregation is that it looks forward to being challenged by progressive sermons that often challenge traditional orthodoxy. The congregation is growing younger and is more ethnically diverse. We are looking to develop further our online presence, so as to enter into discussion with the wider public, pushing for greater inclusiveness in the broader church, and continuing our history of speaking out for those on the margins.

PAX: Progressive Anglican Christians

PAX meets once a month at St Thomas' Anglican Church, Toowong. It provides a wonderful place of safety and inclusion for those who feel they have no voice or no empathy with more traditional church communities. We engage in open and non-judgmental discussion about some of the most complex and potentially explosive subjects the church is facing today.

We use the DVD series *Living the Questions*; however, we also have guest speakers to discuss progressive Christianity, relevant books and even inter-faith dialogue. The group began after one of the members attended a *Living the Questions* course in 2010 organised by the Rector, Tom Sullivan.

We begin every meeting with a shared meal. Once completed, we watch a DVD or hear the guest speaker, and then have about half an hour of discussion. As well as providing a place for fellowship and learning for progressive Anglicans, PAX hopes to develop into a recognised group of action, pushing forward with progressive ideas and ways of 'doing church'. We also hope to engage in inter-faith and multi-faith dialogue as a part of a call to engage in peace-making and social justice.

We also hope to assist in the creation and/or dissemination of much needed resources for the progressive community in Brisbane, such as progressive liturgies and prayer collections, overtly progressive and inclusive churches, and a widespread and easily accessible progressive network within Brisbane, and indeed, Queensland and Australia.

Explorations of Spirituality and Worship

On the first Sunday of each month (except January) a group of people, ranging in number from fifteen to twenty-five, gathers at Hopewell Hospice on the Gold Coast for a group known as 'Explorations of Spirituality and Worship'. There is no formal membership and people attend as they are able.

The title indicates that the time spent together includes discussion and sharing, as well as use of activities such as music, meditation and prayer. Some of those attending are also active in their own church. Others come because they have 'outgrown' their former faith community and are looking for a context that nurtures their spiritual growth. Sometimes a hospice resident has been well enough to attend or a family member has had the support of the group, but most come from the wider community.

Uniting Church minister, Revd Dr Ian Mavor, OAM, and Anglican Lay Chaplain Deirdre Hanna provide leadership of the group.

The group was started in 1999 as a combined Hopewell and Lifeline Gold Coast activity. Each month a set of notes on a particular topic is prepared. These provide a resource from which the group can draw, as well as being available for later reading and study; they also provide a focus for the involvement of the members.

Because the group is under the auspices of a community-based charity and is led by two people with progressive ideas in regard to Christianity and spirituality, the notes and the discussion draw from a range of religious traditions. They also help those attending to reclaim some of the more mystical elements of the Christian tradition, such as forms of meditation.

Topics have included: Spirituality and Illness; Searching for Freedom; Claiming Our Power; Suffering and Grace; and Spirituality and Self-Esteem.

Quest: Connecting
Spirit and Life

The adult education program is a long-established part of The Avenue Uniting Church, Blackburn—going back over forty years. About five years ago we reviewed the purposes of this particular group and decided we needed a name that was less formal than 'adult education', would be more attractive to people starting to think about Christianity, emphasised 'exploring' rather than teaching an established position, focussed on contemporary world views, and connected with life today.

'Quest: Connecting Spirit and Life' is part of the education program of The Avenue. The group meets every Sunday morning from 9.00 a.m. to 10.05 a.m., February–June and September–early December. A church service follows at 10.15 a.m. With about thirty participants, it is the largest program group in the church.

Quest was not and is not initiated by the minister, but has been well supported by the minister, who leads an occasional session. We are fortunate in having scholarly leaders in the congregation and have been successful in attracting excellent guest leaders.

The group is known for its lively discussion. Issues covered include social, environmental, spiritual and religious topics. But most interest is in gaining a better understanding of recent theological thought and seeking more meaningful insights into our relationship with God and the world. Of particular interest is contemporary scholarship to assist understanding the Scriptures. In recent times the Quest group has studied the writings of such people as John Dominic Crossan, Marcus Borg and Harvey Cox. We have used the *Open Christianity Series* of DVDs from the Progressive Christian Network of Victoria.

Despite the early start time; there are about thirty people who are regular in attendance, with a weekly average of 20–25 keen participants. Regular attendees include two members of the Catholic Church and there are occasional participants from another Uniting Church.

Quest has helped in opening up new possibilities for people to discover ways of understanding Christianity and being Christian that do not require them to suppress their normal critical thinking. By expanding the range of ways of being Christian, we make it unnecessary for some people to leave the church because they think they will not be acceptable. There is also a strong commitment to justice and compassion that flows from the discovery that Jesus offers a different vision of a more just and compassionate world.

The venue for the group is also important. The Avenue Centre adjoins the church but is separate from the venue for worship. It is carpeted, has individual chairs, making movement in and out of small discussion groups easy, and has two whiteboards. It has good heating, a PA system and a wall that is suitable for data projection.

Progressive Christianity Network of South Australia

The impetus to form the 'Progressive Christianity Network of South Australia' (PCNetSA) arose out of a visit to Adelaide by Bishop John Shelby Spong in June 2001. The Network is managed by a committee, which operates as a task group of the Effective Living Centre (ELC), an agency of Christ Church Uniting Church in Wayville, an inner-city suburb of Adelaide. Membership of the committee varies (approximately 6–10 members), and is ecumenical.

The Network has no formal membership and charges no membership fees. It maintains a database of interested people and organizations, over five hundred names, with whom it keeps in contact via email and a newsletter. There is usually a small charge for events to cover costs. The Network has access to some funds from ELC but tries to run a yearly program that at least breaks even. Its program consists mainly of forums, with local or visiting speakers, and studies. A year's activities typically include three or four forums and one or two study series.

The forums, mostly on a Friday night but sometimes on a Sunday evening, usually consist of a speaker who gives a presentation, a short supper break for people to meet with each other informally, and finally a question-and-answer/discussion session. On some occasions a forum involves a panel of speakers or is conducted as a discussion between the speaker and an interviewer.

The Network keeps in contact with progressive Christians at the national level and promotes and participates in the national *Common Dreams* conferences. It hosts international speakers whose Australian tour has been organised by the Common Dreams committee. The Network also works cooperatively with other progressive Christian groups to organise jointly sponsored events or to advertise and promote relevant events run by other groups. A newsletter is produced three or four times a year, which contains news of coming events, a book review, a personal account of a progressive faith journey, and other material of interest to progressive Christians. Its website (pcnetsa. org) has information about events, book reviews, lists of resources (including a list of progressive Christian communities or groups in South Australia) and links to progressive Christian websites.

Temple Society Australia

The Temple Society of Australia supports individuals to develop a deeper relationship with their understanding of 'God'. Trust, respect, self-discovery, acceptance and integrity are fostered, and we encourage people to think for themselves. We have no fixed statements of faith. Different formats are provided for religious gatherings because we recognise that everyone has something of the divine within and so is a 'temple' where the 'God spirit' resides.

Our religious leadership is in the hands of lay Elders. Our motto is: *Set your mind on God's kingdom and his justice before everything else and all the rest will come to you as well.* While members have diverse views, our common aim is to work together towards a fairer, more compassionate and sustainable world. A deep-seated sense of community provides us with opportunities to learn from each other.

Our founders (Germany, 1861) split from the Protestant Church, believing love of God and neighbour as oneself could best be practised in communal living and this should start in Jerusalem, the heart of Christianity. They migrated to Palestine in 1868 and established successful community settlements. During World War II, many Templers were transported from Palestine to Australia for internment, where the TSA was constituted in 1950.

We have a full range of regular activities and programs (religious services, social functions, welfare support, an aged-care facility, cultural and heritage events) at our community centres in Bentleigh, Bayswater (Melbourne) or Meadowbank (Sydney). Recently, we changed our operation by creating a focus-based structure. Focus Groups include religious/spiritual, youth, communication and social welfare.

The Temple Society comprises two regions, Germany and Australia. In Australia our adult membership exceeds five hundred. While we celebrated our 150th year in 2011, future challenges include raising our profile in the wider community.

Study Group, Denmark
Uniting Church

The Denmark Uniting Church 'Study Group' had its origins eight years ago, with weekly Lectionary discussions initiated by an Albany 'relief' minister. Church Council members then continued these discussions with a mostly elderly afternoon group and a younger (50+) evening group. The evening group continued as an in-depth discussion group choosing instead to discuss challenging and controversial theological issues.

There has been no involvement from clergy since the relief minister departed. For several years we've been a congregation without ministerial appointment, which has given us more freedom to 'source' material and to take on leadership.

Leadership now usually rotates among the ten to twelve members . . . a quarter of our usual Sunday worship numbers. Meeting frequency varies according to the length of the study material/books being discussed and the time taken to source new material. Individual members take it upon themselves to seek out 'progressive' study material, books, CDs and DVDs, such as: Marcus Borg's *Heart of Christianity*, Michael Morwood's lectures, Dominic Crossan's DVD lectures, and *Living the Questions* CDs, Val Webb's *Like Catching Water in a Net*, Gretta Vosper's *With or Without God* and Bruce Sanguin's *Darwin, Divinity and the Cosmos.*

Sensitivity to where people 'are at' has been important in the conduct of the study group. We've attracted three to four members from fairly traditional theological positions who have been motivated by the group to consider and explore progressive ideas. Over the years deeper relationships have also developed within the group. The 'collective creation' of alternative Church Festival liturgies has been a very meaningful experience for us, and for the congregation.

Wembley Downs Uniting Church

This Church has been an active member of the Uniting Church for many years. It seeks to present the Christian faith in a way relevant to today's world, incorporating knowledge and information not available to those in past times while still holding to the truth of Jesus and the gospels. We are inclusive, welcoming and feel the greatest call for a Christian congregation is to love and support both one another and those in the wider world, while also calling for social and political transformation.

Worship is open, using not just our religious sources but other sacred and secular writings, poetry and songs, video clips and DVDs as well as reflecting on current events to make our faith alive and relevant today. Ecumenism is important and throughout the year we join other churches from different denominations in worship, finding our common ground rather than our differences.

We engage in the progressive journey in a number of ways. We educate ourselves about the wider world by conducting a First Sunday Forum, once a month, which looks at current political and social issues. We run a Triple D group (Debate, Doubt and Dialogue) once a month where discussion and questions about anything is encouraged, and we have a Science and Theology group, which meets in the evening. This group aims to explore our emerging evolutionary story and the way many theologians are incorporating this story into our sacred story.

In addition we run programs throughout the week, using many of the resources made available from such people as Marcus Borg, John Crossan and *Living the Questions* so as to incorporate modern scholarship into our traditional understanding.

Mission in the wider world is very important to us and the congregation is involved in many community projects. The congregation also financially supports many outreach programs such as the youth care and chaplaincy programs run within our state schools.

The driving force in this congregation is our minister, ably supported by a team of faithful people who contribute to our journey towards a more progressive understanding. As a congregation we feel this is the only way for the church to survive and grow in the twenty-first century.

Australian Reforming Catholics

'Australian Reforming Catholics' was effectively launched in the year 2000 when a declaration was made of its values and objectives. The emphasis was on 'reform' to show that radical change is necessary to overcome the abuses of authority in the Catholic Church. The group was established by a number of concerned Catholics who wished to draw others of like mind into discussion and action in order for the Catholic Church to better reflect the spirit and teachings of Jesus in its administration and teaching.

The group has members in most States of Australia and holds an Annual General Meeting each year. This meeting often coincides with a conference on a relevant topic. Its coordinating committee meets regularly to deal with administrative matters and issues raised by members.

Since the members come from various parts of Australia, they are members of many faith communities. This is a lay movement not initiated by priests. However, there are many priests, brothers and nuns who support Australian Reforming Catholics and some of them are members.

Activities include support, communication and education of members through our quarterly newsletter *Arcvoice*, which contains comments and articles on a range of subjects, conferences held when possible on various topics to enable interaction and discussion, comments and press releases to various media on salient matters regarding Church teaching and administration.

The people associated with the group run into the hundreds. Some are paying members (annual subscription), some are non-paying members (members of religious congregations) and many others keep in contact and identify with the group through emails and attendance at our conferences. Committee members are elected at each Annual General Meeting and activities preferred by the members attending are mapped out for the following year.

Any plans are based on the extent to which we grow in membership. Unfortunately so many people who are dissatisfied and disillusioned with the Church tend to leave it instead of coming to an understanding that *they* are the Church and have a right to be heard.

Fresh Steps in Faith. Supporting the Uniting Church in adapting to change

'Fresh Steps in Faith' is an initiative of Rodney Eivers, a member of the Uniting Church of Australia in Queensland. Fresh Steps was chosen as a name as it represented the possibility of taking a new path rather than destroying something that, at its best, has proven of great value to human well-being.

The idea has been developing since 2009, but the company Fresh Steps in Faith Pty Ltd was incorporated in March 2010. It is to some extent an offshoot of the Lay Forum in the Uniting Church, which in turn, was an offshoot of Sea of Faith in Australia Incorporated. It shares some of the objectives of these two groups with two main differences:

- It seeks to provide an opportunity for those inclined to open doctrinal exploration of faith, including what constitutes 'core belief', especially within the Uniting Church.
- It is a supporter and an active participant in many of the public gatherings nurturing progressive Christianity in Queensland. It plays a part in committees organising such gatherings.

A range of progressive book titles are held and made available at concession rates to progressive gatherings and correspondents. Probably the most significant venture had been the publication of *Fresh Steps in Faith Magazine*. This email newsletter was distributed fortnightly for most of the year 2010, reaching some 150 people. Most were in Queensland, but an Australia-wide readership was developing. It sought to summarise some of the concepts of progressive Christianity, provide notice of coming events, and provide the medium for some stimulating correspondence.

A recent initiative is an offer to the Uniting Church in Queensland to provide financial support to enable a wider curriculum in our theological institutions. This would be to extend studies into progressive Christianity and perhaps other perspectives such as feminist theology. It must be emphasised this venture is in *support* of the Uniting Church in Queensland. One looks to the day when the official church will share the taking up of some of these proposals as a contribution to nurturing our institution as a revitalised influence for good in Queensland.

Basics and Beyond, Nowra Uniting Church

The stimulus for the group began in late 1996 towards the end of the short-term ministry of a visiting Canadian Minister of the Word. The original suggestion of a group was then strengthened early in 1997 in part as a reaction to the debate in the Uniting Church on sexuality. As that debate developed in the Nowra Uniting Church it became clear there was a need for a regular gathering of members of the local church who would find it helpful to have a place where alternative opinions and ideas could be shared. Thus began a luncheon gathering of people on an informal basis to discuss aspects of the Christian faith and other community issues.

The number of those interested was approximately twelve to fifteen from one congregation, and then that number increased with similarly concerned members of the Berry congregation. Through contacts with friends outside the church more joined this group so that membership includes members of other denominations and some whose allegiance to any church is strained. The group continued as an informal gathering with no formal structure until 2003. About that time it was agreed we should become a recognised group within the Uniting Church and the name of the group 'Basics and Beyond' was adopted to reflect both our connection with conventional religious views and a desire to continue searching for 'yet more truth'.

This process was completed in early 2004. During that year we were in contact with The Centre for Progressive Religious Thought, which was meeting at The Church of St James in Curtin, ACT. They provided support for our group and subsequently we became members of CPRT Canberra. That connection continues. Through that membership we also have contact with the Ryde Group, Centre for Progressive Religious Thought Sydney [Freedom to Explore], and a carload joined us for one of our regular gatherings.

The group operates quite informally. There are no office bearers other than the Coordinator. There is no joining fee or annual subscription. There are twenty-six on the list of contacts and the average attendance is seventeen. Decisions about meeting places in homes of members and topics for discussion are agreed by consensus. Monthly meetings begin with lunch together which is a valuable time to connect and share our experiences.

Discussions are based on issues rather than Bible study. The syllabus of subjects includes learning about other faith communities, and thus we have welcomed into our group people from other faiths to share their beliefs. Within the membership a significant number participate in the formal councils of the Uniting Church or in other congregations. The form of the meeting includes discussions led by a member, DVDs, and visiting speakers.

The support of our group in our individual searches for truth and faith has been paramount. Our group provides a forum where nothing is taboo. People can say what they think without concern about negative responses. Although members of the group generally have a 'liberal' approach to Christianity, there is a wide range of opinions and beliefs along the liberal spectrum. We have had the freedom to express our concerns about all aspects of our past and present beliefs.

The spirituality of the group is extremely important to its members. This is our house church. The group is distanced from formal church affiliation because we can no longer in conscience assent to various creedal statements. The words of hymns and formal prayers sound alien to our spiritual ears, even though a number of our group are regular and supportive members of their churches; there are others who are not. Our group is the only community access to spiritual support and nourishment. All members of our group would agree that the fellowship and intense discussions provide a place where we can continue our search. The context may or may not be Christianity; the search is always the same.

The Centre for Faith, Life and Learning

'The Centre for Faith, Life and Learning' (CFLL) was established over four years ago as a joint venture between East Doncaster Baptist and Templestowe Uniting Churches. From its beginning the Centre offered lectures, workshops and study groups with the intention of bringing a progressive and enquiring approach to Christian learning. The Centre has as its leaders the ministers of both churches and is run by a very active lay committee, again drawn from these churches and other congregations in the area.

The impetus for establishing the Centre was the desire in many churchgoers to explore biblical and theological ideas in a progressive and open manner. While the two churches involved in the establishment of the Centre did have progressive ministers leading them, there was still the sense that a 'safe' forum was necessary to both explore contemporary issues in theology and to have a place where those insights could be shared with others inside and outside of the Christian church.

Over its history the CFLL has offered the local church and the local community a range of evening programs. These have included the *Living the Questions* series; the Progressive Christian Network's *Open Christianity Series*; a study group on Fr Richard Rohr's book *Simplicity*; it has led an open forum on Buddhism, meditation and Hindu thought and practice, and provided its members with an experience of progressive worship. More recently, a very successful event drew forty-five people over two nights to consider a progressive and contemporary approach to understanding a theology of heaven and hell.

Because the group meets irregularly, an active email list is used to keep in touch and advertise coming events. The list has grown to over 150 people who have attended at least one event on the Centre's calendar. This includes people beyond the two congregations, in fact a number who have no church affiliation at all.

The Centre has become important to those who attend as it gives voice to the growing need for a progressive, thoughtful and open approach to Christian faith. There is a strong ecumenical camaraderie in the group often seen around the coffee pot at the break. Provided the Centre remains open to current thinking and pays attention to offering its clientele relevant and helpful topics, it will have a strong future.

Faith Explorers, St John's Uniting Church Mount Waverley

A group was initiated by Lay members of the church approximately fifteen years ago and was titled St John's Book Group. The intention of the group was to objectively investigate the Christian faith and its relationship to other faiths, through the study of modern biblical scholarship.

With the expansion of the group to include members from nearby Uniting churches, access and distribution of multiple copies to members was a practical problem. We changed to viewing and discussing DVDs and videos, and the group name was changed to 'Faith Explorers'. We meet once every six weeks on church property, where we view and discuss the thought of prominent theologians from Australia and overseas. After the viewing we break up into groups of eight or ten with a leader, to discuss prepared questions on the subject matter. This is followed by an informal time of further discussion and supper.

All church members are invited to attend but in fact only liberal or progressive thinking members participate. Leadership of 'Faith Explorers' has been a smooth transition over the years. At the establishment of the group the then minister approved of the idea but was not involved. The present minister of ten years is not supportive. Leadership is therefore entirely lay led, and always has been.

Our plans for the future are to continue in the present format while it serves the needs of the current membership (20–25 members). The greatest benefit of the group's activities is to be able to discuss any areas of doubt or concern and to freely express our beliefs in an open forum, without fear of ridicule or hostility. Additionally, a close personal bond has developed over the years among members of the group.

Explorations, Habitat Uniting Church

'Explorations' is an informal lay-established and lay-led group for those wishing to explore faith, beliefs and relationship/social issues. It aspires to provide a forum for progressive theological thought, valuing the search for understanding, the questions of faith and the breadth of scholarly thought.

Explorations comprise three series per year; each series of three to four weekly sessions held in school terms, with themes and topics arising from the interests of the participants. Sessions are held on Wednesday evenings followed by supper. Overall, we find the timing, content and structure of Explorations suits the progressively inclined component of the congregation.

Explorations grew out of the merger in 2008 of two Uniting Church congregations—the Augustine Centre, Auburn and the numerically larger St David's, Canterbury, which now constitute Habitat Uniting Church.

Explorations has a 'core' group of ten people and a 'floating' component of seven others with an average attendance of twelve people. A charge of $2.00 per person applies to cover the cost of discussion materials, e.g. DVDs, speakers, study notes and supper. It is financially self-supporting.

Most of the people attending Explorations are in 60+-age bracket and reflect the demographics of the Habitat congregation. In the main, though not exclusively, those who attend Explorations sessions are prominent in the life of the overall Habitat community. There is no clergy involvement as the minister is newly arrived and is settling in. Explorations is not clergy-dependant for its leadership or content.

The use of the DVD series *Exploring Open Christianity* presented by the Progressive Christian Network of Victoria has been the basis for group focus and sessions. The DVDs and discussion notes lend themselves to segmentation over three weeks. The task of the current four joint convenors therefore becomes one of publicity, promotion, and setting the framework for each evening and simple supper.

Explorations can be regarded as evolving. It provides a number of benefits to the Habitat community. It acknowledges the existence of diversity in views and understandings and gives validity to questioning one's own life journey and search for meaning. It provides a forum to explore faith, belief, biblical scholarship and issues of importance to the group's participants. It helps to disseminate progressive theological thinking.

A second group also operates within the wider Habitat Uniting, called SOUL FOOD CAFÉ. It meets at the Augustine Centre on the second Sunday of the month and has done so for some ten years. Twenty to twenty-five people from both former congregations enjoy it.

At the beginning of each year, a program is planned. Whoever suggests a visiting speaker usually takes responsibility for contacting them, leading the session and thanking the speaker afterwards. Topics are varied and have recently included "Counselling for Problem Gamblers"; "Grief and Death"; "Storytelling"; "The Star of Bethlehem—Myth or Reality?" The group also celebrates Mother's Day and Shrove Tuesday (Pancake Day).

St Mary's in Exile

On the first Sunday after Easter 2009, about 80 percent of the St Mary's Catholic Community located in South Brisbane, in Queensland, celebrated the Liturgy of the Word and then processed down Peel Street to the Trades and Labour Council (TLC) building a short distance away and completed the liturgy with the Eucharistic meal.

We have been there ever since, celebrating three liturgies each weekend on Saturday night at 6.30 p.m.; Sunday morning at 9.00 a.m. and Sunday evening at 5.00 p.m. Most weekends we would have over four hundred people taking part. People from a number of Christian traditions have joined us.

We have set up a company and currently we are continuing to establish structures that will, hopefully, serve us into the future.

A number of cluster groups meet once a month in people's homes to discuss issues of faith and to deepen a sense of community.

We have called our community 'St Mary's in Exile', since we were exiled from the Roman Catholic Church by the Archbishop. We believe we were denied natural justice when we were judged to be outside the beliefs and practices of the Roman Catholic Church on the reports of a small number of ultra-orthodox Catholics, who were not part of our community but who had 'the ear' of the traditional Cardinals in Rome.

There was wide media coverage on television, radio and the Internet. A book was published entitled *Peter Kennedy: The Man Who Threatened Rome. Australian Story*, an ABC television documentary, was aired in 2009, documenting our journey. Another ABC television program, *Compass*, was screened in May 2011, entitled "The Trouble with St Marys", by filmmaker Peter Hegedus. This documentary follows our story from the time we left St Mary's to where we are today, as seen through the eyes of Peter Hegedus.

Disciples: Kapiti
Progressive Christians

This New Zealand group was established in April 2010 through an email invitation sent by John Murray to people who had flagged an interest in exploring together 'Spiritual Openness'. The group's activities have been based around the eight guidelines of progressive Christianity as propounded by The Centre for Progressive Christianity. It has received encouragement from the Uniting Church minister and by retired clergy, but not by the lay leaders of the community of faith.

The meetings consist of a time for worship in which leadership is shared and a time for open discussion. More than twenty people have attended but not all have continued their involvement. There is a regular attendance of twelve to fifteen members each meeting. The focus of the group has remained constant with its initial aims: to focus on discussion and the sharing of spiritual experiences.

The group has not settled on a name but sees itself as a compassionate group of people, sharing a liberal or progressive Christian perspective. It describes its mission as people who desire to learn how the gospels can assist people to live in a complex modern world.

The Progressive Christian
Network of Victoria

The 'Progressive Christian Network of Victoria' was constituted in June 2006 before a gathering of 145 people. Five years on this network has 350 paying members; it is one of the fastest growing organisations facilitating progressive Christian thought and practice in Australia.

The purposes of the PCNV are to:

- promote progressive Christian thought and practice
- explore the implications of critical biblical scholarship
- explore the alternatives to traditional religious beliefs and practices, and discover new ways to understand religious faith

Its activities are to:

- provide opportunities to share experiences, knowledge and resources
- organise seminars, colloquiums and discussions
- co-ordinate and promote speaking tours by eminent international and Australian progressives
- encourage Australian scholars, to conduct research, to write, to speak and teach on aspects of progressive Christian thought and practice
- interact with organisations at the national and international level to pursue common aims

The PCNV is non-denominational and it reaches out to other faith traditions in a spirit of ecumenism.

Nine or ten events are staged each year including, formal lectures, panel discussions, and workshops. The leaders normally are local or Australian progressives. Over the short life of the PCNV, about forty of these events have been held. They are generally well supported (an audience of 100–125 is usual). Visits by eminent international scholars have been promoted and these events have attracted audiences of several hundreds.

A regular newsletter is published which communicates news of the PCNV's activities. It also contains reviews of books, study resources and occasional opinion pieces. An attractive and frequently visited website has been established which contains links to other progressive organisations, an e-commerce site (selling audio recordings of PCNV events, books and other materials) and an online registration facility for forthcoming events.

Books and study resources with progressive Christian themes are not always readily available in Australia and, in the case of new releases, there is often a considerable delay before they come available. To fill this void, the PCNV has developed a book retailing operation, which is well supported by our members and the public. Audio and, on some occasions, DVD recordings are made of most events, and these products become a valuable resource for progressives to use.

◆ ◆ ◆

Summary

Requests for information were sent to forty groups or congregations in Australia and New Zealand who referred to themselves in one way or another has being 'progressively Christian'. There is no national list in either country of progressive groups, and so we had to rely on contacts through word-of-mouth. In a number of Australian states there were state bodies or networks where there were affiliate groups and from these we established a number of contacts. The two international conferences *Common Dreams 1* and *Common Dreams 2* also provided a list of contact people. These group or congregational contacts were requested to provide, in narrative form, information regarding their development and reasons for their initiation and progress or lack of it. They were provided with a wide-ranging checklist of headings to guide their deliberations.

It is important to recognize that in the antipodes there is an attitude of self-deprecation to the value of knowledge through experience. Often my requests for information was met with, "Why do you want information from us? We aren't doing anything special."

Of the forty requests for information, there were responses from twenty-six groups ranging across the denominations of Catholic, Anglican, Baptist, Temple Society, Presbyterian and Uniting Church. The groups comprised people from different denominations and from no religious affiliation. Some groups like Quest did not wish to use the name 'progressive', but their content and educational practices were similar to many other progressive groups. These responses are a small sample, but in our understanding they do reflect the 'grassroots' progressive movement in Australia and New Zealand.

The size of the group was considered important, and most hovered between fifteen and twenty-five members. This allowed for individual participation and for the development of their personal spiritual journey and personal friendships. Some groups were experiencing a recent change in their demographics in that they were attracting a younger, more ethnically diverse membership. Almost all of the groups were dependent on lay leadership in what is clearly a lay-led development.

The principal strength of these groups is that they are vibrant discussion groups exploring contemporary scholarship in a safe, open and inclusive environment. An atmosphere where nothing is 'taboo', where 'hostility' and 'ridicule' is not tolerated, and where open and frank exchange of ideas is encouraged. There was an intentional commitment to hospitality characterised by the inclusion in many situations of a shared meal.

A common thread in all groups was the importance of embracing a faith that has 'intellectual integrity'. Those who joined these groups were seeking an opportunity to share their concerns that 'contemporary knowledge' and 'personal life experience' had brought them into conflict with a traditional interpretation of their faith. These progressive groups are providing an opportunity to safely share with those who have had a similar experience, whilst acknowledging the diversity of their personal journeys.

Certainly there were concerns about the future direction of many of the groups. Even the growth of the groups was considered a concern in the belief this could take away the value of the personal and informal nature of most groups. Others expressed concern the group may morph into the organised institutional approach that many found unhelpful in institutional religion, while others were seeking younger leaders to ensure the groups ongoing activities. Maintaining a balance to ensure no one person or viewpoint excluded others from participating was an expressed concern.

Content of and accessibility to appropriate resources such as DVDs, study books and reliable book review resources, especially those with an Australian theological emphasis, were a concern for many. Resources of practical coherent liturgies that allowed for the expression of these new discoveries in faith was also needed.

In some cases the state bodies such as PCNV and PCNetSA were able to provide access to some of these resources and in the case of PCNV developing their own educational material was seen a positive step forward. However, we cannot replace the importance of the support and influence from our colleagues in North America, Canada, and the United Kingdom.

As one Australian colleague remarked, we are experiencing not so much the development of a national organisation but something akin to an overflowing river when it enters a flood plain as it seeks the path of least resistance to find its journey. It is important, however, to recognise that even though some of these congregations and groups have met with stout resistance they have actually flourished— a justification for some that what they are trying to achieve in the way of change is important.

Clearly, this movement provides an opportunity for people to explore their faith in a safe environment as they share their experiences with people who have similar concerns. For many there is a sense of belonging and acceptance within the group and a belief they are no longer alone.

For others their involvement has meant progress on their journey for 'intellectual integrity'. A journey which has enabled them to bring together experience and the recent knowledge of New Testament scholarship, with their liturgical practice in a coherent and for many, a more meaningful encounter. Those whom Bishop John Shelby Spong refers to as 'believers in exile' or the 'church alumni', have found justification in the new scholarship for their felt concerns of alienation from Christian orthodoxy. In many ways the written reports did not do justice to the true colour of the enthusiasm that this movement has created. People talked passionately about experiencing a transformation on reading the works of the Jesus Seminar scholars. One group leader spoke about experiencing a 'renaissance' on hearing a presentation by Spong.

More research needs to be done if we are to understand how progressive Christianity impacts on communities of faith. However, the value of the information presented here is that the development of small local interest groups has responded, in many cases very effectively, to a need for the exploration of questions of faith and the opportunity to share this journey in a safe place with people who have a similar interest.

Resources Toolbox

COMPILED BY REX A. E. HUNT

A collection of hymns, liturgies, prayers, and a few known web/ blog sites, which may be helpful when exploring 'progressive' Christianity.

1. Progressive Hymns . . .
(New Lyrics to Traditional Music)

Andrew Pratt

Here Is a Canvas
Tune: 11.10.11.10
Here is a canvas as broad as creation,
here is a palette of life and of light.
Here God is painting through each generation,
mixing fresh pigments to move or delight.

Artists have joined in the bright celebration,
capturing images, pictures that shine;
telling new stories, recording our hist'ry,
moments of harmony, dancing through time.

Others reflecting, exploring and shaping,
seek to imagine, to let colours flow,
using their skills as they share in creation,
changing perspectives as images grow.

Now let us join in this same acclamation,
challenge perceptions and offer new ways,
new ways of seeing to share re-creation,
now in this place, in this time, in our days.

© *Andrew Pratt 24/4/2010*

Commissioned for Gravelhole Methodist Church Arts Festival at Royton Methodist Church, Oldham.

At the Learning Curve's Beginning
Tune: Metre 8.7.8.7

At the learning curve's beginning,
hardly knowing where we head,
finding how to learn, while living,
grasping all that's seen or said.

Looking through the sky that's soaring,
waiting at the ocean's shore,
filled with wonder at the seeing,
sensing God will offer more;

Filled with praise for revelation,
and for all we've yet to find.
Praise to God the source of wisdom,
and for each enquiring mind.

© *Andrew Pratt 9/1/2008*

We Cannot Make Distinctions
Tune: 'Intercessor', 11.10.11.10

We cannot make an easy, safe distinction,
all people are our neighbours, none denied;
the voices of all nations heard beside us:
all sisters, brothers, none we should deride.

The wall between the peoples has been broken,
in love of God divisions disappear;
as seen in Christ we recognise our neighbours
We greet unusual faces without fear.

We celebrate each difference God has given;
each nation, black and white, both straight and gay;
the able and the challenged God has offered
that we might share together, learn and pray.

We meet with those who paint a different picture,
who value God in words not yet our own,

in dialogue we offer one another
a vision we could never find alone.

This God we seek is greater than each difference,
the source and ground of all variety,
the centre and the soul of all creation
erasing hate with love to set us free.

© *Andrew Pratt 2008*

Help Us Trace Your Rainbow Colours
Tune: 'Stuttgart', 8.7.8.7
Help us trace your rainbow colours
through these days of change and choice,
holding firmly to your promise:
all the world can praise, rejoice.

In a world of contradictions
let your justice change our ways,
then with mercy fire compassion,
let no bias mar our praise.

Let us nurture fresh expressions,
different ways of being church,
sharing love and understanding,
joining people in their search.

Let us go with common purpose,
though distinctive from our birth;
welcome all to share our vision,
go as one to all the earth.

Through diversity and difference,
rainbow colours of our race,
let us share without distinction,
God's demanding, loving grace.

© *Andrew Pratt 9/7/2008*

We Cannot Gloat
The death of Osama bin Ladin
Tune: 'Abingdon', 88 88 88
"Do not gloat when your enemy falls; when he stumbles, do not let your heart rejoice." —Proverbs 24:17

We cannot gloat: a time for grief,
another mother's son is dead,
and if that son has killed and maimed,

it is the better least is said;
but let us mourn for all the loss,
and stand in shadow of the cross.

We mourn for victims we have loved,
and for the orphans yet unborn;
for those for whom a searing pain
greets this and every rising dawn,
and then we bow our heads and pray
that peace might drench the world today.

And to that end we pledge our lives,
our words, our actions and our deeds,
as following the Prince of Peace,
we'll work for peace till peace succeeds,
in breaking every barrier down,
that love may be our goal and crown.
© *Andrew Pratt 2/5/2011*

Jim Burklo

Love Now Ascending
Tune: 'Holy, Holy, Holy', Nicaea

Holy, holy, holy, love now ascending
Early in the morning our song shall rise to you
Holy, holy, holy, joy that has no ending
Giving, forgiving, breathing life anew.

Holy, holy, holy, love without a limit
Care that binds creation in sacred unity
Holy, holy, holy, birthing every minute,
Christ, Love's revealer, sets our spirits free.

Holy, holy, holy, infinite compassion,
Makes a place for every soul in God's eternal reign
Holy, holy, holy, truth beyond religion,
Love that endures should nothing else remain.

Holy, holy, holy, raise your voice in singing,
Join the cosmic chorus in praise of Love divine,
Holy, holy, holy, God beyond all naming,
Echoes our song in harmony sublime.
© *Jim Burklo*

George Stuart

In This Sacrament with Water

Suitable for a Baptism
Tune: 'Ar Hyd Y Nos' 84 84 8884

In this sacrament with water
God can be seen;
In each human son and daughter
God can be seen;
When love streams from fathers, mothers,
Gen'rously from sisters, brothers,
When compassion flows from others
God can be seen.

God in love's refreshing water
Brings us to life;
God in love's creative water
Brings us to life;
Water, vital for our growing,
Health and energy bestowing,
Like God's love, in overflowing
Brings us to life.

Joining in this solemn moment
Our spirits rise;
As we pledge our shared commitment
Our spirits rise;
Through this joyous celebration
We receive God's affirmation;
So it is with all creation
Our spirits rise.

© *George Stuart*

Pam Raff

My Song is of Love

On behalf of the Rockhampton Progressive Group
Tune: 'Love Unknown', 66 66 4444

My song is of the Love
not known or understood
a mystery that surrounds
us all yet dwells within.
Where e'er we go
what e'er we do
it is through love
that we are free.

We find in those we meet
companions for the way
gender and colour will
no longer bring discord.
Together we
drag barriers down
and strive to help
divisions heal.

Men, women, children all
can build a better place
a place where everyone
can find true harmony.
From birth till death
may our lives show
the mystery
that we call Love.

© *Pam Raff*

2. Responsive Prayers/Reflections . . .

Keith Rowe

(i)   Voice 1   Mystery beyond the reach of human words,
silence more eloquent than a Shakespearean sonnet,
nearer than our breathing—GOD.
      All   **We know the word;**
we are touched by the presence,
yet we only dimly understand what we know.

Voice 2   May the gentle beauty of this place,
the pleasure of our gathering, become
a doorway into deepening appreciation
of the mystery we call GOD.
      All   **May our music take us deeper into mystery, our**
thinking be shaped by insights not yet explored.

Voice 1   May our prayers become extensions
of our love for the world,
holding friends and nations,
the grieving and the joyful
within the mystery of GOD.
      All   **May words read from the Bible**
become more than words on a page;

may they become for us a stairway
into wisdom beyond our normal reach.

Voice 2 God, spirit, energy within life,
weaver of beauty, drawing humanity
together into a single family,

All   **Hold us in our weakness,**
direct our strength and fill us
with love that persists.

Voice 1 Mystery at the heart of life,
Father, Mother, Lord, Wind, Spirit,
Yahweh, Allah, Brahman we immerse ourselves
in the sea of life and love
that is your presence around us.

All   **Amen. Amen.**

(ii) Voice 1 Ever present God,
Like water bubbling down a mountain stream;
washing clean what has been soiled;
carving new channels for the river of life;
soothing the thirst of explorers,
pilgrims and trampers . . .

(Sung response)
"I sing the grace of God within you"
I sing the grace of God within you,
I know that grace within my soul;
and when we honour God in each other
we bring together one gracious whole . . .

Voice 1 Like wind blowing through the valleys of Aotearoa;
disturbing, disruptive intensity;
or gently reviving zephyr;
blowing us together into communities
of compassion and hospitality . . .

(Sung response)
"I sing the grace of God within you"
I sing the love of Christ within you,
I know that love within my soul;
and when we honour Christ in each other
we come together, one loving whole . . .

Voice 1 Like a giant Kauri watching over northern forests;
guardian of ancient wisdom;
sanctuary where the small and vulnerable
find protection;

beauty and stability;
enduring strength persisting over the centuries.

(Sung response)
"I sing the grace of God within you"
I sing the Spirit's life within you,
I know that life within my soul;
and when we honour life in each other
the Spirit forms one living whole.

Voice 2   God in the faces of your people;
a rich tapestry of cultures, religions,
nationalities and ages;
holding difference together within a single family;
luring us all towards a shared and generous future.
All   **Open the windows of our minds, our imaginations**
and our deepest sensitivity,
so we may know ourselves
   to be embraced by grace,
   touched with possibility, and
invited to share in the creation of new futures.

3. A Liturgy for Holy Communion Celebrating Pluralism . . .

Rex A. E. Hunt

This liturgy was first celebrated at The Centre for Progressive Religious Thought, Canberra, Australia. It was inspired by many others, including Carter Heyward, L Bruce Miller, Michael Morwood, Shirley E Murray, David Bumbaugh, John Shelby Spong, and the Iona Community.

Welcome to the Table

Voice 1   At this table we give thanks for
justice, love, peace and freedom.
Men   *At this table we give thanks for friends and strangers*
together in community in this safe place.
Women   AT THIS TABLE WE WELCOME OLD AND YOUNG.
Voice 2   A place at the table. And all are invited.

Thanksgiving

Voice 1   We give thanks for the unfolding of
matter, mind, intelligence, and life

that has brought us to this moment in time.

All   **We celebrate our common origin
with everything that exists.**

Voice 1   We celebrate the mystery we experience
and address as 'God',
ground and sustainer of everything that exists,
in whom we live and move and have our being.

Voice 2   And we acknowledge this mystery embodied
in every human person,
aware that each one of us gives God
unique and personal expression.

All   **God is everywhere present.
In grace-filled moments of sharing.
In carefully created communities
of loving solidarity.**

Voice 1   We are one with everything, living
and nonliving, on this planet.

All   **Connected. Interrelated. Interdependent.**

The Story

Voice 1   We remember the stories from our tradition . . .
How on many occasions Jesus would share
a meal with friends.
Bread and wine shared in community.

Voice 2   For everyone born, a place at the table . . .

Voice 1   How the bread would be taken,
a blessing offered, and then shared between them.
And all of them ate.

Voice 1   How some wine would be poured out,
a blessing offered, and then passed between them.
And all of them drank.

Voice 2   The bread and the wine symbolised human lives
interconnected with other human lives,
and the power of giving and receiving.

Voice 1   May the passion for life as seen in Jesus,
and in the lives and struggles of many other
committed and faithful people then and now,
enable us to dare and to dream and to risk . . .

All   **Together may we re-imagine the world.**

Voice 1   Together may we work to make all things new.

All   **Together may we celebrate the possibilities
and hope we each have and are called to share.**
Voice 2 For everyone born, a place at the table . . .

Bread and Wine
Bread is broken several times
Voice 1 We break the bread for the broken earth,
ravaged and plundered for greed.
All   **May there be healing of our beautiful blue and
green planet.**

Voice 1 We break this bread for our broken humanity,
for the powerful and the powerless
trapped by exploitation and oppression.
All   **May there be the healing of humanity.**

Voice 1 We break this bread for those
who follow other paths:
for those who follow the noble path of the Buddha,
the yogic path of the Hindus;
the way of the Eternal Guru of the Sikhs;
and the descendants of Abraham,
the children of Hagar and Sarah.
All   **May there be healing where there is pain and
woundedness.**

Voice 1 We break this bread
for the unhealed hurts and wounds
that lie within us all.
All   **May we be healed.**

Wine is poured into the cup.
Voice 2 This is the cup of peace and of new life for all.
A sign of love for the community of hope.
All   **A reminder of the call
to live fully,
to love wastefully, and
to be all that we can be.**

Communion
Voice 1&2   To eat and drink together reminds us
of the deeper aspects of human fellowship,
for from time immemorial
the sharing of bread and wine
has been the most universal of all symbols
of community.

The bread and wine will be served in the four corners of the worship space.

After Communion

Voice 2 Divine Presence in all of life,
we give thanks that we have gathered together
in this sacred place.

All **We rejoice in the giftedness of each person here.**
We are grateful for who we are for each other.
May we continue to be truly thankful
in all we do and in all we become.

4. A Liturgy for the Celebration of Birth/Life . . .

Andrew Pratt

Presentation

Voice 2 The birth of children has been celebrated by parents
and families since the dawn of human communities.

Voice 1 We never possess our children.
They are individuals from before their birth.
We offer them the inheritance of our genes.
We nurture them in the light of our experience.
We bring them up in hope.
But we never possess them.

Voice 2 Children are born for freedom,
born to grow,
born to learn,
born to reach beyond this time,
beyond our present experience.

Voice 1 Today is just a time of beginnings,
a time to express our commitment
to hold and to care,
to nurture and to teach,
that one day we may let go.

Voice 2 Parents have the main care of a child
but no parent should ever be alone.
We are here today to signify our support
and our commitment
to share in the care of this child,

with her/his parents (*name*) and (*name*),
her/his brothers/sisters (*name*) and (*name*).

We have a duty of care to all children
with whom we have contact and so

All   **We pledge ourselves to love and to nurture,
to care and support,**
to cherish and value this child, and to support
(*names of parent[s]*) **in her/his upbringing.**

Naming

Voice 1   Let us claim a name for this child which is a sign
that she/he is an individual, a person,
in her/his own right . . .

Born here,

All   **we welcome you.**
Gift and grace,
gift to us and life to nurture.

All   **And so we give thanks,
and we name you (*full name*).**

We claim for you all that is worthy of humanity,

All   **Voice of which you are worthy.**
We promise to nurture you,

All   **to love you.**

We promise to set before you
knowledge and mystery,
certainty and those things still left to fathom,
things known by fact and faith,
the things believed
and things we hold with faltering trust;
for yours is the world
and together we'll share it.

All   **These things we promise you.**

Voice 2   Come then, child, and join this happy journey,

All   **sing along with all of us
and learn the steps of life.**
Others may now greet the child or make further affirmations.

A Candle

A candle is lit.
May this candle signify the light
to guide your path through life,

that you may never walk in darkness or be lost.

All   **We pledge ourselves to keep our promises**
for (NNN) for now and for always.

© *Andrew Pratt 2011*

5. Inspired by The *'Abba'* Prayer . . .

Jim Burklo

Dear One,
closer to us than our own hearts,
farther from us than the most distant star,
you are beyond naming.

May your powerful presence become obvious
not only in the undeniable glory of the sky,
but also in the seemingly base
and common processes of the earth.

Give us what we need, day by day,
to keep body and soul together,
because clever as you have made us,
we still owe our existence to you.

We recognize that to be reconciled with you,
we must live peaceably and justly with other human beings,
putting hate and bitterness behind us.

We are torn between our faith in your goodness
and our awareness of the evil in your creation,
so deliver us from the temptation to despair.
Yours alone is the universe
and all its majesty and beauty.

So it is. Amen.

Pam Raff

On behalf of The Rockhampton Progressive Group

Living presence
life fire of the universe
blessed be the energising spirit that

draws all living beings into unity and
urges earthly creation towards its greatest fulfilment
as it moves and blends within its universe.

We give thanks that our earth has
provision for all that we need and we
commit ourselves to frugality of desire.

We regret our selfishness and greed
that harms others and willingly forgive
any hurt done to us.

We align ourselves with universal wisdom as our guide,
rejecting all abusive behaviour and
seeking life in its variety and abundance
throughout the whole of our lives.

6. A Celebration/Affirmation of Faith . . .

Pam Raff

On behalf of the Rockhampton Progressive Group

Voice 1 Let us together acknowledge our responsibility
to protect the earth and its inhabitants . . .
Over millions of years, this earth has experienced
ongoing change.

Voice 2 We are in awe of the miracle of life in all its forms.
We gaze in wonder at the sky that shows us an
expanding universe
beyond our knowledge and understanding.

Voice 3 We rejoice in the natural beauty of the earth—its
mountains, its oceans, its forests, its plains.
We marvel at the profusion and diversity
of animal life inhabiting the earth.

Voice 4 We respect the different cultures of the people of the
earth and accept the right of all
to live in a manner
that is of significance to them.

We recognise the right of people to live with dignity,
with adequate shelter, food, and clothing.

Voice 5 We acknowledge the desire of people for safety,
for freedom, for health, for education, for work.
We accept our responsibility to provide sustenance
to those in need.

Voice 1 We join together in making this pledge
in the confidence of that which unites us all:

All **The humanity we share . . . demands a fair portion
of earth's bounty
as the birthright of all.
The humanity we share . . . demands freedom
from abuse as the privilege of all.
The humanity we share . . . demands forgiveness
for wrongs suffered as the resurrection
for all (restoration of all).**

7. Non-Theistic Prayers . . .

Rex A. E. Hunt

Inspired by many others.

(i)   How good it is to be alive!
To feel the beat of our own hearts,
the pulsing of life in our veins,
the rhythm of our breathing.

So we come into the silence of this time of prayer and reflection
with gratitude for the gift of life this day.
(Silence)

In a universe so vast, may we be helped to sustain
a good sense of who we are,
and a good sense of worth in ourselves.

When time and events and people go by so fast,
help us to know the power in pausing,
and in pausing,
help us to find our life renewed.

(Silence)

We give thanks for the beauty of the created world . . .
We lament there are places where the environment
    is willfully destroyed
    or carelessly neglected.
May we learn to cherish and care for the earth,
to share all resources justly with all people.

We give thanks for the richness and diversity of human life . . .
We lament there are many
    who lack the necessities of daily life,
    who face danger, conflict or persecution.
May we learn the ways of justice,
and that violence and oppression may cease.
(Silence)

We live in a divided world,
a world where people have lost faith in political protest
    and resort to blowing up themselves
        and the neighbors they hate;
a world where soldiers are called peace-keepers
    and bombs are dropped in the name of national
    and international security.

As God longs for peace, may we find the wisdom
to see all sides of each issue.

As God longs for healing and wholeness,
may we find the love to persevere when all else fails.

This is our prayer.

(ii)   A sense of Creativity is among us
            in the changing of the seasons . . .
    Let the slowly changing leaves of autumn
    speak quieting words to our inner-most selves.

    Let the breeze of these early autumn mornings
    bring a vitality and hope to our lives.

    Let the symbols of this place: candle, bread and wine,
    speak strength and courage to our hearts and minds,
            as we come, and as we go.
    (Silence)

In the silence and acceptance of this sacred place
we look inward at ourselves:
    the advantages we have been given,
    the opportunities we have seized.

May we have a sense of gratitude for the gifts that are ours:
    knowledge, skills, insights.

Yet may we also be nudged
        to see new perspectives,
        to give back,
        to reach out,
sharing our talents, our riches, and ourselves
with those who are discouraged, disheartened,
        or simply unaware.

May we be more open, tolerant and charitable
        toward one another,
and all with whom we share this globe
of love and laughter and tears.
(Silence)

May our attention be grabbed.
And may we be seized with the miracle of life itself,
that we might be filled with
        new passion,
        new resolve, to take the next step,
risking the way of Jesus.

This is our prayer.

9. Blessings/Benediction . . .

Jim Burklo

May the peace of God surround you
Like the trees of the forest
May the peace of God warm you all over
Like the sun in the sky
May the peace of God swell and roll over you
Like a wave in the sea
May the peace of God fill you
Like the cool wind
May the peace of God be with you

10. Web Sites Worth Exploring Further . . .

(In no particular order)

ProgressiveChristianity.Org, USA
http://progressivechristianity.org

Common Dreams Progressive Religion Conference, Australia/NZ
http://commondreams.org.au

Westar Institute/Jesus Seminar, USA
http://www.westarinstitute.org/

FaithFutures Foundation/Jesus Data base, USA
http://www.jesusdatabase.org/index.php?title=Main_Page

Permission to Speak: Progressive Christianity and Spirituality, UK
http://www.permissiontospeak.org.uk/

Living the Questions, USA
http://www.livingthequestions.com/xcart/home.php

Progressive Christian Network, Victoria, Australia
http://www.pcnvictoria.org.au/

Progressive Christianity Network, South Australia, Australia
http://www.effectiveliving.org/pages/pcnet.htm

Progressive Christianity Network, UK
http://www.pcnbritain.org.uk/

Open Christianity Network, Ireland
http://www.ocnireland.com/

The Canadian Centre for Progressive Christianity, Canada
http://progressivechristianity.ca/prc/

Eremos. Exploring Spirituality, Australia
http://www.eremos.org.au/

The Centre for Progressive Religious Thought, Australia

Canberra, ACT:
http://www.progressivereligion.org.au/

Sydney, NSW:
http://www.cprtfreedomtoexplore.org/

Progressive Spirituality Network, Brisbane, Australia
http://www.progressivespirituality.net/

Radical Faith, UK
http://homepages.which.net/~radical.faith/index.htm

The St Andrew's Trust for the Study of Religion & Society, NZ
http://satrs.standrews.org.nz/

St Mark's Centre for Radical Christianity, UK
http://www.stmarkscrc.co.uk/

Lay Forum.
Open dialogue and Inclusive action in the Uniting Church in Australia,
Queensland Synod, Australia
http://www.layforum.unitingchurch.org.au/

Progressive Christians Uniting, USA
http://www.progressivechristiansuniting.org/

Homebrewed Christianity, USA
http://homebrewedchristianity.com/

'Emergent' Christianity sites, 'Big Tent' Christianity, USA

http://www.emergentvillage.com/
http://apprising.org/
http://www.bigtentchristianity.com/

The Great Story, USA
http://thegreatstory.org/

Evolution Weekend. The Clergy Letter Project, USA
http://www.theclergyletterproject.org/

Earth Bible, Australia
http://www.flinders.edu.au/ehlt/theology/ctsc/projects/earthbible/
earthbible_home.cfm

Process and Faith, USA
http://www.processandfaith.org/

Sea of Faith, UK
http://www.sofn.org.uk/

Sea of Faith, Australia
http://www.sof-in-australia.org/

Sea of Faith, NZ
http://www.sof.org.nz/

Modern Churchperson's Union, UK
http://www.modchurchunion.org/

Season of Creation (Liturgical), Australia
http://seasonofcreation.com/

The New Zealand Hymn Book Trust, NZ
http://www.hymns.org.nz/

Pluralism Sunday. Celebrating the many paths to God, USA
http://pluralismsunday.org/

John Shelby Spong. A New Christianity for a New World, USA
http://johnshelbyspong.com/

Rex A. E. Hunt. Progressive Sermons, Liturgies, Prayers. Australia
http://www.rexaehuntprogressive.com/

Michael Morwood, Australia/USA
http://www.morwood.org/index.html

Gretta Vosper, Canada
http://www.grettavosper.ca/

Val Webb, Australia
http://www.valwebb.com.au/

Bruce Sanguin, Canada
http://ifdarwinprayed.com/

Andrew Furlong, Ireland
http://myhome.iolfree.ie/~andrewfurlong/

Paul Alan Laughlin, USA
http://laughlinonline.net/homepaulblue.html

Marcus J. Borg, USA
http://www.marcusjborg.com/

Don Cupitt, UK
http://www.doncupitt.com/doncupitt.html

Barbara Wendland Connections, USA
http://www.connectionsonline.org/

Diarmuid O'Murchu, Ireland
http://www.diarmuid13.com/

Matthew Fox, USA
http://www.matthewfox.org/

Spiritual But Not Religious (SBNR) Blog, USA
http://www.sbnr.org/

John Shuck. Religion For Life, USA
http://www.religionforlife.com/

"Musings". Jim Burklo Blog, USA
www.tcpc.blogs.com/musings

Andrew Pratt. Hymns & Books Blog, UK
http://hymnsandbooks.blogspot.com/

Jesus, Jazz & Buddhism. Jay McDaniel, USA
http://www.jesusjazzbuddhism.org/home.html

Contributors

REVD DR JOHN BODYCOMB, has been a parish minister in Australia, New Zealand and the USA. He has served as a Christian educator, University Chaplain and Dean of a theological school, where he taught sociology and preaching. He is an authority on church growth and decline.

REVD PROFESSOR GARY D. BOUMA is Emeritus Professor of Sociology and UNESCO Chair in Intercultural and Interreligious Relations—Asia Pacific at Monash University and Chair, Board of Directors for The Parliament of the World's Religions 2009.

REVD JIM BURKLO is the Associate Dean of Religious Life at the University of Southern California in Los Angeles, USA.

THE VERY REVD DR PETER CATT is Dean of St John's Anglican Cathedral, Brisbane, QLD.

REVD DAVID CLARK was a New Zealand Presbyterian minister at the Community of Saint Luke, Remuera, Auckland, Aotearoa New Zealand, for twenty years. He died in March 2012.

DR JOHN DOMINIC CROSSAN, Professor Emeritus of Biblical Studies at DePaul University, Chicago, USA, is the former co-chair of the Jesus Seminar, and a former chair of the Historical Jesus section of the Society of Biblical Literature.

REVD PROFESSOR SIR LLOYD G. GEERING, ONZ, GNZM, CBE is Emeritus Professor of Religious Studies at Victoria University, Wellington, Aotearoa New Zealand, and a Fellow of Westar Institute/Jesus Seminar.

REVD DR NORMAN HABEL, AM, is Professorial Fellow at Flinders University in Adelaide, and a pastor of The Lutheran Church of Australia.

DR ROY W. HOOVER is Weyerhaeuser Professor of Biblical Literature and Professor of Religion Emeritus, Whitman College, Washington, USA, and a Fellow of the Westar Institute/Jesus Seminar.

REVD REX A. E. HUNT is a retired Uniting Church in Australia minister, Founder and Life Member of The Network of Biblical Storytellers Australia/New Zealand, Founding Director and Life Member of The Centre for Progressive Religious Thought in Australia, and an Associate of the Westar Institute/Jesus Seminar.

REVD DR GREGORY JENKS is an Anglican priest, Academic Dean and Lecturer in Biblical Studies at St Francis Theological College, Brisbane, QLD, and a Senior Lecturer in the Charles Sturt University School of Theology. He is a Fellow of the Westar Institute/Jesus Seminar and a Co-Director of the Bethsaida Excavations in Israel.

251

DR PAUL ALAN LAUGHLIN is Professor and former Chair of the Department of Religion and Philosophy, Otterbein College, Westerville, OH. He is a Fellow of the Westar Institute/Jesus Seminar.

REVD IAN LAWTON is Executive Minister and Minister for Theological Inquiry at C3 Exchange (formerly Christ Community Church) in West Michigan, USA.

REVD CANON DR NIGEL LEAVES is on the staff of St Francis Theological College and Canon of St John's Anglican Cathedral, Brisbane, Australia. He is an Academic Associate of Charles Sturt University.

REVD DR MARGARET MAYMAN is Senior Minister at St Andrew's on The Terrace in Wellington, Aotearoa New Zealand. She has taught Feminist Theology, Ethics and Religious Studies in the USA and NZ. She founded Christians for Civil Unions and advocated for the passage of the Civil Union Act (2004) in New Zealand.

MICHAEL MORWOOD, a former Catholic priest, is the author of several books and is well known internationally for his work in the area of adult faith formation in Australia and USA.

REVD CLAY NELSON is Priest Associate at St Matthew's-in-the-City (Anglican) in Auckland, Aotearoa New Zealand.

REVD DR LORRAINE PARKINSON, a retired Uniting Church Minister, was Chair for ten years of the UCA Victorian and Tasmanian Synod's Working Group on Christian-Jewish Relations, and served for eight years as a member of the UCA Assembly national dialogue group with the Executive Council of Australian Jewry. She is also a member of the Council of Christians and Jews.

REVD FRED PLUMER was the founding Pastor of Irvine United Church of Christ, in Irvine, California, USA. Since 2005 he has served as President of the Board of The Center for Progressive Christianity USA, while being an active member of the Executive Council of TCPC since 1996.

REVD DR ANDREW PRATT, a Lecturer at Luther King House, the Partnership for Theological Education—an ecumenical Christian theological college in Manchester UK—is recognized as one of Great Britain's foremost contemporary hymn-writers. He is an ordained minister of the Methodist Church in the United Kingdom.

REVD DR NOEL PRESTON, AM, a retired Uniting Church in Australia minister, is Adjunct Professor in the Key Centre for Ethics, Law Justice and Governance, Griffith University, QLD. He is also a member of the Advisory Panel of Green Cross Australia and the Committee of Earth Charter Australia.

REVD DR KEITH ROWE has served as parish minister, theological teacher and church leader in the Methodist Church of New Zealand and the Uniting Church in Australia. A former Principal of Trinity Methodist Theological College, Auckland, he served as President of the Methodist Church of New Zealand.

REVD BRUCE SANGUIN is a minister of the United Church of Canada at Canadian Memorial Church and Centre for Peace in Vancouver, British

Columbia, Canada, and a member of the British Columbia Association for Marriage and Family Therapy.

REVD JOHN SHUCK is Pastor of the First Presbyterian Church in Elizabethton, Tennessee, USA. He is an ordained minister of the Presbyterian Church (USA), and an Associate of the Westar Institute.

REVD JOHN W. H. SMITH is a Uniting Church in Australia minister in part-time parish ministry. As a trained social worker he is best known for his pioneering work with children, especially those in need of care and protection, including young offenders. He has also worked with adults who have intellectual disabilities. He is an Associate of the Westar Institute/Jesus Seminar.

JOHN THORNLEY, from New Zealand, has had a varied working life: teaching, social working and publishing. He is the publisher/editor of *Music in the Air* (exploring the creative arts and spirituality), and co-manager, with his wife Gillian, for the New Zealand Hymnbook Trust.

DESHNA UBEDA is Associate Director and Web Producer at (the former) Centre for Progressive Christianity, now called ProgressiveChristianity.Org, in the USA. She is the project manager and editor for the Children's Curriculum Project.

REVD DR JAMES VEITCH is currently lecturing in the Centre for Defence and Security Studies at Massey University, NZ. He is the former Associate Professor in the Strategic Studies Program of the School of Government, Victoria University of Wellington, and New Zealand Co-Chair of the Council for Security Cooperation in Asia Pacific. An ordained Presbyterian minister in Aotearoa New Zealand, he is a Fellow of Westar Institute/Jesus Seminar.

DR VAL WEBB's professional career spans microbiology, business, public relations, writing, art and theology. She has taught religious studies at the University of Minnesota and Augsburg College, USA, and at Whitley College, Melbourne, VIC, together with visiting lectureships at other Australian colleges.

DR MICHAEL ZIMMERMAN is Professor of Biology at Butler University, Indianapolis, USA. A Fellow of the American Association for the Advancement of Science, he is also Founder (2006) and Executive Director of The Clergy Letter Project—an annual celebration of Evolution, Science and Religion.

Bibliography

Adams, G. *Christ and the Other.* Farnham: Ashgate, 2010.

Adams, M. McC., and R. M. Adams, eds. *The Problem of Evil.* Oxford Readings in Philosophy, Oxford: Oxford University Press, 1990.

Alves, R. *The Poet, the Warrior, the Prophet.* The Edward Cadbury Lectures. London: SCM Press/Trinity Press International, 1990.

Aretius, B. *A Short History of Valentinus Gentilix: The Tritheist, Tried, Condemned.* Ann Arbor: University of Michigan Press, 2009.

Armstrong, K. *The Case for God: What Religion Really Means.* London: The Bodley Head/Random House, 2009.

_____. *The Battle for God. Fundamentalism in Judaism, Christianity and Islam.* London: HarperCollins, 2000.

_____. *The Bible: A Biography.* New York: Atlantic Monthly Press, 2007.

_____. *A History of God: The 4,000-Year Quest of Judaism, Christianity and Islam.* London: The Bodley Head/Random House, 1993.

Badger, C. *The Reverend Charles Strong and the Australian Church.* Melbourne: Abacada Press, 1971.

Bailey, R. *New Light on George Fox and Early Quakerism: The Making and Unmaking of God.* San Francisco: Mellen Research University Press, 1992.

Bawer, B. *Stealing Jesus: How Fundamentalism Betrays Christianity.* New York: Three Rivers Press, 1998.

Benedikt, M. *God Is the Good We Do: Theology of Theopraxy.* New York: Bottino Books, 2007.

Bercot, D. W. *Will the Real Heretics Please Stand Up: A New Look at Today's Evangelical Church in Light of Early Christianity.* Tyler: Scroll Publishing Company, 1989.

Berger, P. *The Heretical Imperative: Contemporary Possibilities of Religious Affirmation.* New York: Doubleday, 1980.

Beutner, Edward F. "The Haunt of Parable" in *Listening to the Parables of Jesus.* Ed. E. F. Beutner. Jesus Seminar Guides. Santa Rosa: Polebridge Press, 2007.

Blackman, E. C. *Marcion and His Influence.* Eugene: Wipf & Stock Publishers, 2004.

Birch, L. C. *Science and Soul.* Sydney: UNSW Press, 2008.

Black, K. *A Healing Homiletic: Preaching and Disability.* Nashville: Abingdon Press, 1996.

Boer, R. "Bilbies, Gumnuts and Thanksgiving, or the Commodified Religious Imagination in Australia and America" in *Australian Religious Studies Review* 13, no. 1, (Autumn 2000): 40–55.

Boomershine, T. E. *Story Journey: An Invitation to the Gospel as Storytelling*. Nashville: Abingdon, 1988.

Borg, Marcus J. *The God We Never Knew: Beyond Dogmatic Religion to a More Authentic Contemporary Faith*. New York: HarperSanFrancisco, 1997.

————. *The Heart of Christianity: Rediscovering a Life of Faith*. New York: HarperSanFrancisco, 2003.

————. *Meeting Jesus for the First Time: The Historical Jesus and the Heart of Contemporary Faith*. New York: HarperCollins, 1994.

————. *Jesus: Uncovering the Life, Teachings and Relevance of a Religious Revolutionary*. New York: HarperSanFrancisco, 2006.

————. *Reading the Bible Again for the First Time: Taking the Bible Seriously but Not Literally*. San Francisco: HarperSanFrancisco, 2001.

————. *Speaking Christian: Why Christian Words Have Lost Their Meaning and Power—And How They Can Be Restored*. New York: HarperOne, 2011

————. and J. D. Crossan. *The First Christmas: What the Gospels Really Teach About Jesus' Birth*. New York: HarperOne, 2007.

————. and J. D. Crossan. *The Last Week: A Day-by-Day Account of Jesus's Final Week in Jerusalem*. New York: HarperCollins. 2006.

————. and N. T. Wright. *The Meaning of Jesus: Two Visions*. New York: HarperSanFrancisco, 1999.

Boulton, D. *Who on Earth Was Jesus: The Modern Quest for the Jesus of History*. Winchester: John Hunt Publishing, 2008.

Bouma, G. *Being Faithful in Diversity: Religions and Public Policy in Multifaith Societies*. Brooklyn Park: ATF Press, 2011.

Bourgeault, C. *The Wisdom Jesus: Transforming Heart and Mind; A New Perspective on Christ and His Message*. Boston: Shambhala, 2008.

Bowden, J. *Dictionary of Theology*. London: SCM Press, 1983.

Brueggemann, W. *Hopeful Imagination*. Philadelphia: Fortress Press, 1986.

Burklo, J. *Birdlike and Barnless: Meditations, Prayers and Songs for Progressive Christians*. Haworth: Saint Johann Press, 2008.

Campbell, J. *The Hero with a Thousand Faces*. New Jersey: Princeton University Press, 1968.

Campbell, T. A. et al. *Wesley and the Quadrilateral: Renewing the Conversation*. Nashville: Abingdon Press, 1997.

Carr, W. *Brief Encounters: Pastoral Ministry through Baptisms, Weddings and Funerals*. Rev. ed. New Library of Pastoral Care series. London: SPCK, 1994.

Chittister, J. et al. *The Tent of Abraham: Stories of Hope and Peace for Jews, Christians, and Muslims*. Boston: Beacon Press, 2006.

Christ, C. P. *She Who Changes: Re-Imagining the Divine in the World*. New York: Palgrave Macmillan, 2003.

Clayton, P. *Transforming Christian Theology*. Minneapolis: Fortress Press, 2010.

The Clergy Letter Project. 2004. www.theclergyletterproject.org.

Cobb Jr., J. B. "In What Ways Can Whitehead's Process Philosophy Assist Process Theologians to Understand the Doctrine of Atonement?" Pro-

cessandfaith.org: August, 1998. http://processandfaith.org/writings/
ask-dr-cobb/1998-08/atonement. Accessed January 2011.

_____. *Lay Theology*. St Louis: Chalice Press, 1994.

_____. *Postmodernism and Public Policy*. Albany: State University of New York Press, 2002.

_____. "The Presence of the Past and the Eucharist" in *Process Studies* 13 (1883): 3.

_____, *Reclaiming the Church: Where the Mainline Church Went Wrong and What to Do About It*. Louisville: Westminster/John Knox, 1997.

_____, ed. *Resistance: The New Role of Progressive Christians*. Louisville: Westminster/John Knox, 2008.

_____, and D. R. Griffin. *Process Theology: An Introductory Exposition*. Louisville: Westminster, 1976.

Countryman, L W. and M. R. Ritley. *Gifted by Otherness: Gay and Lesbian Christians in the Church*. NY: Morehouse Publishing, 2001.

"Covenanting for Justice in the Economy and the Earth: The Accra Declaration of the World Alliance of Reformed Churches" in *Resistance*. Ed. John B. Cobb, Jr. Also available at www.ch/documents/ACCRA-pamphlet.pdf. 2004.

Cox, H. "Living in the New Dispensation" in *Atlantic Monthly*, March, 1999.

_____. *When Jesus Came to Harvard: Making Moral Choices Today*. Boston: Houghton Mifflin Co., 2004.

Crossan, J. D. *The Birth of Christianity: Discovering What Happened in the Years Immediately After the Execution of Jesus*. New York: HarperSanFrancisco, 1999.

_____. *God and Empire: Jesus against Rome, Then and Now*. San Francisco: HarperSanFrancisco, 2007.

_____. *The Greatest Prayer: Rediscovering the Revolutionary Message of The Lord's Prayer*. New York: HarperOne, 2010.

_____. *Jesus: A Revolutionary Biography*. San Francisco: HarperSanFrancisco, 1994.

_____, and J. Read, *In Search of Paul* New York: Harper One, 2005.

Crumlin, R. *Images of Religion in Australian Art*. Sydney: Kensington Bay Books, 1988.

Cupitt, D. *The Meaning of the West: An Apologia for Western Christianity*. London: SCM Press, 2009.

_____. *Reforming Christianity*. Santa Rosa: Polebridge Press, 2001.

_____. *Theology's Strange Return*. London: SCM Press, 2010.

_____. *What Is a Story?* London: SCM Press, 1991.

Daly, H. E, and J. B. Cobb Jr. *For the Common Good: Redirecting the Economy toward Community, the Environment, and a Sustainable Future*. Boston: Beacon Press, 1994.

Davies, O. *Meister Eckhart: Mystical Theologian*. London: Society for Promoting Christian Knowledge, 1991.

De Borchgrave, H. *A Journey into Christian Art*. Minneapolis: Fortress Press, 2000.

Delio, I. *Christ in Evolution*. Maryknoll: Orbis, 2008.

Deppermann, K. "Melchior Hoffman and Strasbourg Anabaptism" in *The Origins and Characteristics of Anabaptism*. Ed. M. Lienhard. Hague: Nijhoff, 1977: 216–19.

Dermond, S. *Calm and Compassionate Children: A Handbook*. Berkeley: Celestial Arts, 2007.

Dewey, A. et al. *The Authentic Letters of Paul: A New Reading of Paul's Rhetoric and Meaning*. Salem: Polebridge Press, 2010.

Dossey, B. M. *Florence Nightingale: Mystic, Visionary, Healer*. Springhouse: Springhouse Corp, 2000.

Dowd, M. *Thank God for Evolution: How the Marriage of Science and Religion Will Transform Your Life and Our World*. New York: Plume/Penguin Group, 2007.

Drury, J. *Painting the Word: Christian Pictures and Their Meanings*. New Haven: Yale University Press, 1999.

Duffy Toft, M. et al. *God's Century: Resurgent Religion and Global Politics*. New York: W. W. Norton & Co., 2011.

Duggan, D. L. *Constantine's Bible: Politics and the Making of the New Testament*. Philadelphia: Fortress, 2006.

Dunderberg, I. *Beyond Gnosticism: Myth, Lifestyle, and Society in the School of Valentinus*. New York: Columbia University Press, 2008.

Eck, D. 1993. *Encountering God: A Spiritual Journey from Bozeman to Banares*. Boston: Beacon Press, 1993.

Edwards, D. *Ecology at the Heart of Faith*. Maryknoll: Orbis Books, 2006.

Ehrman, B. D. *The New Testament: A Historical Introduction to the Early Christian Writings*. 3d ed. Oxford: Oxford University Press, 2000.

_____. *Lost Christianities: The Battles for Scripture and the Faiths We Never Knew*. Oxford: University Press, 2003.

Eisland, N. L. *The Disabled God: Toward a Liberatory Theology of Disability*. Nashville: Abingdon, 1994.

Ellison, M. M. *Erotic Justice: A Liberating Ethic of Sexuality*. Louisville: Westminster John Knox Press, 1996.

Epperly, B. *Process Theology: A Guide for the Perplexed*. London/New York: T & T Clark International, 2011.

Evans, C. H. *Liberalism without Illusions: Renewing an American Christian Tradition*. Baylor University Press, 2010.

Evans, R. F. *Pelagius: Inquiries and Reappraisals*. Eugene: Wipf & Stock Publishers, 2010.

Finlan, S. *Options on Atonement in Christian Thought*. Minnesota: Liturgical Press, 2007.

Fox, M. *A New Reformation: Creation Spirituality and the Transformation of Christianity*. Rochester: Inner Traditions/Bear & Co., 2006.

_____. *Original Blessing: A Primer in Creation Spirituality*. New York: Jeremy P. Tarcher/Putnam, 2000.

_____. *The Coming of the Cosmic Christ*. New York: Harper & Row, 1988.

Fromm, E. *The Art of Loving*. New York: Perennial, 1989.

Funk, R. W. *A Credible Jesus: Fragments of a Vision*. Santa Rosa: Polebridge Press, 2002.

_____. *Honest to Jesus*. San Francisco: HarperSanFrancisco, 1996.

_____. *Jesus as Precursor*. Rev. ed. Sonoma: Polebridge Press, 1994.

Funk, R. W., R W. Hoover, and the Jesus Seminar, eds. *The Five Gospels: The Search for the Authentic Words of Jesus*. New York: Macmillan, 1993.

Funk, R. W., and the Jesus Seminar, eds. *The Acts of Jesus: The Search for the Authentic Deeds of Jesus*. New York: Macmillan Press, 1998.

_____. *The Once and Future Jesus: The Future of Jesus, the Church of the Future, and the Future of Faith*. Santa Rosa: Polebridge Press, 2000.

Funk, R. W., B. B. Scott, and J. R. Butts, eds. *The Parables of Jesus: Red Letter Edition*. The Jesus Seminar series. Sonoma: Polebridge Press, 1988.

Gamble, R. M. *The War for Righteousness: Progressive Christianity, the Great War, and the Rise of the Messianic Nation*. Wilmington: Intercollegiate Studies Institute, 2003.

Gatti, H. *Giordano Bruno and Renaissance Science*. Cornell University Press, 2002.

Geering, L. *2001: A Faith Odyssey*. Wellington: St. Andrew's Trust for the Study of Religion & Society, 2001.

_____. *Christianity without God*. Santa Rosa: Polebridge Press, 2002.

_____. *Coming Back to Earth: From gods, to God, to Gaia*. Santa Rosa: Polebridge Press, 2009.

_____. *God in the New World*. London: Hodder & Stoughton, 1968.

_____. *Is Christianity Going Anywhere?* Wellington: St Andrew's Trust for the Study of Religion & Society, 2004.

_____. *Such Is Life!: A Close Encounter with Ecclesiastes*. Wellington: Steele Roberts, 2010.

Gold, M., ed. *Crisis: 40 Stories Revealing the Personal, Social, and Religious Pain and Trauma of Growing Up Gay in America*. Austin: Greenleaf Book Group Press, 2008.

Goldstone, L. and N. Goldstone. *Out of the Flames: The Remarkable Story of a Fearless Scholar, a Fatal Heresy, and One of the Rarest Books in the World*. New York: Broadway Books, 2003.

Gonzalez, J. L., and C. G. Gonzalez. *Heretics for Armchair Theologians*. Louisville: Westminster John Knox Press, 2008.

Good, J. *The Dishonest Church*. Scotts Valley: Rising Star Press, 2003.

Goodenough, U. *The Sacred Depths of Nature*. New York: Oxford University Press, 1998.

Gould, S. J. "Nonoverlapping Magisteria". *Natural History* 106 (1997): 16–22.

Gray, J. *False Dawn: The Delusions of Global Capitalism*. London: Granta Books, 2002.

Greeley, A. "Homilies". http://www.agreeley.com/homilies.

Greer, R.A. "Introduction". *Origen: An Exhortation to Martyrdom, Prayer, and Selected Works*. Mahwah: Paulist Press, 1979.

_____, trans. *Origen: An Exhortation to Martyrdom, Prayer, and Selected Works*. Mahwah: Paulist Press, 1979.

Griffin, D. R., ed. *Deep Religious Pluralism*. Philadelphia: Westminster John Knox Press, 2005.

―――. *Two Great Truths: A New Synthesis of Scientific Naturalism and Christian Faith*. Louisville: Westminster John Knox, 2004.

Griffin, G. "The Colour of Joy" in *Jesus Christ for Us: Reflections on the Meaning of Christ Appropriate to Advent and Christmas*. Ed. N. Watson. Melbourne: JBCE, 1982.

Habel, N. *An Inconvenient Text: Is A 'Green' Reading of the Bible Possible?* Adelaide: ATF Press, 2009.

Haïk-Vantoura, S. *The Music of the Bible Revealed*. Berkeley: Bibal, 1991.

Hamilton, A. "Democracy in the Church" in *Eureka Street 21*, 14. 20 July 2011. http://www.eurekastreet.com.au/article.aspx?aeid=27273. Accessed July 2011.

Hamilton, C. *Growth Fetish*. Crows Nest: Allen & Unwin, 2003.

Hampson, M. *Last Rights: The End of the Church of England*. London: Granta, 2006.

Hardwick, C. D. *Events of Grace: Naturalism, Existentialism and Theology*. Cambridge: Cambridge University Press, 1996.

Harper, T. "New Creeds" in *The Emerging Christian Way*. Ed. M. Schwartzentruber. Kelowna: Copper House/Wood Lake Publishing, 2006.

Hedrick, C. W, ed. *When Faith Meets Reason: Religion Scholars Reflect on Their Spiritual Journeys*. Santa Rosa: Polebridge Press, 2008.

―――. *Many Things in Parables: Jesus and His Modern Critics*. Louisville: Westminster/John Knox Press, 2004.

Heilbron, J.L. *Galileo*. New York: Oxford University Press USA, 2010.

Herzog II, W. R. *Parables as Subversive Speech: Jesus as Pedagogue of the Oppressed*. Louisville: Westminster/John Knox Press, 1994.

Hick, J. H, and Knitter, P. F, eds. *The Myth of Christian Uniqueness: Toward a Pluralistic Theology of Religions*. Eugene: Wipf & Stock, 2005.

Hill, J. A. *Ethics in the Global Village: Moral Insights for the Post-9/11 USA*. Santa Rosa: Polebridge Press, 2008.

Hillar, M. and C. Allen. *Michael Servetus: Intellectual Giant, Humanist, Martyr*. Lanham: University Press of America, 2002.

Holloway, R. *Between the Monster and the Saint: Reflections on the Human Condition*. Melbourne: Text Publishing, 2008.

―――. *Doubts and Loves: What is Left of Christianity*. London: Canongate, 2001.

Hoover, R. W., ed. *The Historical Jesus Goes to Church*. Santa Rosa: Polebridge Press, 2004.

―――. "The Jesus of History: A Vision of the Good Life" in *Profiles of Jesus*. Ed. R. W. Hoover. Santa Rosa: Polebridge Press, 2002.

―――, ed. *Profiles of Jesus*. Santa Rosa: Polebridge Press, 2002.

Horsley, R. A. "The *Sicarii*: Ancient Jewish 'Terrorists'", in *The Journal of Religion* 59, no. 4 (October 1979): 435–458.

Idle, C. "George Matheson, 1842–1906: One Man, Two Halves, Three Hymns?" *Grace Magazine*. http://www.gracemagazine.org.uk/articles/historical/matheson.htm. Accessed November 2010.

Jenks, G. C. *The Once and Future Bible: An Introduction to the Bible for Religious Progressives.* Eugene: Wipf & Stock, 2011.

Johnson, E. A. *Quest for the Living God: Mapping Frontiers in the Theology of God.* New York: Continuum Publishing, 2007.

_____. "The Word Was Made Flesh and Dwelt Among Us: Jesus Research and Christian Faith" Pp. 146–166 in *Jesus: A Colloquium in the Holy Land.* Ed. D. Donnelly. New York: Continuum 2001.

A Joyful Path: Progressive Christian Spiritual Children's Curriculum. The Inner Wisdom Series. Produced by The Center for Progressive Christianity USA, 2010.

Kaufman, G. D. *God, Mystery, Diversity: Christian Theology in a Pluralistic World.* Minneapolis: Fortress Press, 1996.

_____. *In the Beginning ... Creativity.* Minneapolis: Fortress Press, 2004.

_____. *In Face of Mystery: A Constructive Theology.* Cambridge: Harvard University Press, 1993.

_____. *Jesus and Creativity.* Minneapolis: Fortress Press, 2006.

King, K. *The Gospel of Mary of Magdala: Jesus and the First Woman Apostle.* Santa Rosa: Polebridge Press, 2003.

_____. "Letting Mary Magdalene Speak". *BeliefNet.* http://www.beliefnet. com/Entertainment/Movies/The-Da-Vinci-Code/Letting-Mary-Magdalene-Speak.aspx. 2003. Accessed February 2007.

King, U. *The Search for Spirituality: Our Global Quest for a Spiritual Life.* New York: Bluebridge, 2008.

Knitter, P. F., and C. Muzaffar, *Subverting Greed: Religious Perspectives on the Global Economy.* Maryknoll: Orbis, 2002.

Krishna, A. *One Earth One Sky One Humankind: Celebration of Unity in Diversity.* Jakarta: PT Gramedia Pustaka Utama Publishing, 2009.

Kugler, R., and P. Hartin. *Introduction to the Bible.* Grand Rapids: Eerdmans, 2009.

LaPlante, E. *American Jezebel: The Uncommon Life of Anne Hutchinson, the Woman Who Defied the Puritans.* New York: HarperCollins, 2005.

Laughlin, P. A. *Remedial Christianity: What Every Believer Should Know about the Faith, but Probably Doesn't.* Santa Rosa: Polebridge Press, 2000.

Leaves, N. *Religion Under Attack: Getting Theology Right.* Salem: Polebridge Press, 2011.

_____. "A Journey in Life" in *When Faith Meets Reason: Religion Scholars Reflect on their Spiritual Journeys Ed.* C. Hedrick. Santa Rosa: Polebridge Press, 2008.

_____. *The God Problem: Alternatives to Fundamentalism.* Santa Rosa: Polebridge Press, 2006.

van Leeuwen, T. M. *Arminius, Arminianism, and Europe: Jacobus Arminius (1559/60–1609).* Boston: Brill Academic Publishers, 2009.

Loader, W. *Jesus and the Fundamentalism of His Day: The Gospels, the Bible and Jesus.* Melbourne: UnitingEducation, 1997.

Ludwig, T. M. *The Sacred Paths: Understanding the Religions of the World.* 4th ed. New Jersey: Pearson Prentice Hall, 2006.

MacLean, M. "Worship: Pilgrims in the Faith" in *The Emerging Christian Way: Thoughts, Stories and Wisdom for a Faith of Transformation.* Ed. M. Schwartzentruber. Kelowna: Copper House/Wood Lake Publishing, 2006.

Marxsen, W. *The Beginnings of Christology, Together with the Lord's Supper as a Christological Problem.* Philadelphia: Fortress Press, 1979.

McCall, T. *Which Trinity? Whose Monotheism?: Philosophical and Systematic Theologians on the Metaphysics of Trinitarian Theology.* Grand Rapids: Wm. B. Eerdmans Publishing, 2010.

McGaughy, L. "Infancy Narratives in the Ancient World" in *The Fourth R* 5, no. 5 (1992): 1–3.

McGinn, B. *The Mystical Thought of Meister Eckhart: The Man from Whom God Hid Nothing.* New York: Herder & Herder, 2001.

McKenzie, S. L. *How to Read the Bible: History, Prophecy, Literature; Why Modern Readers Need to Know the Difference and What it Means for Faith Today.* New York: Oxford University Press, 2009.

McKibben, B. *Eaarth: Making a Life on a Tough New Planet.* Melbourne: Black Inc., 2010.

McLennan, S. *Jesus Was a Liberal: Reclaiming Christianity for All.* New York: Palgrave McMillan, 2009.

Mesle, C. R. 1993. *Process Theology: A Basic Introduction.* St. Louis: Chalice Press, 1993.

Miles, C. A. *Christmas Customs and Traditions: Their History and Significance.* New York: Dover Publications, 1976. Originally published in 1912.

Miller, R. J., ed. *Born Divine: The Births of Jesus and Other Sons of God.* Santa Rosa: Polebridge Press, 2003.

———. *The Future of the Christian Tradition.* Santa Rosa: Polebridge Press, 2007.

———. *The Jesus Seminar and its Critics.* Santa Rosa: Polebridge Press, 1999.

Morwood, M. *Children Praying a New Story: A Resource for Parents, Grandparents and Teachers.* South Bend: Kelmor Publishing, 2009.

———. *Praying a New Story.* Richmond: Spectrum Publications (Australia) and Orbis Books (USA), 2003.

Murray, S. E. *Touch the Earth Lightly.* Carol Stream: Hope Publishing, 2008.

National Academy of Sciences. *Science, Evolution, and Creationism.* Washington: National Academies Press, 2008.

Neff, C., and W. O. Packull. "Hoffman, Melchior (*ca.* 1495-1544?)" in *Global Anabaptist Mennonite Encyclopedia Online.* 1987. http://www.gameo. org/encyclopedia/contents/H646.html. Accessed September 2010.

Nelson-Pallmeyer, J., and B. Hesla. *Worship in the Spirit of Jesus: Theology, Liturgy and Songs Without Violence.* Cleveland: Pilgrim Press, 2005.

New Zealand Hymn Book Trust: *Alleluia Aotearoa* (1993), *Carol Our Christmas* (1996), *Faith Forever Singing* (2000), *Hope Is Our Song* (2009). Palmerston North: NZHBT.

Nissenbaum, S. *The Battle for Christmas: A Cultural History of America's Most Cherished Holiday.* New York: Vintage Books, 1996.

Numbers, R.L. *Galileo Goes to Jail and Other Myths about Science and Religion.* Cambridge: Harvard University Press, 2009.

Ogden. S. *Love Upside Down: Life, Love and the Subversive Jesus.* Alresford: O-Books, 2011.

Ong, W. J. *Orality and Literacy: The Technologizing of the Word.* New York: Metheun & Co., 1982.

Outler, A. C. *John Wesley.* Oxford: Oxford University Press, 1964.

Pagels, E. *Adam, Eve, and the Serpent.* New York: Vintage Books, 1988.

_____. *Beyond Belief: The Secret Gospel of Thomas.* New York: Random House, 2003.

_____. *The Gnostic Gospels.* New York: Vintage Books, 1979.

Pailin, David A. *A Gentle Touch: From a Theology of Handicap to a Theology of Human Being.* London: SPCK, 1992.

Parkinson, L. *The World According to Jesus … His Blueprint for the Best Possible World.* Richmond: Spectrum Publications, 2011.

Patterson, S. J. *Beyond the Passion: Re-Thinking the Death and Life of Jesus.* Minneapolis: Augsburg Fortress, 2004.

_____. "Was the Resurrection Christianity's Big Bang?" in *The Fourth R* 24, no. 3 (2011).

Peters, K. E. *Dancing With the Sacred: Evolution, Ecology, and God.* Harrisburg: Trinity Press International, 2002.

Picirilli, R. E. *Grace, Faith, Free Will: Contrasting Views of Salvation.* Nashville: Randall House Publications, 2002.

Pierson, M. *The Art of Curating Worship: Reshaping the Role of the Worship Leader.* Minneapolis: Sparkhouse Press, 2010.

Polanyi, M. *The Tacit Dimension.* New York: Doubleday, 1967.

Polkinghorne, J. *Belief in God in an Age of Science.* 2d ed. New Haven: Yale University Press, 2003.

Pratt, A. *Reclaiming Praise: Hymns from a Spiritual Journey.* London: Stainer & Bell, 2006.

_____. *Whatever Name or Creed: Hymns and Songs.* London: Stainer & Bell, 2002.

Prat, F. "Origen and Origenism" in *The Catholic Encyclopedia.* New York: Robert Appleton Company, 1911. http://www.newadvent.org/cathen/11306b.htm. Accessed August 2010.

Preston, N. *Beyond the Boundary: A Memoir Exploring Ethics, Politics and Spirituality.* Burleigh: Zeus Publications, 2006.

Rasor, P. *Faith without Certainty: Liberal Theology in the 21st century.* Boston: Skinner House Books, 2005.

Rauschenbusch, P, ed. *Walter Rauschenbusch, Christianity and the Social Crisis in the 21st century: The Classic that Woke Up the Church,* New York: Harper One, 2007. Originally published in 1907.

Reston, J. *Galileo: A Life.* New York: HarperCollins, 1994.

Reynolds, N. B., and Durham, W. C, ed. *Religious Liberty in Western Thought.* Grand Rapids: Eerdmans, 2003.

Robinson, J. A. T. *The Human Face of God.* London: SCM Press, 1973.

————. *Honest to God*. London: SCM Press, 1963.

Robinson, J. M. *The Nag Hammadi Library in English*. 3d rev. ed. New York: HarperOne, 1990.

Roll, S. K. *Toward the Origins of Christmas*. Kampen: Kok Pharos Publishing House, 1995.

Rowland, I. D. *Giordano Bruno: Philosopher/Heretic*. Farrar, Straus, and Giroux, 2008.

Saliers, D. *Music and Theology*. Nashville: Abingdon, Nashville, 2007.

Sanguin, B. *Darwin, Divinity, and the Dance of the Cosmos: An Ecological Christianity*. Kelowna: CopperHouse/Woodlake Publishing, 2007.

————. *The Emerging Church: A Model for Change and a Map for Renewal*. Kelowna: CopperHouse/Woodlake Publishing, 2008.

————. *If Darwin Prayed: Prayers for Evolutionary Mystics*. Vancouver: ESC Publishing, 2010.

Schüssler Fiorenza, E. *In Memory of Her: A Feminist Theological Reconstruction of Christian Origins*. New York: Crossroad Publishing, 1989.

Schwartzentruber, M., ed. *The Emerging Christian Way: Thoughts, Stories, and Wisdom for a Faith of Transformation*. Kelowna: Copper House/ Wood Lake Publishing, 2006.

Scott, B. B. *Hear Then the Parable. A Commentary on the Parables of Jesus*. Minneapolis: Fortress Press, 1989.

————. "Introduction: What Did Jesus Really Say?" in *The Parables of Jesus: Red Letter Edition*. Ed. R.W. Funk et al. The Jesus Seminar series. Santa Rosa: Polebridge Press, 1988.

————, ed. *Jesus Reconsidered: Scholarship in the Public Eye*. Jesus Seminar Guides. Santa Rosa: Polebridge Press, 2007.

————. "Jesus Seminar: Retrospect and Prospect". Paper delivered at the 20th Anniversary Fall Meeting of the Westar Institute/Jesus Seminar. Direct from the author.

————. "The Reappearance of Parables" in *Listening to the Parables of Jesus*. Ed. E. F. Beutner. Jesus Seminar Guides. Santa Rosa: Polebridge Press, 2007.

————. *Re-Imagining the World: An Introduction to the Parables of Jesus*. Santa Rosa: Polebridge Press, 2001.

————, ed. *The Resurrection of Jesus: A Source Book*. Jesus Seminar Guides. Santa Rosa: Polebridge Press, 2008.

————. *The Trouble with Resurrection: From Paul to the Fourth Gospel*. Salem: Polebridge Press, 2010.

Shea, J. *Starlight: Beholding the Christmas Miracles All Year Long*. New York: Crossroads, 1993.

Smith, D. E., and H. E. Taussig. *Many Tables: The Eucharist in the New Testament and Liturgy Today*. Eugene: Wipf and Stock Publishers, 2001.

Smith, H. *The Illustrated World Religions: A Guide to Our Wisdom Traditions*. New York: HarperSanFrancisco, 1994.

Smith, M. H. "Israel's Prodigal Son: Reflections on Reimaging Jesus" in *Profiles of Jesus*. Ed. R. W. Hoover. Santa Rosa: Polebridge Press, 2002.

Smith, R. G. *Secular Christianity*. London: Collins, 1966.

Spong, J. S. *Eternal Life: A New Vision.* New York: HarperCollins, 2009.
_____. *Jesus for the Non-Religious: Recovering the Divine at the Heart of the Human.* New York: HarperCollins, 2007.
_____. *A New Christianity for a New World: Why Traditional Faith is Dying and How a New Faith Is Being Born.* New York: HarperSanFrancisco, 2001
_____. *Rescuing the Bible from Fundamentalism: A Bishop Rethinks the Meaning of Scripture.* San Francisco: HarperOne, 1992.
_____. *Why Christianity Must Change or Die: A Bishop Speaks to Believers in Exile.* New York: HarperSanFrancisco, 1998.
Sproul, R.C. *Willing to Believe: The Controversy over Free Will.* Grand Rapids: Baker Books, 2002.
Stone, J. *Religious Naturalism Today: The Rebirth of a Forgotten Alternative.* Albany: State University of New York Press, 2008.
Strong, C. *Christianity Re-Interpreted and Other Sermons.* Melbourne: George Robertson and Company, 1894.
Stuart, E. et al. *Religion is a Queer Thing: A Guide to the Christian Faith for Lesbian, Gay, Bisexual and Transgendered People.* Cleveland: Pilgrim Press, 1997.
Stuart, G. *Singing a New Song: Traditional Hymn Tunes with New Century Lyrics.* Vol. 2. Toronto (NSW): Stuart, 2009.
Tabbernee, W. *Prophets and Gravestones: An Imaginative History of Montanists and Other Early Christians.* Peabody: Hendrickson Publishers, 2009.
Tatman, L. "Atonement" in *An A to Z of Feminist Theology.* Ed. L. Isherwood and D. McEwan. Sheffield: Sheffield Academic Press, 1996. 10–12
_____. "Crucifixion". Pp. 37–38 in *An A to Z of Feminist Theology.* Ed. L. Isherwood and D. McEwan. Sheffield: Sheffield Academic Press, 1996.
Taussig, H. E. *In the Beginning Was the Meal: Social Experimentation and Early Christian Identity.* Minneapolis: Fortress Press, 2009.
_____. *A New Spiritual Home: Progressive Christianity at the Grass Roots.* Santa Rose: Polebridge Press, 2006.
Taylor, P. *Talking to Terrorists: A Personal Journey from the IRA to Al Qaeda.* New York: HarperCollins, 2011.
Teilhard de Chardin, P. *Christianity and Evolution.* San Diego: Harcourt Brace Jovanovich, 1969.
_____. *Hymn of the Universe.* London: Collins, 1961.
Thorsen, D. A. D. *The Wesleyan Quadrilateral: Scripture, Tradition, Reason and Experience as a Model of Evangelical Theology.* Lexington: Emeth Press, 2005.
Tillich, P. J. *The Courage to Be.* New Haven: Yale University Press, 1952.
Tolle, E. *A New Earth: Awakening to your Life's Purpose.* London: Penguin, 2008.
Trevett, C. *Montanism: Gender, Authority and the New Prophecy.* Cambridge/New York: Cambridge University Press, 2002.
Tyson, J. B. *Marcion and Luke-Acts: A Defining Struggle.* Greenville: University of South Carolina Press, 2006.
Veitch, J. *Jesus of Galilee, Myth and Reality: Five Gospels in One Volume; The Five Gospels in Modern Translation Arranged Chronologically.* Red Beach: ColCom Press, 1994.

————. *Nothing Will Ever Be the Same Again: New Zealand Presbyterians in Conflict, September 1965-November 1967.* Unpublished ThD thesis, 1999.

————. *The Origins of Christianity and the Letters of St Paul.* Vol. 1 of *The New Testament in Modern Translation Arranged in Chronological Order.* Red Beach: ColCom Press, 1994.

————. "Revelation and Religion in the Theology of Karl Barth" in the *Scottish Journal of Theology* 24, no. 1 (1971).

————. "Spotlight on Saint Paul" in *Rediscovering the Apostle Paul.* Ed. B. B. Scott. Jesus Seminar Guides. Salem: Polebridge Press, 2011.

————, and J. Martin. *The Death of Osama bin Laden and the Future of Al-Qaeda.* Dhaka: Bangladesh Institute of Peace and Security Studies, 2011.

Vermes, G. *The Resurrection: History and Myth.* London: Penguin Books, 2008.

Vosper, G. *With or Without God. Why the Way We Live is More Important than What We Believe.* Toronto: HarperCollins, 2008.

Wallace, W. L. *The Mystery Telling: Hymns and Songs for the New Millennium.* Kingston: Selah Publishing, 2001.

Webb, V. *Florence Nightingale: The Making of a Radical Theologian.* St. Louis: Chalice Press, 2002.

————. *In Defense of Doubt: An Invitation to Adventure.* St. Louis: Chalice Press, 1995.

————. *Like Catching Water in a Net: Human Attempts to Describe the Divine.* New York: Continuum, 2007.

————. *Stepping Out with the Sacred: Human Attempts to Engage the Divine.* New York: Continuum, 2010.

———. *Why We're Equal: Introducing Feminist Theology.* St. Louis: Chalice Press, 1999.

Wheatley, M. J. *Leadership and the New Science: Discovering Order in a Chaotic World.* 3d ed. San Francisco: Berrett-Koehler Publishers, 2006.

Whitehead, A. N. *Process and Reality.* New York: The Free Press, 1978.

————. *Science and the Modern World.* New York: Mentor, 1948.

Wieman, H. N. *Intellectual Foundation of Faith.* London: Vision Press, 1961.

Wilber, K. *A Sociable God: Toward a New Understanding of Religion.* Boston: Shambhala, 2005.

Williams, P. "The Jesus Agenda: Christianity for a New Century" in *The Fourth R* 23, no. 1 (Jan/Feb 2010): 15–19, 24.

Williams, R. *Arius: Heresy and Tradition.* Revised edition. Grand Rapids: Wm. B. Eerdmans Publishing, 2001.

Wilson, B. *How Jesus Became Christian.* Canada: Random House, 2008.

Winship, M. *The Times and Trials of Anne Hutchinson: Puritans Divided.* Lawrence: University Press of Kansas, 2005.

Wright-Neville, D. P. *Dictionary of Terrorism.* Oxford: Polity, 2010.

Yolin, J., and L. Ingle. *Friend: The Story of George Fox and the Quakers.* Philadelphia: The Quaker Press, 2005.

Zimmerman, M. "Redefining the Creation/Evolution Controversy" in *The Huffington Post.* 3 March 2010. http://www.huffingtonpost.com/michael-zimmerman/redefining-the-creationev_b_484691.html.